ISBN: 9781290768672

Published by:
HardPress Publishing
8345 NW 66TH ST #2561
MIAMI FL 33166-2626

Email: info@hardpress.net
Web: http://www.hardpress.net

THE LIBRARY
OF
THE UNIVERSITY
OF CALIFORNIA
LOS ANGELES

WILLIAM GEORGE'S SONS LTD
89 PARK STREET, BRISTOL 1

DANIEL O'CONNELL

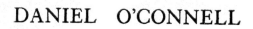

DANIEL O'CONNELL:
HIS EARLY LIFE,
AND
JOURNAL, 1795 TO 1802.

BY

ARTHUR HOUSTON, LL.D., DUBLIN,

One of His Majesty's Counsel

" Let all the ends thou aim'st at be thy country's,
Thy God's, and truth's."
—KING HENRY VIII., Act 3, Sc. 2

LONDON: SIR ISAAC PITMAN & SONS, LTD.,
1, AMEN CORNER, E.C.   1906

BRADBURY, AGNEW, & CO. LD., PRINTERS,
LONDON AND TONBRIDGE.

INTRODUCTION

———◆———

THE Journal of Daniel O'Connell, so far as it is extant, is now for the first time published in its entirety, with the omission of the name of one person, and of a paragraph containing an uncomplimentary reference to the personal appearance of a lady. Select passages from it appeared in the tenth volume of the *Irish Monthly*, about twenty-four years ago, but did not attract as much attention as they deserved. Mr. Macdonagh, in his *Life of O'Connell*, has drawn largely on the *Irish Monthly*. The extracts from the Journal to be found in these two works, besides omitting much that is of importance and interest, are given without those explanations which are necessary for a due appreciation of this valuable fragment. The Editor hopes that the notes which are appended to each entry and the observations made in this Introduction, taken in conjunction with the sketch of O'Connell's life up to the date when the Journal commences which follows it, will supply the deficiency.

At first blush the Journal is disappointing. It is

singularly wanting in references to the matters upon which one would naturally expect it to enlarge, O'Connell's call to the Irish bar, his early successes, the rebellion of 1798, the Union, for example. With the exception of the rebellion of 1798, which is mentioned as having been the subject of a conversation between O'Connell and his friend Richard Newton Bennett, not one of these things is alluded to.

But if the Journal fails to satisfy the reader's curiosity upon matters such as these, it makes up for the omission by giving him full information as to the works which O'Connell studied between the ages of twenty-one and twenty-seven, that is to say, the most impressionable period of a man's life, and by letting him into the secret of the objects which O'Connell set before him and the principles by which he proposed to regulate his conduct.

The following is a classified list of the works mentioned by O'Connell in the Journal :—

Biography.

Boswell's *Life of Johnson ;* Condorcet's *Life of Turgot ;* Johnson's *Life of Cowley ;* Murphy's *Life of Johnson ; Milton's Life ; Plutarch's Life ;* Rousseau's *Confessions.*

Fiction.

Caleb Williams ; Hugh Trevor ; The Ring ; The Man of Feeling.

History.

Adams's *History of Republics* ; Barthélémy's *Travels of Anacharsis* ; Gibbon's *Decline and Fall of the Roman Empire* ; Henry's *History of England* ; Mirabeau's *Cour de Berlin* ; Whitaker's *History of Manchester*.

Law.

Blackstone's *Commentaries on the Laws of England* ; Boote's *Historical Account of a Suit at Law* ; Coke's *Commentary on Littleton's Treatise on Land Tenures* ; *Cruise on Fines* ; *Cummin on Fee Tail*.

Natural Science.

Buffon's *Natural History* ; Dutens' *Les Origines des Découvertes attribuées aux Modernes* ; Hall's *Encyclopædia*, title " Aerology " ; *Memoires de l'Académie des Sciences*, article on observations made on the planet Jupiter and its satellites by Cassini.

Poetry.

Akenside's *Pleasures of Imagination* ; Cowley's *Poems* ; Johnson's *London* and *Vanity of Human Wishes* ; Macpherson's *Ossian* ; Milton's *Paradise Lost* ; Pindar's *Poems* ; Shakespeare ; Voltaire's *Tragedies*.

Political and Social Science.

Adam Smith's *Wealth of Nations* ; Bolingbroke's *Answer to the " London Journal "* ; Bolingbroke's

Vindication; Colquhoun's *Police of London;* Godwin's *Political Justice;* Hume's *Essays; The Jockey Club; Manual of Liberty;* O'Brien's pamphlet against the Ministry entitled *Utrum Horum; The Rolliad;* Voltaire's works ; Wolstonecraft's *Vindication of the Rights of Women.*

Theology.

The Bible ; Blair's *Sermons ;* Paine's *Age of Reason; Recueil Nécessaire;* Zapata's *Questions.*

Miscellaneous.

Bayle's Dictionary ; Collins's *Account of New South Wales; Encyclopædia Britannica,* title " Gladiator " ; *Encyclopédie,* title " Gladiateur " ; Gibbon's *Miscellaneous Works ;* Grose's *Antiquities of Ireland; Plan of a Dictionary,* by Dr. Johnson *; Transactions of the Royal Irish Academy ;* a play the name of which is not given.

During the period embraced by the Journal O'Connell doubtless studied other works besides those enumerated in the foregoing list, for there are wide gaps in the Journal, one extending from January 13th to December 31st, 1798, and another from January 2nd, 1799, to June 4th, 1802. Besides, he mentions in the entry under date December 12th, 1795, that he intends to record only the important ones among the books which he reads.

The most striking fact that appears from a perusal of the above list is that O'Connell studied such works as Paine's *Age of Reason* and the *Recueil Nécessaire*. That they had a transient influence on his mind is obvious, not merely from the observations made upon them in the Journal and the remark made by Miss Hunter that "in fifty years he would doubt whether he was a man or a cabbage-stump, so much was he inclined to scepticism," but from such passages as these. Speaking of the second part of Paine's *Age of Reason*, he says: "It has put the foundation of the religious question of the Christians in a point of view in which a judgment is easily formed on its solidity. I now have no doubts on this head. I may certainly be mistaken. But I am not wilfully mistaken, if the expression has any meaning. My mistakes I refer to the mercy of that Being who is wise by excellence. To the God of nature do I turn my heart; to the meditation of His works I turn my thoughts. In Him do I find my soul saturated. He will not, justice tells me, punish for a darkness, if such it be, that cannot be removed; He will not punish for the unbiassed conviction of the soul. To affirm the contrary would, in my apprehension, be to calumniate." Again he exclaims, "Oh, ETERNAL Being, Thou seest the purity of my heart, the sincerity of my promises. Should I appear before Your august tribunal after having performed them, shall I not be entitled to

call for my reward ?   Will the omission of a superstitious action, will the disbelief of an unreasonable
dogma, that day rise in judgment against me?
Oh, God, how hast Thou been calumniated!"
" Religious subjects," he writes on January 20th,
1796, " engross much of my attention.   The prejudices of childhood and youth at times frighten and
shake the firmness of my soul.   These fears, these
doubts, perhaps imply a libel on the First
Cause. . . . It is impossible that He whose justice
is *perfect* should punish with eternal torments the
belief which is founded on conviction."   His reflections on death, inspired by the last moments of
the expiring year 1795, show that he doubted the
immortality of the soul.   After dilating on the
dissolution of the body into its component elements,
he proceeds, " But the mind, the mind !   Through
what variety of untried being is that to roam ?
What changes is it to suffer ?   Does it perish as a
dependant on the corporal system ? . . . Our best
surmises are founded on an analogy.   Now what
analogy can there be between any part of corporal
existence and the state of the mind when separated
from the body, supposing separation actually takes
place ? "

It can hardly be doubted that when the passages
above quoted were penned O'Connell was inclined
to that deism which Paine and those of his school
preached.   It is needless to say that such studies had
no permanent effect on the religious convictions of

the Liberator, who lived and died a most devout Catholic, and maintained that errors in faith were more dangerous than errors in morals. But they probably had a good deal to do with that large tolerance that he extended to those who differed from him in matters of belief, for, however much he may subsequently have dissented from the conclusions drawn by Paine and the contributors to the *Recueil Nécessaire*, he could hardly help being convinced of the purity of their motives and their sincerity in the pursuit of what they believed to be truth.

The study of such works on political philosophy as Godwin's *Political Justice* left, however, a more permanent impression on O'Connell's mind.

Godwin's work appeared in 1793, a most inauspicious time for a treatise which assailed monarchy, aristocracy, property, and everything that the French revolution swept away, and that the ruling classes in England were straining every nerve to maintain. But while Godwin attacked these venerable institutions as being pernicious, he denounced the idea of unnecessarily resorting to force for their destruction. He relied almost entirely on the influence of reason. "If," he says, "the cause we plead be the cause of truth, there is no doubt that by reasonings, if sufficiently zealous and constant, the same purpose may be effected in a mild and liberal way. In a word, it is proper to recollect here what has been established as to the doctrine of force in general, that it is in no case to be employed but where every other means is ineffectual." This was practically the attitude which O'Connell took up. "The altar of liberty," he writes on December 29th, 1796, "totters when it is cemented only with blood." But he carried the doctrine too far when, in after-life, he laid down the principle that the best possible political revolution was not worth the shedding of a single drop of human blood, an idea which he may have imbibed from Rousseau, who said that the justest revolution would be bought too dearly by the blood of a single citizen.

His success in obtaining Catholic emancipation appeared to justify the view that Godwin put forward and O'Connell adopted. But when it was applied in the case of the repeal of the Union, it failed, and its failure broke O'Connell's heart. Godwin pointed to the American revolution and the French revolution as examples of changes brought about without the use of force to any considerable extent, the public mind having been previously educated up to the necessary point. O'Connell's "Agitate! agitate!" was only the maxims of Godwin put into a terse form.

No one who reads the Journal can have a doubt of the loftiness and purity of O'Connell's motives as a public man. It was not intended for publication. It was kept partly for amusement, but chiefly for self-improvement. He writes, "Since I commenced this Journal at Chiswick I have felt many salutary effects from thus taking a retrospective view of my conduct. I study much more than I did before." On another occasion he says, "I know that to persevere in it"—the resolution to write up the Journal regularly—"would be of the greatest utility to me. Did I regularly record the day, shame would prevent me from being negligent. The perusal of my Journal would be the best reward of my diligence, the surest punishment of idleness."

To his Journal, as to a trusted friend, he confides the secrets of his heart, and there we may read his character as in a mirror. He chides himself for his slothfulness, his indulgence in sleep, his inattention to matters of business, his propensity to untruth, his inclination to intemperance. He makes resolutions to reform in these matters, and records his success or failure.

Two great principles he lays down for his own guidance : the practice of private virtue and the promotion of his country's good. Writing on March 25th, 1797, he says, " Virtue, thou certainly art more than a name. Thou bestowest firmness and quietude on the heart of mortal, whilst thou exaltest his conceptions. . . . After having, in the conviction of my soul, made this eulogium on virtue, let me tremble whilst I ask myself how much of myself entered into my desire or dread of a revolution. Oh, if I was possessed of virtue, I would wish for the happiness alone of mankind. If I possessed virtue, I would meet every event without shrinking." He says again on the last day of the year 1798, " I have several resolutions formed. . . . My first resolution is no less than to be *virtuous*. This includes everything. . . . I know that to be virtuous is to be happy. Everything that is contrary to our happiness is necessarily and of consequence contrary to virtue." He repeats these sentiments again in a subsequent entry, and in one of the latest he ever made bewails the weakening which he imagines he feels in his love for virtue.

But perhaps the most interesting passages in the Journal are those in which he declares the principles by which he will regulate his conduct in public life. O'Connell, like other great men, early felt the stirrings of ambition in his breast. They appeared when he was but a child, as an incident narrated below and his own statement to O'Neill Daunt attest. In a letter to his uncle written on December 10th, 1795, he owns to having " a glowing and enthusiastic ambition." In his Journal he frankly confesses his love of fame. " I know," he writes on January 25th, 1797, " that praise is useless to the dead, yet I would not die unknown." But the ambition which he felt, and which he cherished, had nothing sordid or selfish about it. The entry under date January 7th of the same year contains this passage : " I would, and I trust I will, serve man. I feel, I really feel, the sacred and mild warmth of true patriotism. I will endeavour to make the narrow circle of my friends happy, I will endeavour to give cheerfulness and ease to the peasantry over whom I may command, I will endeavour to give liberty to my country, and I will endeavour to increase the portion of the knowledge and virtue of humankind." "Sometimes," he writes —"and indeed this happens most frequently—I am led away by vanity and ambition to imagine that I shall cut a great figure on the theatre of the world; sometimes I fear that I shall never be able to rise to mediocrity. *But this I always think, that nothing could shake the steadiness with which I would pursue the good of my country.*" On February 20th, 1797, O'Connell listened to a debate in the Irish House of Commons. On the same evening he records his impressions of the oratory of Sir Lawrence Parsons, and adds, "I too will be a member. Young as I am, unacquainted with the ways of the world, I should not even now appear contemptible. I will stead-fastly and perseveringly attach myself to the real interests of Ireland. I shall endeavour equally to avoid the profligacy of corruption and the violence of unreasonable *patriotism*. Of real patriotism moderation is the chief mark."

Surely in these passages this youth of twenty-one places before himself a noble and lofty ideal. How comprehensive are his aims. All mankind he will seek to serve by endeavouring to increase the knowledge and virtue of the human race. His country he will seek to serve by attaching himself to her real interests and promoting them, not by wild projects of rebellion or revolution, but by gradual and peaceful reform. The tenantry over whom he may exercise control he will seek to serve by making their lives comfortable and pleasant. His friends, a comparatively narrow circle when he wrote, but a wide one when he became more widely known, he will seek to serve by endeavouring to make them happy. He sums it all up in one sentence, where he says, while lamenting the death of a friend of his boyhood and moralising on the shortness of life, " I will make my heart a heart of love."

It falls to the lot of few men, if indeed it falls to the lot of any, to realise their ideals. O'Connell did not quite succeed in realising his. But he had a large measure of success. After a score of years of strenuous exertion, he achieved the political emancipation of his co-religionists. Before another score of years had passed he had sunk beneath the weight of the huge task he set himself half a century before, and had died in the endeavour to give liberty to his country. But the labour of the closing years of his life has not been in vain. He found the peasantry of Ireland broken in spirit, despairing; he left them courageous and hopeful, ready to follow, as they have followed, the leaders who have pursued the same paths of peaceful and constitutional agitation which it is the great merit of O'Connell to have marked out. The fervour of his eloquence, the fire of his enthusiasm, the force of his energy, and the brightness of his example, infused life into the dry bones of Irish Nationality, which to-day is a greater power than it ever was, except, perhaps, when, in 1782, Ireland wrung from the Parliament of England the independence of her own. What may be the result of the long struggle for Irish autonomy no one, so far as the near future is concerned, can venture with confidence to predict. But that it is destined ultimately to succeed no one who is acquainted with the past, and can read the signs of the times, will venture to deny.

The reference to corruption in the last of the extracts above made is noticeable. Unacquainted, as O'Connell says he was, with the ways of the world, he evidently was aware how great a part "the profligacy of corruption" played in the politics of Ireland. He declared his intention of eschewing it. No man's hands were ever freer from corruption than his. He would never accept rank or place. In a letter written to Edward Dwyer from London, which is without date, but bears the London postmark, December 4th, 1830, he says, "The Irish appointments are not yet made out. . . . You will of course hear a good deal about me—I fancy Mahony wrote to Conway that I was to become a *tame elephant*—but they know little of me. Bah ! What do I care for all they could give me except the liberty of Ireland ? That, and that alone, is my bribe. Whenever you hear that I am accepting office, pledge yourself to its being false. I would ·take office for only one purpose, for which the times are not ripe—that is, the amicable settlement of the terms on which the Union was to be repealed." That either title or place was offered to him at this time is apparent from the letter to O'Connell from his wife, which is also undated, but bears the Dublin postmark of December 3rd, 1830, and is copied in full in a note to the entry under date December 13th, 1795. On May 27th, 1833, he wrote to Fitzpatrick, " How can you be so weak as to credit any idle story of my being to be called to the English bar, or to stay in this country? I am wedded to Ireland for life, whatever may be my dower. I do believe that if I chose I could be Master of the Rolls in *this* country. But keep this fact to yourself. I would not accept the office of English Chancellor. In short, my ambition and my pride, as well as my first and most sacred duty, bind me to struggle for her, and I will struggle for her." How well the sentiments expressed in this letter accord with the resolve recorded by the writer six-and-thirty years before.

In his letter to the Earl of Shrewsbury defending his claim to the repeal rent, he writes, " The year before emancipation, though wearing a stuff gown, and belonging to the outer bar, my professional emoluments exceeded £8,000, an amount never before realised in Ireland in the same time by an outer barrister.

" Had I adhered to my profession, I must have

been called within the bar, and obtained the precedency of a silk gown. The severity of my labour would have been mitigated, whilst the emoluments would have been considerably increased. I could have done a much greater variety of business with less toil, and my professional income must have necessarily been augmented by probably one half.

" If I had abandoned politics, even the honours of my profession and its highest stations lay fairly before me.

" But I dreamed a day-dream—was it a dream? That Ireland still wanted me; that although the Catholic aristocracy and gentry of Ireland had obtained most valuable advantages from emancipation, yet the benefit of good government had not reached the great mass of the Irish people, and could not reach them unless the Union should be made a reality, or unless that hideous measure should be abrogated.

" I did not hesitate as to my course. My former success gave me personal advantage such as no other man could easily procure. I flung away the profession; I gave its emoluments to the winds; I closed the vista of its honours and dignities; I embraced the cause of my country : and, come weal or come woe, I have made a choice at which I have never repined, nor ever shall repent.

" High professional promotion was placed within my reach. The office of the Lord Chief Baron of the Exchequer became vacant. I was offered it, or had I preferred the office of the Master of the Rolls, the alternative was proposed to me. It was a tempting offer. Its value was enhanced by the manner in which it was made, and pre-eminently so by the person by whom it was made—the best Englishman that Ireland ever saw, the Marquis of Normanby. But I dreamed again a day-dream—was it a dream?—and I refused the offer. And here am I now taunted, even by you, with sordid motives."

It was in 1838 that he received the offer of being made Chief Baron. "On the morning that he received it," says O'Neill Daunt (*Personal Recollections*, i. 36), "he walked to the window, saying, 'This is very kind, very kind indeed, but I haven't the least notion of taking the offer. Ireland could not spare me now. Not but that, *if she could*, this office would have great attractions for me. . . . In fact, I should enjoy the office exceedingly on every account if I *could* but accept it consistently with the interests of Ireland, but I cannot.'"

"I'll take nothing for myself while Ireland wants me," said O'Connell to a friend who suggested that a seat in the House of Lords, with the title of Viscount O'Connell, would be a glorious termination to his political career.

Though O'Connell felt able to say of himself to O'Neill Daunt, "If I know myself well, I really do think I never did any one action with a view to fame," yet there can be no doubt but that he had a healthy desire for distinction, but distinction won in the field where success was gained by honourable and peaceful means, and meant a triumph for the cause of his country, and the liberties of mankind. "What thou wouldst highly, that wouldst thou holily," might with justice have been written of O'Connell.

His devotion to liberty is shown by the Journal to have been real and passionate. In the first entry that is extant he displays his contempt for those who would persuade him that the slave loved his chains and mourned over their loss. One of the books that he read through was *The Manual of Liberty*. Over and over again he records his attachment to the great principle of human freedom. On December 29th, 1796, he writes, "I love, from my heart I love, liberty. I do not express myself properly. Liberty is in my bosom less a principle than a passion. . . . The liberty which I look for is that which would increase the happiness of mankind. In the service of that liberty I have devoted my life and whatever portion of talents I may have or acquire." On January 22nd in the following year he tells us that he and Dawson and Bennett "talked some pure, because moderate, democracy," and then follows this outburst: "Hail, Liberty! How cheering is thy name. How happy would mankind be if thou wert universally diffused." On March 24th he writes again, "I love liberty—and this is a moment fit for indulging reflection on that subject—I love liberty as conducive to increase the portion of human happiness."

These were not mere words. O'Connell never lost an opportunity of putting the principles here enunciated into practice. When, for example, the fate of the English Reform Bill of 1832 hung in the balance, O'Connell boldly pronounced in its favour, and it was carried by the votes of his followers in the House of Commons, though this particular Bill was afterwards thrown out on an amendment. At a meeting of the National Political Union held in January, 1832, O'Connell was urged to oppose the Bill because equal justice was not done to Ireland. He refused. "I will ever," said he, "assist those who are struggling for freedom, no matter what their creed, nation, or class may be, without reference to its effect on our claims."

Many other instances of O'Connell's active support of the principles enunciated in his Journal might be given. Thus on May 17th, 1830, he spoke in favour of the Bill for the removal of Jewish disabilities. "He should," he said, "support the Bill on the principle of toleration, if that were not an improper word to be used on such an occasion. Perhaps he should have said the principle of right." He was in favour of universal suffrage and vote by ballot, as his speech on the National Petition delivered on May 3rd, 1842, and his speech on the Address delivered on August 27th, 1847, will attest. He was, as

O'Neill Daunt records (*Personal Recollections*, ii.
112), in favour of international arbitration, one of
his day-dreams being that the Pope should be the
arbitrator.

O'Connell said that all the principles of his subsequent political life were contained in his first speech,
namely that which he made in opposition to the
Union on January 13th, 1800.   It would be
equally true to say that those principles were contained in his Journal.   Political consistency is not
necessarily a virtue, for it may be, and often is, the
outcome of prejudice, or self-interest, or obstinacy,
or ignorance, or stupidity.   But when it is the off-
spring of sound principles, rooted in honest conviction, the result of study and reflection, and when
it is displayed in the face of obloquy, and at the
cost of great personal sacrifices, then it is indeed a
noble trait of character.   To political consistency of
this lofty type could O'Connell justly lay claim.

Whether the study of Adam Smith's *Wealth of
Nations* extended beyond that part of the work
which deals with the benefits derived from division
of labour does not appear from the Journal.   But
it seems probable that he read beyond this point, as
he was strongly in favour of Free Trade, so far, at
any rate, as regarded corn.   His letter to the Earl
of Shrewsbury, who sought by means of a pamphlet
that he published to enlist the Catholics on the side
of the corn laws on religious grounds, is one of
the most brilliant attacks on Protection and one of

the most powerful defences of free trade in food ever penned. O'Connell denounced in scathing language the attempt thus made by this Catholic nobleman to uphold what he described as "the hard-hearted iniquity of the corn laws," "the grinding bread-tax." In his speech on the Address, August 27th, 1841, he said, "Indeed, Ireland illustrates the fallacy of some of the topics used by the supporters of these laws. It is said that they increase the rate of wages. If they have that operation anywhere, surely it is in Ireland. Ireland has the full benefit of the corn laws, and yet *there* is the rate of wages lower than in any part of the kingdom. Ireland is an agricultural country: you have taken care that she shall not be a manufacturing country; but people see distinctly that corn laws do not raise the rate of wages, and they feel, and I feel, that it is a robbery upon the operative to make him pay more for his bread than his earnings enable him to pay."

Having regard to the part which duelling played in O'Connell's public life, the passage in his Journal dealing with this practice possesses considerable interest. He had a quarrel with a Mr. Douglas Thompson, the son of a brewer in Chiswick, who sent him a letter demanding an explanation of some strong language that O'Connell had used towards him. Having no "friend" available to carry a message, O'Connell called on Thompson in person, and discussed the matter standing at the street door of Thompson's father's house. Thompson was so little satisfied with their interview that he rushed into the house and got a cane, with which he struck O'Connell, who, though much his superior in strength and armed with a heavy cane, did not return the blow, but contented himself with seizing his assailant. The sequel will be found described in the Journal under the date December 29th, 1795, and subsequent entries. His observations on this incident are curious and characteristic. He discusses duelling in quite a philosophic spirit. " I reflect with pleasure," he says, "on the courage which I *felt* on this occasion. All I have to fear is precipitation in plunging myself in future quarrels. I know that duelling is a vice ; yet there is a charm in the independence which it bestows on a man that endears it even to many thinking minds. I have, however, made a resolution not to fight a duel from the time that I become independent of the world." The courage which O'Connell felt on this occasion he displayed on that of his famous duel with D'Esterre ; but that species of courage he renounced for ever after. In his speech on the police trials in Ireland, replying to Doherty, the Irish Attorney-General, he said, "I will not be deterred from doing my duty fearlessly by any man, however he may be supported. In saying *fearlessly* I allude not to that species of courage which is recognised in a court of honour, and of which I know nothing. There is blood upon this hand ; I regret it deeply, and he knows it. He knows that

I have a vow in heaven, else he would not have ventured to address to me such language, or to use those taunts which in this House he has safely resorted to."

It has been thought advisable to prefix to the Journal a sketch of O'Connell's life during the period anterior to the commencement of that record of his sayings and doings, so as to enable the reader better to appreciate what he will there find set down by the Liberator himself. This, with the Journal itself and the notes appended to it, will form as complete a biography of O'Connell during the first six or seven-and-twenty years of his life as can be compiled from the materials available for the purpose.

The Editor has to express his thanks to Mr. John Murray for permission to quote from Fitzpatrick's *Correspondence of Daniel O'Connell*, to Mrs. Morgan John O'Connell for permission to quote from *The Last Colonel of the Irish Brigade*, to the Rev. Matthew Russell, S.J., for permission to quote from the *Irish Monthly*, to Cassell & Co., Ld., for permission to quote from *The Life of Daniel O'Connell*, by MacDonagh, to Mr. T. Fisher Unwin for permission to quote from *A Life Spent for Ireland*, to Mr. Peter Rayleigh for permission to quote from his *History of Ye Antient Society of Cogers*, and to Mr. Daniel O'Connell of Darrynane, and many friends for valuable information and assistance.

SKETCH OF THE LIFE OF DANIEL O'CONNELL UP TO THE DATE OF THE COMMENCEMENT OF HIS JOURNAL.

Birth and Parentage.

DANIEL O'CONNELL was born on August 6th, 1775, and was therefore in his one-and-twentieth year when the first entry in his Journal was made. He was the eldest son of Morgan O'Connell, of Carhen, in the county of Clare, a gentleman farmer, and Catherine O'Mullane, of Whitechurch, county Clare. The other sons were Maurice, John, and James, the last mentioned of whom was created a baronet in 1869. His parents were married in April, 1771, in the Protestant church of the Holy Trinity, Cork.[1] The licence granted by the Protestant bishop is dated April 16th, 1771, and is preserved in the Record Office, Dublin, where it was discovered by Mr. Valentine Coppinger, an Irish barrister. All Catholics who expected to inherit landed property took out these Protestant licences, but were married by their own priests.[2] Why the marriage of

[1] *Life of Daniel O'Connell*, by MacDonagh, p. 4.
[2] *The Last Colonel of the Irish Brigade*, by Mrs. Morgan John O'Connell, vol. i. p. 158.

O'Connell's father and mother should have been solemnized in a Protestant place of worship, as well as by a clergyman of their own Church, which no doubt it was, it is not easy to understand. But the object may have been to avoid the risk occasioned by the Irish statute 19 Geo. III. c. 19, which enacted that every marriage celebrated by a popish priest between a Papist and a person that had been, or had professed to be, a Protestant, at any time within twelve months of such celebration, should be null and void.

The great Tribune came of an ancient stock. There is said to be in the British Museum an original manuscript in Irish—though the Editor has not been able to trace it—which records that in the year 1245 a Daniel O'Connell advanced, at the head of a considerable body of men, to the north of Ireland, to repel the incursions of an invading force from the land of Morven, supposed to be Scotland; that he defeated the invaders, and having become on friendly terms with them, fell in love with one of their people, a beautiful maiden, named Agandecca; that, her affections having been already bestowed, she repelled his advances, and that he resolved to carry her off, but was foiled by her flight into her own country, where he did not think it prudent to pursue her.[1]

---

[1] *Memoirs, Private and Political, of Daniel O'Connell*, by Huish, p. 8. See below, n. *m*, p. 131.

Mrs Morgan O'Connell.
Mother of Daniel O'Connell
Reproduced by permission
From an unpublished picture in the possession of
Sir Morgan Ross O'Connell, Bart. of Lake View Co. Kerry.

The names Morven and Agandecca appear in Macpherson's *Ossian*. The name O'Connell, or rather O'Conal, appears in a commission issued by Edward III. in 1337 to Hugh O'Conal to reduce some refractory tribes in Limerick. It recurs in public records in the years 1372, 1421, and 1490. One of the family, named Maurice, took up arms in defence of the pretender Perkin Warbeck, but was pardoned in 1496. A Morgan O'Conal undertook to pay a rent of twenty pence Irish to Henry VIII. as a recognition of his authority, and was High Sheriff of Kerry in the following reign. His son Rickard served in the army of Queen Elizabeth against the rebels of Desmond. One of the family, named Daniel, of Ahavore, held. aloof from the rebellion of 1641, and so saved his property in Iveragh.[1]

An ancestor of the Liberator fought at the head of a regiment for James II., a fact to which he referred in his speech in the House of Commons made on July 31st, 1840, in support of the Melbourne Ministry.

The O'Connells were originally settled in Limerick, but were compelled to retreat to Iveragh, in the county of Kerry. On December 14th, 1653, an ancestor of the Liberator, Maurice, of Caherbearnagh, was transplanted by Cromwell in extreme old age. He died on the way, but his family proceeded into exile, with their

---

[1] *Life and Times of Daniel O'Connell*, by O'Flanagan, vol. i. pp. 14, 15; Burke's *Landed Gentry*.

servants, flocks, and herds, and settled in a district called Briantree, or Brentree, near Lisdoonvarna, in the county of Clare.[1] A descendant of this Maurice known as Donal Mor, or Big Daniel, of Darrynane, married Mary O'Donoghue, known as Maur-ni-Dhuiv, or Mary of the Dark Folk, granddaughter, or at any rate a blood relation, of Donal Mahony, of Dunloe, whom Froude (*English in Ireland*, vol. i. p. 452) refers to as the terrible Papist that ruled South Kerry with his four thousand followers.[2] Donal Mor it was who in 1740 built that house at Darrynane[3] which was destined to become a

---

[1] *The Last Colonel of the Irish Brigade*, vol. i. p. 2 ; vol. ii. p. 312. Fifty-nine persons are said to have accompanied Maurice. He is buried in a rude tomb, bearing, in Irish, the inscription, " The burial tomb of the O'Connells, lords of Braintree. Pray for Raghnall, the Brave O'Connell" (*ib.* vol. ii. p. 18). According to Burke (*Landed Gentry*) this branch became extinct in 1749 on the death of Rickard O'Connell, of Brentree. He traces the descent of Daniel O'Connell to John O'Connell, of Ahavore and Darrynane, father of Daniel, who married Maur-ni-Dhuiv.

[2] *The Last Colonel of the Irish Brigade*, vol. i. pp. 7, 51 ; vol. ii. p. 203.

[3] The etymology of this word is debatable. O'Connell derived it from the two Irish words *darragh*, an oak, and *inane*, ivy—the Ivied Oaks (*Personal Recollections*, i. 168). O'Flanagan disputes this derivation, and suggests that it comes from words which signify a solitary oak forest (*Life and Times of Daniel O'Connell*, i. 4, note). Mrs. Morgan John O'Connell thinks it means St. Finan's Oak Wood (*The Last Colonel of the Irish Brigade*, i. 5). Fitzpatrick says " Darrinane, the Oak Grove of Finan, whose ancient church is shown a few miles

historical edifice. Of the union of Donal Mor and Maur-ni-Dhuiv there were issue twenty-two children, twelve of whom, four sons and eight daughters, grew up. John, the eldest of the sons, died in youth. The second of them, Maurice, was familiarly known as Hunting-cap, "Murrish-a-Cauppeen," from the velvet headgear which, after a tax had been put upon beaver hats, he invariably wore. Mrs. Morgan John O'Connell, in the Preface to her interesting *Life of General Count O'Connell*, gives the following graphic account of Hunting-cap:—" His " —Count O'Connell's — " brother Maurice, witty, wealthy, and wise, was a remarkable man in his own way. He lived in seeming seclusion and voluntary obscurity, yet amassed a great fortune in spite of the anti-Popery laws, and carried on a most interesting political correspondence with the leading Protestants of his county. We find him about to be tried for his life in 1782, and appointed a deputy governor for Kerry a few years later."[1] He

from the O'Connell residence " (*Correspondence of Daniel O'Connell*, p. 3). The word comes apparently from *Doire Fhionain*, the " Fh " being silent.

[1] *The Last Colonel of the Irish Brigade*, vol. i. p. viii. The obscurity in which the wild and remote region of Kerry was at this time wrapped was very favourable to the acquisition of property by Catholics living there. Its effect in this direction will appear from an extract from a Kerry paper accounting for the omission of the O'Connells from Smith's *History of Kerry*, quoted by O'Flanagan (*Life and Times of Daniel O'Connell*, p. 3). Smith was hospitably entertained by O'Connell's grandfather,

married, but had no children, and watched over the fortunes of his nephews, of whom the illustrious Daniel was one. Many references will be made to him in the course of this sketch, as he had a great influence on the career of the subject of it.

The third of the sons of Donal Mor and Maur-ni-Dhuiv who reached man's estate was Morgan, the father of Daniel O'Connell.

The fourth was General Count O'Connell, whose name is also closely associated with the career of the Liberator. He entered the service of France in 1761, being then in his sixteenth year. Four of his cousins sailed from Darrynane harbour in the same ship that, if we are to believe the poem from which an extract is given below, bore away eighteen Irish recruits for the French army. Maur-ni-Dhuiv, a woman of great talent, reckoned among her gifts that of song, and one of her efforts was a lament composed on the departure of the vessel which

who gave him valuable information about the county. Smith offered to insert in his history a tribute to the virtues and heroism of the clan Connell. The offer was declined. His host made answer, " We have peace and comfort here, Mr. Smith. We love the faith of our fathers, and amidst the seclusion of these glens enjoy a respite from persecution. If man is against us God is for us. He gives us wherewithal to pay for the education of our children in foreign lands, and enough to assist their advancement in the Irish Brigade ; but if you mention me or mine the solitude of the sea-shore will no longer be our security. The Sassenach will scale the moun-tains of Darrynane, and we shall be driven upon the world without house or home."

conveyed her son to the scene of his future distinctions. It was written in Irish. The following
lines, from a translation made by Father Charles
O'Connor, Kerry, will enable the reader to understand the feelings with which the exiled Celt and
the kinsfolk he left behind regarded the race by
which they were ruled :—

" To your bark, brave boys, haste !
    In our haven's deep strait is a sail ;
  On through the shallows and o'er the watery waste
    For France, with my blessing on the gale !
  To the land of the lily bear the shamrock of our isle ;
    May they bloom above the blood-stained rose !
  Ye are safe upon the wide sea : the cruiser lags a mile ;
    God be praised ! ye have baffled your foes.

       *   *   *   *   *

" My sons and my nephews, we are one ;
    One red stream is flowing in our veins :
  My blessing, then, will follow with the radiant sun,
    And my fervent prayers when dark night reigns.
  Ye go your ways. A greater chief from me shall yet be born
    To triumph over ocean's haughty lord.
  Remember in your hearts the Sassenach's foul scorn ;
    In his breast find a sheath for your sword."[1]

The " greater chief " was indeed born. He
triumphed over " ocean's haughty lord." But it
was a peaceful triumph, won, not by finding in his
breast a sheath for the sword, but by planting there
some small sense of the injustice which drove the
flower of the Irish race into the service of his

---

[1] *The Last Colonel of the Irish Brigade*, i. 68.

bitterest foe. The " greater chief " was essentially a man of peace, a friend of law and order, a lover of justice, passionately devoted to liberty, as even the fragmentary Journal that he kept as a record of his actions and his opinions will testify. By his energy and his eloquence, gifts which he inherited from Maur-ni-Dhuiv, he secured for Catholics on both sides of the Irish Sea that religious equality which had been denied them for three dark centuries.

Count O'Connell was first attached to the regiment of the Royal Swedes ; but in October, 1769, he entered the Irish Brigade, then commanded by Colonel Meade, and afterwards, in 1775, incorporated with the Irish infantry regiment of Berwick. He subsequently went back to the Royal Swedes as lieutenant - colonel. The foreign regiments in the French service were disbanded about 1791. The Count joined the Royalist forces, escaped to England in 1792, and engaged in the formation of the (English) Irish Brigade, which took service in the West Indies.[1]

Infancy and Childhood.

Daniel O'Connell is said to have been born in the hut of a ferryman, his mother having been taken suddenly ill on hearing of the tragic death of a near

[1] *The Last Colonel of the Irish Brigade*, i. pp. 72, 148 ; ii. 97, 107, 142.

relative.[1] But he gave a different account to O'Neill Daunt: "O'Connell and I were standing on the high grounds at Hillgrove which overlook his birthplace. Carhen House, where his father lived, is now in ruins. He pointed to the crumbling walls, and said, 'I was born there, but not in the house whose ruins you see. I was born in a house of which there is now no vestige, and of which the materials were used in constructing the house now dilapidated.'"[2]

O'Connell was sent to nurse to the wife of his father's herdsman, who lived in a cabin on the Iveragh mountains, and remained until he was in his fourth year.[3]

O'Connell's earliest recollection was of an incident that occurred in 1778, when he was only three years old. The celebrated Paul Jones having got the command of three French vessels of war to cruise in the Irish seas and the English Channel, arrived off the headlands of Kerry, where he was becalmed. The tide was running strongly between the Skelligs rocks and Valentia harbour, and his ships were in so dangerous a position that boats were sent ahead to tow them out to sea. A breeze sprang up, and signals were made for the boats to

---

[1] MacDonagh, *Life of O'Connell*, p. 4.
[2] *Personal Recollections*, vol. ii. p. 118. O'Connell's parents lived for a short time after their marriage at Darrynane (*Last Colonel of the Irish Brigade*, ii. 161).
[3] MacDonagh, *Life of Daniel O'Connell*, p. 8.

cast off and come alongside. His vessels were partially manned, however, by English and Irish sailors who had been taken prisoners, and had either been compelled to serve, or had elected to do so in order to escape the horrors of their prison at Brest. Two of the boats' crews, consisting of some of these prisoners, disregarded the signals and pulled for shore. They reached Valentia harbour, and were hospitably entertained by a gentleman of the neighbourhood, who, however, sent to Tralee, and obtained a military guard, to whom he delivered them up. O'Connell was taken in his nurse's arms to see them marched away from Tralee. One of them made a great impression on him. This man, who seemed, as O'Connell put it, to be "the lawyer of the party," declaimed loudly, from the back of the grey nag he was riding, against the injustice done him and his shipmates.[1]

MacDonagh relates two incidents that occurred in the infancy of O'Connell. "Just before he left the dwelling of the herdsman a wedding took place there. It was attended by a crowd of the neighbours, with the usual drinking and merrymaking. He returned to Carhen a precocious and observant child, and noticing how frequently parties assembled under its hospitable roof for dinner or dance, he asked his mother in Irish, 'Is there a wedding here every night?' On another occasion his father inquired

[1] *Life and Speeches of Daniel O'Connell*, by John O'Connell, p. 4.

of the child whether he had ever fresh mutton for dinner at Teiromoile, the place where he had been nursed. 'Yes,' he replied. 'Where did you get it ? ' asked his father. 'Oh,' said the child, who still regarded the kind folk in the herdsman's hut as his real parents, ' my dad brought in one of Morgan O'Connell's sheep, and killed it.' The father laughed heartily. ' I now know,' said he, ' the fate of my missing sheep.' " [1]

Irish was naturally what one may call his foster-mother tongue, and he spoke it fluently enough to address public meetings in that language.[2] But he did not regret its gradual disuse among the peasantry. " I am sufficiently utilitarian," he said in a conversation at Sir Edward (then Mr.) Bulwer's house, " not to regret its abandonment. A diversity of tongues is no benefit ; it was first imposed on mankind as a curse at the building of Babel. It would be of vast advantage to mankind if all the inhabitants of the earth spoke the same language. Therefore, though the Irish language is connected with many recollections that twine round the hearts of Irishmen, yet the superior utility of the English tongue, as the medium of all modern communication, is so great that I can witness without a sigh the gradual disuse of the Irish." [2]

O'Connell was from his childhood a studious boy. It is told of him that, at the age of four, he learned

[1] MacDonagh, *Life of Daniel O'Connell*, p. 8.
[2] *Personal Recollections*, i. 15.

his letters from David Mahony, one of those itinerant teachers known as "hedge-school masters," who, in the time of the penal laws, went from place to place instructing the Catholic peasantry, and often their betters, in Latin and mathematics, as well as other branches of learning. Dr. Smith, the historian of Kerry, who visited Darrynane in 1751, says of the inhabitants of that county, " The common people are extremely hospitable and courteous to strangers. Many of them speak Latin fluently, and I accidentally arrived at a little hut, in a very obscure part of this country, where I saw some poor lads reading Homer, their master having been a mendicant scholar at an English grammar school at Tralee." [1] Education seems to have been cheap in those days in Ireland. Among the items in the account book of John O'Connell, Daniel O'Connell's uncle, is the following :—" Paid Jasper Lisk, the schoolmaster, for teaching my boy to read, write, and siffre, for a twelvemonth, 1s. 1d." [2]

Curious to relate, the hedge-school still survives in Ireland. Mr. Dalton, one of the inspectors of national schools, in his report printed in the appendix to the last report of the Commissioners of National Education in Ireland, writes,—

" I know of only one locality in the circuit to which the national school system has not yet penetrated;

[1] *The Last Colonel of the Irish Brigade,* i. 4.
[2] *Ib.* 23.

and an application for a building grant in this case was reported on by me during the year. The place is a remote but thickly populated district in the county Clare. It is a peninsular ridge of land running out into the waters of the Shannon ; and the people—half cotters, half fishermen—are cut off a good deal from intercourse with the world around. A hedge-school of the primitive type has been in existence here for, perhaps, a century or more. I visited this institution last year ; and I was much interested, and not a little surprised, to find upwards of thirty boys and girls, assembled under the roof of a little hut, receiving a rudimentary education after a fashion that, I should have imagined, had become obsolete even in the time of their grand-parents. Why it is that this survival of the hedge-school days has held its ground so long before the march of the national school system I cannot explain ; but I could not help feeling that a peculiar and a pathetic interest now attaches to it—an interest recalling the educational and social con-ditions of a period of the country's history that has left depressing memories behind, and blended also with something of the curiosity excited by the discovery of an individual specimen of a living organism after the species had been believed to be extinct.''

The first tutor of the Liberator took the curly-headed blue-eyed boy upon his knee, and combed his tangled locks, with so much more gentleness than the little fellow had been accustomed to when that operation was performed, that he gained the child's confidence and secured his attention while he imparted his first lesson.[1] This was no doubt the occasion upon which O'Connell was taught the alphabet. " I learned the alphabet in an hour. I was in my childhood remarkably quick and persevering. My childish propensity to idleness was overcome by the fear of disgrace. I desired to excel, and could not brook the idea of being inferior to others."[2]

As early as the age of nine O'Connell preferred reading to play. The first book he ever read was Captain Cook's *Voyages round the World.* " I read it," he told O'Neill Daunt, "with intense avidity. When the other children would ask me to play with them I used to run away and take my book to the window that is now converted into a press in the housekeeper's room at Darrynane. There I used to sit with my legs crossed, tailor-like, devouring the adventures of Cook. His book helped to make me a good geographer. I took an interest in tracing his voyages on the map. That was in 1784. I do not think I ever met a book that took a greater grasp of me. There I used to sit reading it, sometimes crying over it, whilst the other children were playing."[3] According to Hamilton, he composed a

---

[1] *Life and Speeches of Daniel O'Connell,* p. 6.
[2] *Personal Recollections,* i. 116.
[3] *Ib.* ii. 78.

drama on the fortunes of the house of Stuart at ten years of age.[1]

O'Connell at the age of nine was not only studious, but ambitious, as will appear from the following incident, which occurred at that early period of his life. A party of friends were one day assembled round his father's table, when the conversation turned on the merits of the leading statesmen of the day: Flood, and Grattan, and Charlemont. The services and eloquence of Grattan became the subject of discussion. As the guests were pretty equally divided on this, a warm debate ensued, during which O'Connell was observed sitting dreamily in an arm-chair, lost in thought. The unwonted gravity of the child's countenance, his abstracted air, attracted the attention of a lady, who said to him suddenly, "What ails you, Dan? What are you thinking of?" He turned, and looking at her, said, "I'll make a stir in the world yet."[2] He said to O'Neill Daunt, "When walking through the streets, soon after some meeting at which I had attracted public notice, I saw a magazine in a window containing a portrait of Counsellor O'Connell. I said to myself with a smile, ' Here are my boyish dreams of glory realised.' I need not tell you that in 1810 I had long outgrown that species of ambition."[3]

[1] Hamilton, *Life of O'Connell*, p. 3.
[2] O'Flanagan, *Life and Times of O'Connell*, i. 27 ; Cusack, *The Liberator : his Life and Times*, 43.
[3] *Personal Recollections*, i. 101.

But, indeed, before he was nine years old, when he was seven—"yes," as he tells us, "as long as I could recollect—I always felt a presentiment that I should write my name on the page of history." "I hated," he says, " Saxon domination; I detested the tyrants of Ireland."[1]   It was the example of his uncle, General Count O'Connell, who left Ireland at the age of fifteen and rose rapidly, that inspired him with an ambition to distinguish himself; but he always had one object in his ambitious views, and that was to do something for Ireland.[2]

In 1785, when less than ten years old, he was witness to a scene of sustained and systematic drunkenness that made a deep impression on his mind.   He was staying at the house of a friend near the seaside.   A sloop came in the whole crew of which got drunk every night, Monday night on wine, Tuesday night on punch, Wednesday night on wine, Thursday night on punch, and so on, the only variety consisting in the alternation.[3]

When he was a child, his father had a narrow escape of being murdered.   A gang of cow-stealers, called Crelaghs, that used to steal cows in Galway

---

[1] *Personal Recollections*, i. 48.

[2] *Ib.* ii. 119. O'Connell, when speaking to Daunt on this subject, stated that his uncle left Ireland at the age of fourteen. But this was a mistake. He was born in 1745, and sailed in 1761, before he was sixteen. He got his commission in the spring of the latter year (*Last Colonel of the Irish Brigade*, ii. 67).

[3] *Personal Recollections*, i. 155.

and Clare and sell them in Kerry, and *vice versâ*, stole fourteen cows belonging to O'Connell's father, who at once collected a body of men and surrounded the hut, in the mountains of Glencara, where they lived. After a desperate struggle, two of the marauders were captured, but the others escaped and continued their depredations. These resolved to avenge themselves on the captor of their comrades. When he was riding out one day he was apprised of their design, and warned to go by a different road from that which he was pursuing. He did so, but encountered the ruffians, who rushed down the hill and fired at him, but missed. The mare he was riding threw him, and the robbers again fired at him when he was on the ground, but again without effect. He mounted and rode off amid a fusillade, escaping unhurt. These miscreants were screened by the Protestant gentry, "colonels," as they were styled, who alone had the privilege of sitting on the magisterial bench, and were bribed by the Crelaghs. Fortunately, however, they committed the mistake of robbing a Protestant gentleman on the high-road. He promptly got himself made a magistrate, and brought the band to justice; the cattle of the Catholic gentry no longer became the prey of thieves, or helped to swell the incomes of their Protestant neighbours.[1]

[1] *Personal Recollections,* i.

Boyhood.

Much is not known of O'Connell's early boyhood. In 1787, at twelve years of age, he was brought to the assizes at Tralee. Assizes were then, he said, a great mart for all kinds of amusement, and he was greatly taken with the ballad singers. " I liked ballads above all things when I was a boy. It was then I heard two ballad singers, a man and a woman, chanting out a ballad which contained a verse I still remember :—

> " ' I leaned my back against an oak ;
> I thought it was a trusty tree :
> But first it bent, and then it broke ;
> 'Twas thus my love deserted me.'

He sang the first two lines ; she sang the third line ; both together sang the fourth line, and so on through the whole ballad."[1] The Irish ballad singers to this day follow the same practice.

O'Connell told Daunt with great glee an amusing incident that occurred when he was a boy, during one of his visits to his uncle at Darrynane.

The hospitality of Hunting-cap was extended to Protestants and Catholics indifferently, and during

---

[1] *Personal Recollections*, i. 135. The lines are taken from a Scottish ballad :—

> " O waly, waly, up the bank,
> And waly, waly, down the brae "

(Cusack, *The Liberator : his Life and Times*, p. 41, n.).

one of O'Connell's sojourns at Darrynane, while he was a boy, two Protestant gentlemen were on a visit there. On Sunday they were reduced to the alternative of going to mass or doing without public worship, as there was no Protestant church near. They chose to go to mass, and on entering the chapel they fastidiously avoided the holy water which the clerk was sprinkling copiously on all sides. The clerk observed this, and feeling his own dignity, and that of the holy water, compromised by their Protestant squeamishness, he quietly watched them after service, and planting himself behind the sanctuary door, through which they had to pass, he suddenly splashed the entire contents of his full-charged brush into their faces. "I thought," said O'Connell to O'Neill Daunt when telling this anecdote, "I should have choked with laughing. You cannot conceive anything more ludicrous than the discomfited look the fellows had." And his fancy was so tickled with the recollection that he chuckled over it.[1]

It appears from an entry in the Journal under date December 31st, 1796, that O'Connell was at a school where a person named Linahan was a master, and O'Neill Daunt tells the following story, which discloses the name of another person who was concerned in his education, but does not seem to have made as favourable an impression on him as the poor hedge-

[1] *Personal Recollections*, i. 48.

school master. When O'Connell was about sixteen years of age, he joined a party headed by Marcus Sullivan (his cousin, mentioned in the Journal under date December 31st, 1796), of which a school-master named John Burke was one, formed to attack a herd of bulls that ranged the island of Deenish—which lies off the coast of Kerry, about five miles from Darrynane Bay—and generally resisted all attempts made by people to land. The battle raged with varying success. The bulls were ultimately defeated, but largely because they fought among themselves and killed each other. When their number had been reduced to six, Marcus Sullivan fired at the largest of the survivors. The ball, grazing his shoulder and tearing the flesh upwards, did not kill the brute, but rendered him furious. He rushed at Marcus, who could only save himself by flinging his person over a high rock that overhung the sea, to which he clung by holding on to the -long grass which grew in the crevices. The bull dashed headlong over the precipice, clearing Marcus in his descent, and was killed by his fall upon the rock some hundreds of feet beneath. There were then only five bulls. Burke presented his piece at one of them, but the bull came on with a rush, and Burke, in his panic, did not fire, but fled for safety to a crevice where the bull could not follow him. O'Connell, in narrating this incident to O'Neill Daunt, remarked, " We youngsters, who had often been pestered with

Mr. Burke's teachings, were sorry the bothering schoolmaster was not killed."[1] Mr. Burke appears to have been a private tutor who taught O'Connell at home.[2]

O'Connell himself had an opportunity of realising the feelings of a person who, like the "bothering schoolmaster," had to face an angry bull. "Walking from Hillgrove to Cahirciveen," writes O'Neill Daunt, "O'Connell said, 'Do you see that large stone in yonder field? It was the scene of an encounter I had with a bull when I was a lad. He ran after me, and my retreat was cut off by a high ditch, so I faced about and threw a stone at his forehead that stunned him. That gave me time before he recovered himself; and in the meantime a number of boys came to my assistance, and stoned him out of the field.'"[3]

An incident in O'Connell's life at this period throws a curious light upon the manners and customs of the Irish bankers and their clerks at that day. "I recollect," he told Daunt, "when I was a younker, my uncle gave me £300 in gold to get changed into notes in Cotter and Kellet's Bank.

[1] *Memoirs of O'Neill Daunt*, p. 205. O'Connell could hardly have been about sixteen when this occurrence took place. As he was born in August, 1775, he was fifteen in 1790, in which year he was sent to Harrington's, and remained there till he went to St. Omer's. Sixteen is the age mentioned by O'Connell himself.

[2] Hamilton, *Life of O'Connell*, p. 3.

[3] *Personal Recollections*, ii. 120.

The clerk, through stupidity, gave me £400, of which £300 were in small notes, and the rest in a £100 note. I pointed out his blunder, and he in a very surly manner, and without looking at the heap of notes, insisted that I must be wrong, for that he never mistook. I persisted. He was sulky and obstinate. At last our altercation arrested the attention of Cotter, who came over and asked what was the matter. I told him I had got £100 too much. He reckoned the money, and then took off the £100 note, saying ' now it was all right.' I begged he would allow me to retain that note, as my uncle was desirous to get the largest notes he could ; and I assure you it was with no trifling difficulty I could prevail on the old gentleman to take his hundred pounds in small notes." [1]

One more incident in O'Connell's life, only a trifling one indeed, remains to be told before coming to the time when his systematic education began. Some private theatricals were performed at Tralee in which O'Connell acted. Among the performers was a young gentleman named Hickson, whose part consisted of the words, " Put the horses to the coach." It was difficult for him to make a mistake, but he did ; for when his turn came he exclaimed, to the intense amusement of O'Connell, " Put the horses *into* the coach."

The surroundings in which O'Connell was born

---

[1] *Personal Recollections*, ii. 40.

and reared had a profound influence upon his character. Darrynane, where he spent much of his time in boyhood, and to which he loved to retire for rest and recreation amid the cares and anxieties of later life, lies in the midst of wild and romantic scenery. " The dwelling-house," says O'Neill Daunt,[1] " is situated within a few hundred yards of a little bay, which is separated from the harbour of Ballinskelligs by a rocky promontory called the Abbey Island. This promontory is sometimes insulated in particularly high tides. It contains the ruins of an ancient abbey, amongst which are the graves of the O'Connell family.

" Much of the adjacent coast appears to have been upheaved in some desperate agony of nature. It consists of patches of unprofitable boggy surface, alternating with *débris* of native rock. But there are some grand and romantic scenes among the hills and on the cliffs.

" The house is sheltered on the north and west by mountains ranging from 1,500 to 2,000 feet in height. On the east the view is bounded by a chain of high rocks that divide the bay of Darrynane from that of Kenmare. Close to the house is a thriving plantation called the shrubbery, covering some ten or twelve acres of most rocky and irregular tract, through the irregularities of which there are many pretty winding walks. In the midst of this shrubbery, perched high aloft upon an ivied rock, is

---

[1] *Personal Recollections*, i. 159.

D

a small circular turret, commanding over the tops of the young trees a view of the ocean and the neighbouring hills. To this turret Mr. O'Connell frequently retired to cogitate in solitude over his future political movements. He had also a favourite walk in the garden, which is picturesquely situated amongst rocks, and contains some of the finest hollies I have ever seen.

" Darrynane contains tolerable accommodation, although it often proved scarcely sufficient for the numbers attracted by the hospitable habits and political celebrity of the owner. It was built at different periods, and without the slightest regard to any uniform plan of architecture. A room was added whenever there arose a demand for increased accommodation, so that the whole mass presents a curious cluster of small buildings of different dates, heights, and sizes. In the dining-room are portraits of Mr. O'Connell, his lady, and his children. The portrait of the Liberator, although an indifferent painting, is, I understand, the very best likeness ever taken of him."

A memento of the old evil days was preserved at Darrynane in the shape of a piece of the skull of a friar hewn down with the sword while saying mass by a soldier of Cromwell. This relic had early made a deep impression on O'Connell, whose eye had often been fixed upon it.[1] In after years he had it buried in the Abbey.

[1] O'Flanagan, *Life and Times of O'Connell*, i. 27.

In October, 1838, O'Connell wrote to Walter
Savage Landor from Darrynane, " Little do you
imagine how many persons besides myself have
been delighted with the poetic imaginings which
inspired those lines on one of the wonders of my
infancy : the varying sound emitted by marine
shells :—

> [Shake me, and it awakens ; then apply
> Its polisht lips to your attentive ear ;]
> 'And it remembers its august abode,
> And murmurs as the ocean murmurs there.' "

The third and fourth lines only were quoted by
O'Connell ; but we have taken the liberty of inserting the two that preceded them. The letter goes
on, " Were you with me amidst the Alpine
scenery surrounding my humble abode, listening to
the eternal roar of the mountain torrent as it
bounds through the rocky defiles of my native glens,
I would venture to tell you how I was born within
the sound of the everlasting wave, and how my
dreamy boyhood dwelt upon imaginary intercourse
with those who were dead of yore, and fed its fond
fancies upon the ancient and long-faded glories of
that land which preserved Christianity when the
rest of now civilised Europe was shrouded in the
darkness of godless ignorance. Yes, my expand-
ing spirit delighted in these day-dreams, till, catching
from them an enthusiasm which no disappointment
can embitter, nor accumulating years diminish, I
formed the high resolve to leave my native land

D 2

better after my death than I found her at my birth,
and if possible to make her what she ought to be,—

'Great, glorious, and free,
First flower of the earth and first gem of the sea.'

Perhaps if I could show you the calm and
exquisite beauty of these capacious bays and mountain promontories, softened in the pale moonlight
which shines this lovely evening, till all which
during the day was grand and terrific has become
calm and serene in the silent tranquillity of the
clear night—perhaps you would readily admit that
the man who has been so often called a ferocious
demagogue is in truth a gentle lover of Nature, an
enthusiast of all her beauties,

'Fond of each gentle and each dreary scene,'

and catching from the loveliness as well as from the
dreariness of the ocean, and the Alpine scenes with
which it is surrounded, a greater ardour to promote
the good of man in his overwhelming admiration
of the mighty works of God."

This " high resolve," formed in his " dreamy
boyhood," lived through his youth, as many a
passage in the Journal testifies, and was the main-
spring of his actions during a manhood characterised by the most unselfish devotion to Ireland.

Count O'Connell, who did not marry till late in
life, and never had any children, took a great
interest in his relatives, and especially in his nephews,

several of whom he succeeded in establishing
advantageously abroad, after having in many
instances obtained for them *bourses* in those educational institutions in connection with which rich
members of the old Irish Catholic families had
founded *bourses* for the benefit of the sons of those
who were not wealthy enough to provide a Con-
tinental education for them. Among those in whom
the Count took a particular interest were the sons
of his brother Morgan. While they were yet
but children, he writes to Hunting-cap on April 16th,
1783,[1] "Pray, how old are Morgan's sons? Are
they stout and promising?" He was at that
time constantly on the look-out among his own
people for recruits for the Brigade who in figure and
in intelligence would be worthy of commissions in
its regiments, and later he was planning, moreover,
getting one of Morgan's sons into the French navy,
for he writes on October 23rd, 1787, "From
the late changes which have taken place in our
Ministry, it becomes uncertain whether I shall be
able to effectuate my expectation of placing brother
Morgan's son in the navy; but on the arrival ot
the new Minister of that department I shall see
what's to be done in that line, and let you know the
measures to be taken."[2] This project appears to
have failed, or at all events to have been abandoned
for the alternative plan of putting John into the

[1] *The Last Colonel of the Irish Brigade*, ii. 9.
[2] *Ib.* 55.

French army.   But from this course the Count dis-
suaded his brother in a letter of May 28th, 1788, in
which he writes, " With regard to our nephew John,
the son of our brother Morgan, my desire is that
you apply him to some other course of life than
mine.   Some late changes in the military constitution of this country are [so] exceedingly unfavourable
to strangers destitute of fortune, that it's destining
them to certain misery to send them over. .   .   . I
therefore earnestly recommend you to look out for
another course of life for your nephews, for, was I
to begin the world over again, I should never engage
in the military service in the present state of
things." [1]   This advice seems to have been
followed, for, as will be seen hereafter, Daniel and
Maurice were destined for the legal profession, and
Hunting-cap determined to send them abroad for a
year and a half to be educated.   Accordingly he
consulted Count O'Connell as to the best place to
send them.   The Count wrote on June 16th,
1789, that he had made all possible inquiries, and
concluded that " the college of St. Omer's is the
most suitable."   He then adds, " I cu'd wish to
know their age exactly, and shall only make one
observation, viz., that colledge education has the sole
advantage of pushing youth to the study of *belles
lettres* by giving them a knowledge of the Greek
and Latin tongues, a tincture of mathematicks, logic,

---

[1] *The Last Colonel of the Irish Brigade*, ii. 70.

and philosophy, and that one year and a half are far from being sufficient for that purpose, and that if your object is to give your nephews a polite literary education, so as to qualify them to appear in the world with some advantage, that purpose can be fulfilled only by resorting to good company, and at no small expense in this country, and also when reason and understanding have acquired a certain degree of maturity." [1]

Events were, however, moving so rapidly on the Continent at this time that the Count writes again on January 14th, 1790, " I am not of opinion that you should send our young nephews to St. Omer's until tranquillity be more solidly established than it is. I shall let you know in April or May my fixed sentiment in the matter, and if things should not bear a prospect of peace I would be very much at a loss where to send them to. . . . You see, dear brother, that it is no easy matter to determine a proper place to send two children without a governor, and I durst not advise you to dispatch them for any part of the Continent till the present clouds be dissipated." [2]

In consequence, no doubt, of this advice, the boys were sent in the spring of the year 1790 to the school kept by Dr. Harrington at Redington, in Long Island, near Cork, which is said to have been the first opened by a priest after the relaxation of the

[1] *The Last Colonel of the Irish Brigade,* ii. 80.
[2] *Ib.* 34.

penal code in 1782.   O'Connell was, he tells us himself, the only boy at that school that was not beaten,
and that this immunity from punishment he owed to
his attention.   One day he was idle, and his teacher,
finding him imperfect in his lesson, threatened to
beat him.   O'Connell shrank from the indignity,
and asked his teacher not to beat him for half an
hour, saying that if he had not learned his lesson by
that time, he might beat him then.   The respite
was granted, and the lesson, rather a difficult one,
was thoroughly mastered in the time.[1]   Christopher
Fagan, the father of William Fagan, M.P., who was a
schoolfellow of O'Connell's at Harrington's, and in
the same class, told his son that O'Connell did not
display any extraordinary precocity of intellect, and
was but an ordinary scholar.[2]

Count O'Connell in a letter of September 2nd,
1790, repeated his warning against sending
the boys abroad.   "I think," he writes, "you must
lay aside all thoughts of sending our young nephews
over.   I know not either in France or the Low
Countries where you can safely send them."[3]

Despite these warnings, however, Hunting-cap
resolved to send the two brothers to be educated
on the Continent by the Jesuits, who originally had
a colony at St. Omer's.

[1] *Personal Recollections*, i. 116.
[2] *The Life and Times of Daniel O'Connell*, by William Fagan,
i. 7.
[3] *The Last Colonel of the Irish Brigade*, ii. 90.

In the end of the year 1790 the boys embarked
at the Cove of Cork in a brig bound for London,
and landed at Dover. The tide being out, they
had to go ashore in a boat. It capsized in the
surf, and Daniel got a ducking.[1] From Dover they
took the packet to Ostend, and proceeded thence
by *diligence*. Sitting opposite to Daniel was a
Frenchman who indulged in violent abuse of
England. O'Connell seemed perfectly satisfied,
and the Frenchman, astonished at his apathy,
after talking a long time, lost patience, and cried,
" Do you hear ? Do you understand what I am
saying, sir?" " Yes," replied O'Connell, " I com-
prehend you perfectly." " And yet," rejoined his
fellow-traveller, "you are not angry." " Not in
the least," said O'Connell. " How," asked the
Frenchman, " can you so tamely bear the censures
I pronounce against your country ? " " Sir," said
O'Connell, " England is not my country. Censure
her as much as you please ; you cannot offend me.
I am an Irishman, and my countrymen have
as little reason to love England as yours, perhaps
less."[2]

A little before this time the Jesuits had removed
from St. Omer's to Liège, so the boys went
there from Ostend by Treykschuyt. When they
arrived they found that Daniel was too old to be
admitted, and they therefore retraced their steps as

[1] *Life and Speeches of Daniel O'Connell*, p. 6.
[2] *Personal Recollections*, ii. 26.

far as Louvain, where they waited for six weeks, until fresh instructions came from home. While there they attended the university schools, and had recourse to the library of the Dominicans, to whom they had letters, and who were very civil to them, as were also the Franciscans.[1] Daniel O'Connell made so good a use of his opportunities that he rose to a high place in a class of one hundred and twenty students.[2]

The boys were directed to go to the English college at St. Omer's. This institution, of which they were destined to be among the last inmates, was founded by Philip II. in 1592, with the object of affording to English and Irish Catholics that higher education which was denied them in their native country. It boasted of many distinguished *alumni*. Among them was Kirwan the traveller, who was a fellow-student of O'Connell. It was closed in 1793, and converted into a military hospital.[2]

The boys travelled from Louvain to Ostend, and thence to St. Omer's by Jurens and Dunkirk. They entered the college in January, 1791. They appear to have been well taught, well fed, and well cared for. O'Connell writes to his uncle Maurice

---

[1] See a letter from Maurice to his uncle, dated January 17th, 1791—1792, written from St. Omer's, which is printed in vol. x. of the *Irish Monthly*, and *Life and Speeches of Daniel O'Connell*, p. 7.

[2] *O'Connell et le Collège Anglais à Saint-Omer*, par Louis Cavrois, 2nd ed. p. 69.

on February 3rd that they were taught the Latin
and Greek authors, French, English, and geography,
besides getting lessons during recreation hours in
music, dancing, fencing, and drawing. Maurice
mentions in the letter above quoted that they were
obliged to speak French.[1]   Daniel appears to have

[1] Fitzpatrick, *Correspondence of Daniel O'Connell*, i. 2.   See
also the following letter from Maurice to his uncle of January
17th, 1792, printed in the *Irish Monthly*, vol. x. p. 336:—

" MY DEAR UNCLE,—I received your affectionate letter
of the 22nd ult., and take the first opportunity of answering it.
The letter which came to your hands last month was, I assure
you, given by me to the President on the 29th or 30th of
October, who said he would write some lines in the end of it,
which, until I received yours, I thought he had done, and
also sent you the college bill and his directions.   For our
college duties I refer you to the letter Dan wrote you on
December 5th.   When I wrote first, I was not acquainted with
them.   Our route from Louvain to Ostend you have seen in
the directions given us in Cork.   The expense was about two
guineas each.   From Ostend we came to Jurens, from thence
to Dunkirk, from thence to this town, the expense two
pounds ten shillings each.   We attended the university schools
whilst at Louvain, and had recourse to the library of the
Dominicans (to whom we had letters), who were very civil to
us, as were also the Franciscans.   I should have mentioned
these circumstances if I had thought you would have been
pleased with it.   I hope you will have no cause to be offended
with me for the future.   I assure you, my dear uncle, the ties
of gratitude, duty, and affection bind me too close to you that I
should willingly give you the least pain, and I find myself very
unhappy at being the cause of your past trouble.   I hope our
future conduct will be such as to merit your entire approbation.
The hope of giving you satisfaction will be a greater induce-
ment to our labouring to fulfil our college duties than the

had lessons in music, for he speaks of his violin in a letter to his uncle of March 21st, 1793, referred to below. It has been frequently alleged that O'Connell had no ear for music, and could not distinguish "Garryowen" from "Rule, Britannia." But if he learned the violin, an instrument that requires in the performer a perception of the most delicate gradations of sound, such is not likely to have been the case.

Daniel studied grammar and poetical composition at St. Omer's, if we are to credit M. Louis Cavrois.[1]

Mathematics was an extra, and cost £12 a year to learn. In a letter of February 3rd, 1791—1792, O'Connell says he had received a letter from his uncle in Paris desiring them to learn mathematics, logic, and rhetoric, but had told him that if he wished them to follow that system of education it would be better to send them elsewhere. "Not that I find the smallest fault with this college, where

profit arising to ourselves thereby. We are all obliged to speak French. Our regulations are well observed, and our living sufficiently good. Give my duty to my grandmother, father, and mother, my love to my brothers and sisters and to all other friends.

"I remain, my dear Uncle,
"Your grateful and dutiful nephew,
"MAURICE O'CONNELL.
"ST. OMER'S, *January 17th*, 1792."

[1] "Daniel fit a Saint-Omer ses classes de grammaire et de poésie" (p. 8).

everything that is taught is sufficiently attended to, the boys taken good care of, and the living good enough." They had theatricals also. He writes in the same letter, " Before the places "—at examination—" are read out there is a scene or two of a play acted on a small stage in the college by one of the first four schools, and of them there are eight in the year; of consequence we compose eight times. There is a whole play acted in the month of August." He adds, " As our trunk was too large to get into our dormitory, we were obliged to get a small wooden box from the Procurator, nailed against the wall of the play-yard. These are here called houses. We keep in it the books and other little things we brought with us." [1]

They had, as he tells his uncle in a letter of June 30th, 1792, a country house in connection with the school, situated in a beautiful valley about a mile from the town, to which all the boys went once a fortnight, and remained a day. " This," he remarks, " renders the summer very agreeable." His school went there on July 1st, 1792, and remained four days, " which are by far the pleasantest." After the preceding Easter examinations the boys began on a new footing. " We now read," he says in a letter of April 16th, 1792, " Mignot's harangues, Cicero, and Cæsar. These are our Latin authors, though they are read over

[1] Fitzpatrick, *Correspondence of Daniel O'Connell*, i. 2.

without any study beforehand. Cæsar is given chiefly to turn into Greek. Our Greek authors are Demosthenes, Homer, and Xenophon's *Anabasis*. Our French one is Dugaro's *Speeches*." He adds in a postscript, " Philosophy is not taught publicly in this college. We have had leave to eat meat during this Lent." [1]

Whether O'Connell learned any mathematics while at St. Omer's is doubtful. The boys were certainly taught arithmetic, for he mentions in the letter of June 6th that he was " in interest." [2] That he was quick at figures is evident from an incident related by himself of a case in which a client of his was sued for a sum of £1,100. While his colleagues were endeavouring to get a verdict by abusing the plaintiff's attorney, he extracted from the books of the defendant figures which showed that the plaintiff owed him £700, a fact of which he convinced the jury, who were much annoyed that they could not find a verdict against the plaintiff for that amount. [3]

O'Connell seems to have made good progress at St. Omer's. In the letter of February 3rd, 1791— 1792, already quoted, he tells his uncle that he had got second in Latin, Greek, and English, and eleventh in French. His study of the last-mentioned language left traces in his pronunciation, for Fagan

[1] Fitzpatrick, *Correspondence*, i. 3.
[2] *Ib.* 4.
[3] *Personal Recollections*, ii. 96.

mentions that he pronounced some words with a French accent, such, for example, as " empire " and " charity," and others having an affinity with their French originals. This, according to Fagan, gave a musical turn to his expressions and an interest to his tones which in after-times went far to increase the captivating effects of his eloquence. The last words he uttered in public were spoken in French. They were in reply to Count de Monta-lambert, who headed the deputation that presented O'Connell with an address from the Catholics of France when he was in Paris on his way to Rome. He spoke but briefly, for, as he said, sickness and emotion closed his mouth.[1] He spoke French fluently, but he refused on one occasion to go over to conduct a case in France, on the ground of want of sufficient command of the language.

English composition does not appear to have been neglected at St. Omer's, for while there O'Connell wrote an essay upon the systems of education pursued in England and France respec-tively which was a very creditable effort for a lad of his years.[2] His two close-pressing rivals while at St. Omer's were the Right Rev. Dr. Walsh, afterwards Bishop of the Midland district of England, and Christopher Fagan, who became a

[1] " My Father as I remember him," by Daniel O'Connell, *Temple Bar*, vol. cxviii. p. 221.

[2] *Memoirs, Private and Political, of Daniel O'Connell*, by Huish. He prints the essay in full.

general in the East India Company's service and Judge-Advocate of the Indian forces.[1]

O'Connell did not neglect athletic exercises while he was at St. Omer's, and he appears to have inspired a wholesome dread of his prowess as a pugilist among his fellow-students. We may be sure that he never used his strength as a bully. He was assuredly the protector of the weak against the strong. An anecdote is told of him that is very significant of his courage and coolness. He inflicted bodily chastisement upon one of his fellow-students for some offence. The offender complained that the French were not in the habit of settling their differences with their fists. O'Connell inquired how they settled them, and on being told that it was with sword or pistol he went away and returned with *one* sword and *one* pistol, the choice of which he offered to his opponent, who, however, declined this rather unusual mode of duelling. But O'Connell was never afterwards provoked to a quarrel, which he would have been quite ready to settle in the fashion, whatever it might be, which his antagonist preferred.[2]

M. Louis Cavrois, in his *O'Connell et le Collège Anglais à Saint-Omer* (p. 82), gives an extract from *Gloires Nouvelles de Catholicisme*, of which the following is a translation :—" The young Daniel,

[1] *Life and Speeches of Daniel O'Connell*, by John O'Connell, p. 7.

[2] Huish, *Memoirs, Private and Political, of Daniel O'Connell*.

by the exceptional retentiveness of his memory, by
the solidity of his judgment, by the quickness of his
intelligence, by the wealth of his imagination, left
all his fellow-students far behind, and obtained
at St. Omer successes as rapid as they were
astonishing. Let us add that, profoundly religious,
but without fanaticism ; pious, but without hypo-
crisy ; lofty of character, but without pride ; strict in
morals, but without austerity ; jovial, but without
dissipation ; docile, but without fickleness [*légèreté*] ;
firm, but without obstinacy ; respectful, but without
servility ; obliging, but without obsequiousness, he
knew how to secure, along with the admiration, the
love of everybody, so that each deemed himself
happy in his friendship and honoured by his
society." If this portrait is not exaggerated—and
from Dr. Stapylton's estimate of O'Connell, quoted
below, the boy was indeed the father of the man—it
becomes easy to understand and appreciate those
passages in his Journal in which he gives vent to
his feelings upon the high themes of virtue, and
liberty, and patriotism.

The Rev. Dr. Stapylton, afterwards Bishop
and Vicar Apostolic of the Midland district of
England, was then president of the college ; and
in reply to an inquiry made by their uncle Maurice
in January, 1792, gave the following account of the
two nephews :—" I begin with the younger, Maurice.
His manner and demeanour are quite satisfactory.
He is gentlemanly in his conduct, and much beloved

by his fellow-students. He is not deficient in abilities, but he is idle and fond of amusement. I do not think he will answer for any laborious profession ; but I will answer for it he will never be guilty of anything discreditable : at least, such is my firm belief. With respect to the elder, Daniel, I have but one sentence to write about him ; and that is that I never was so much mistaken in my life unless he be destined to make a remarkable figure in society."

The difference in disposition between the two brothers here indicated is shown also in the letters of Count O'Connell of December 11th, 1793, and January 26th, 1794, quoted below (p. 47).

Whether it was on account of the troubled state of France at that time, or because philosophy and, perhaps, other branches of learning were not taught at St. Omer's, O'Connell, no doubt at the instance of one or other of his uncles, made inquiries about the college at Douay, for he writes in the letter of June 30th, 1792, " I have learned some other particulars relative to the College Douay since my last, which is that French is paid no great attention to there, nay almost totally neglected. Arithmetic also, it is said, will soon be entirely laid aside."[1] It was resolved that they should go to Douay, and, in accordance with a letter from their uncle Maurice, dated July 17th and received exactly a month later, the boys left St. Omer's on August 18th, 1792, for

---

[1] Fitzpatrick, *Correspondence*, i. 4.

the English college at Douay, where they arrived
the same day. They had brought £10 with them
to St. Omer's as pocket-money, which, as O'Connell
tells his uncle Maurice in a letter of April 16th, 1792,
the President gave the Procurator, to be doled out
to them at the rate of sixpence a fortnight.
Although this must have left a considerable balance
to their credit, and although the Procurator knew
that they would want no inconsiderable sum on
their arrival, all he gave them for their journey to
Douay was a crown apiece. They started before
breakfast, and arrived penniless, to find, to their
astonishment, that the only furniture in their rooms
was a bed for each, as every student was supposed
to bring with him money to furnish his room. They
had no previous intimation that they would have to
provide their own furniture, and they spent their
first night at their new abode in great distress.
Daniel took ill, and had to go to the infirmary; so
it was Maurice who wrote home describing the
situation. A fellow-countryman named Duggan,
from Newmarket, county Cork, came to their rescue.
He advised them to go to the President and explain
their position, which they did, with the result that
he advanced them a guinea and a half, with which
they bought most of the little things necessary for
their rooms, such as looking-glasses, candlesticks,
basins, etc. They had also to spend four shillings
each on buckles, as those worn at St. Omer's were
small iron ones. This exhausted the loan, but

their newly found friend forced them to accept a temporary advance of half a guinea, with which they provided themselves with knives, forks, etc., for refectory. The sums so borrowed would have enabled them to carry on till they should hear from their uncle, but meantime the Procurator, M. Baymont, sent for Daniel and told him that, as he depended on the credit his uncle Maurice had given him, he would provide them with furniture, so they got a desk, a table, " a small table for washing and poudering," and four chairs.

In a letter which is undated, but endorsed September 4th, 1792, Maurice asks for £12 or £13, requests his uncle to mention what he wished them to learn, " as musick, etc.," and promises to send the college rules in his next.[1] It appears that his uncle gave Daniel leave to learn music, for he had a violin when he was leaving Douay. As to philosophy and rhetoric, the course in those subjects had begun the previous Whitsuntide, and Daniel tells his uncle in a letter of September 14th that they had already learned the first principles of the latter, and before they got an answer from him would be able to study it privately for themselves. He points out that if they went into philosophy they would save a whole year ; that they were already studying it in their leisure hours, Mr. Duggan having got them books. He suggests therefore

[1] *The Last Colonel of the Irish Brigade*, ii. 105.

that it would be better for them to go straight into philosophy than remain any longer in rhetoric, as they could get lessons wherever they studied the law, and learn more rhetoric in a month than in a whole year at Douay.[1] It would appear from this letter that both the brothers were originally intended for the legal profession, a fact which shows how groundless is the idea that Daniel was intended for the Church, as many suppose, notwithstanding that O'Connell himself emphatically contradicted it in a letter to the *Dublin Evening Post* of July 17th, 1828.

The commissariat at Douay does not appear to have been altogether satisfactory. The *pension* was twenty-five guineas a year, but Daniel writes in the letter last quoted, "We get very small portions at dinner. Most of the lads (those on bourses excepted) get what they call 'seconds'—that is, a second portion every day—and for this they pay £3 or £4 a year extra ordinary. We would be much obliged to you for leave to get them, but this as you please." In another place he says, "We are obliged to pay for the washing ourselves. At St. Omer's everything was done for the boys; here the boys are obliged to do everything for themselves." But he hastens to add, "This colledge is much better in every respect than the other."

The students at Douay were at this period apprehensive for their safety, fearing that the

---

[1] Fitzpatrick, *Correspondence*, i. 5.

revolutionaries would break in and massacre them ; but they seem never to have been exposed to any real danger. Once, indeed, Daniel O'Connell and some of his companions got a fright when walking for recreation. A waggoner of the army of Dumouriez espied them and shouted, "Voilà les jeunes Jesuites, les Capucines, les recolets." The students fled in panic to the college, which they reached in safety without being pursued.[1] It became impossible, however, for the boys to remain at Douay. On January 17th, 1793, O'Connell wrote to his uncle at Darrynane, "The present state of affairs in this country is truly alarming. The conduct the English have pursued with regard to the French in England makes us dread to be turned off every day. In case of a war with England this is almost inevitable."[2] Louis XVI. was guillotined on January 21st, 1793. The two boys quitted Douay on the same day, and journeyed to Calais. Their carriage was attacked on the way by Republicans, who reviled them, calling them "young priests" and "little aristocrats." The soldiers struck the head of the vehicle several times with their musket stocks as it was starting.[3] When they arrived at Calais

[1] *Personal Recollections*, i. 103. Dumouriez won the battle of Jemappes on November 6th, 1792. Jemappes is in Belgium, thirty-six miles from Douay.

[2] Fitzpatrick, *Correspondence*, i. 7.

[3] Macdonagh, *Life of O'Connell*, p. 17 ; John O'Connell, *Life and Speeches of Daniel O'Connell*, p. 9 ; *Personal Recollections*, i. 103.

the news came that the King had been executed.
The tragic event naturally created great excitement
among the passengers aboard the packet for Dover,
who included the two O'Connells. It is said that
as soon as the packet was under way Daniel
plucked from his hat the tricolor cockade which he
had worn for safety on his journey, and threw it
into the sea, and that some fishermen reverently
rescued it, cursing him the while. The horror
among the passengers created by the tidings of the
French king's death was deepened by an incident
that occurred on the voyage. While they were
discussing and denouncing the barbarous act, two
gentlemen entered, and one of them mentioned that
they were present at the execution, having bribed
two of the National Guard to lend them their
uniforms, at the same time exhibiting a handkerchief stained with the blood of the ill-fated monarch.
An Englishman asked how, in Heaven's name, they
could bear to witness such a hideous spectacle.
The answer astounded the hearers. "For the love
of the cause," was the reply. The two voluntary
witnesses of the " hideous spectacle " were the
brothers Sheares.[1]

From the Journal, entry No. 37, under date
December 31st, 1796, it appears that the lads were
to have gone to Ireland with Darby Mahony and

[1] *Personal Recollections*, ii. 95. It was John Sheares, the
elder of the brothers, who dipped his handkerchief in the King's
blood (Fagan, *Life and Times of Daniel O'Connell*, p. 27).

Marcus Sullivan, but that Count O'Connell intervened, with the result that they were sent to Fagan's, which, it is to be supposed, was the school to be mentioned presently.

Count O'Connell made his escape out of France in the middle of July, 1792, and arrived in London about the end of October.   Soon after the boys left Douay the college was suppressed, and converted into a military barrack.   Daniel writes to his uncle Maurice from London on March 29th, 1793, " I send you by my uncle Dan's orders, though it is not a month since Maurice wrote, the accounts as they came from Douay.   We left most of our furniture, together with my violin, to be sold ; but they have been seized by the municipality, as was every other article which had no particular owner then present, all such goods being considered national property.   When we came to London we had every single article of wearing apparel to buy, and as things are excessively dear here, a large sum of money is soon expended."   He adds in a postscript, "We are satisfied in every respect with our present situation." [1]

It appears from a letter from Daniel to his uncle Maurice, dated October 21st, 1793,[2] that Daniel was sent to school to a Mr. Fagan.   A reference to this fact will be found in the Journal under date December 31st, 1796.   He remained at Mr. Fagan's

[1] Fitzpatrick, *Correspondence*, i. 7.
[2] *Ib.* i. 8.

till a short time before this letter was written. The school was broken up owing to the paucity of pupils, Daniel and a Mr. Waters, nephew of Count Waters, being the only constant boarders there for some time. Daniel went to the house where Maurice had been placed. He learned logic while at this school, for he told his uncle in the same letter that Mr. Fagan thought that on the whole it would turn out much to his advantage, as he had got pretty near the end, and got over almost, if not all, its difficulties.

How the lads were getting on at this time is seen from a letter written by the Count to their uncle Maurice of December 11th, 1793 : " Our two nephews are well and improved in their carriage and demeanour. Dan is indeed promising in everything that is good and estimable, and I hope Maurice will conform to your commands and merit your goodness." [1]

The contrast between the terms in which the Count speaks of his two nephews is significant. Maurice had evidently run counter to Hunting-cap's wishes in some way. Probably he refused to follow the law as a profession. However this may be, he was called to Darrynane. The Count writes on January 26th, 1794, " Our nephews are both well. Maurice will return home with Dan Mahony. . . . Dan shall be entered next week at the

[1] *The Last Colonel of the Irish Brigade*, ii. 121.

Temple, and remove from the present *pension* where he now is to a house more convenient for attending the courts. Mr. Duggan is already a boarder there, and the price is not unreasonable. I have every expectation that our nephew Dan will show himself worthy of your unequalled favours, and I likewise cherish hopes that under your own eye Maurice will acquire that steadiness and solidity of judgment suited to the situation you intend him for." [1] What this situation was can only be a matter of conjecture. Maurice wanted to be a soldier. He had his way, and perished, as recorded in the Journal, in the pestilential climate of St. Domingo.

Count O'Connell was not accurate in saying that the Inn in which Dan would be entered was the Temple. As a matter of fact, he was entered at Lincoln's Inn on January 30th, 1794. He was also entered as a student at Gray's Inn on April 26th, 1796, and kept one term there. Although Inns were established in Ireland for the benefit of students of the law so far back as the reign of Edward I., no Irish lawyer could practise at the bar from the year 1542 down to a recent time without keeping terms at an English Inn. Reference to this matter will be found in a note to the entry under date February 18th, 1796. Why O'Connell entered as a student at Gray's Inn it is

The Last Colonel of the Irish Brigade, ii. 145.

hard to see. Possibly it may have been because his friend Richard Newton Bennett belonged to that Inn, having been admitted on May 7th, 1793.

The arrangement that O'Connell should move from the boarding-house where he was living in January, 1794, to another where Mr. Duggan was already a boarder, seems to have been abandoned, or at any rate to have been adhered to for only a very short time, for Count O'Connell writes to his brother Maurice on March 12th in that year, " Our nephew Dan has been entered at the Temple with the requisite formalities, and is now in private lodgings. I really think from what I have learned, and from what I can compute, that he would be unable to support himself in the most modest gentility under £120 English per annum." [1] The word " English " was inserted because the currencies of the two countries were not assimilated at this time, the English pound sterling bearing to the pound Irish the ratio of thirteen to twelve. From a letter quoted below it would appear that the thrifty old gentleman demurred to this expense.

Some references to O'Connell occur in the Count's letters to Hunting-cap written in the period immediately preceding the commencement of the Journal. In that of March 12th, 1794, already quoted, he writes that "Maurice carries you a translation of the memoir I drew up of the plan of operations for

---

[1] *The Last Colonel of the Irish Brigade*, ii. 148.

the campaign of 1794." Maurice, as appears from the same letter, was to set out with Dan Mahony that afternoon for Dublin, and thence immediately for Cork. On August 21st following he writes, " Poor Dan, our nephew, has had a severe fit of sickness, but is now recovered, and returned to town."[1] That his recovery was maintained appears from a letter of November 6th, in which the writer says, "Dan is very well."[2] In his letter of the 29th of the same month he says, " Dan is in my room, and begs his love and respects to you. He has moved near Lincoln's Inn, and is settled in a family much to his satisfaction."[2]

At this period the half-formed political opinions of O'Connell assumed a definite shape. He had returned from Douay almost a Tory; but the trial, in the autumn of 1794, of Hardy, the secretary of the London Corresponding Society, for high treason, which O'Connell attended, resulted in fully and finally converting him to popular opinions and principles and confirming his natural detestation of tyranny and his desire of resisting it.[3]

O'Connell lived in a *cul de sac* off Coventry Street, London, in 1794.[4] This probably was the place referred to in the Count's letter of November 29th,

---

[1] *The Last Colonel of the Irish Brigade,* ii. 151.
[2] *Ib.* 153.
[3] *Life and Speeches of Daniel O'Connell,* by John O'Connell, p. 11.
[4] *Personal Recollections,* i. 277.

1794, quoted above (p. 49), and is not unlikely to have been Mrs. Tracey's, mentioned in the title-page of the Journal, for no change of residence is referred to in any of the Count's letters after that date.

Early in 1795 steps were taken to enter O'Connell as a student in Dublin. The Count writes on February 26th, " The day after I had written to you I called on Mr. Franks [the family solicitor], and have taken care that every requisite information be given him in writing for the purpose of enabling him to have Nephew Dan entered in Dublin next term, which he pledges himself to do. He showed me a memorial which he presented to that end, in which were several blanks, which I filled in, namely the name of his mother before her marriage, whether he be the eldest son of Mr. Morgan O'Connell, where he had been educated, etc. I fortunately was able to answer all these questions, by which all further difficulties are removed. Dan's letter to Mr. Franks came to Dublin at a time when he was absent; therefore the disappointment, or rather the delay, cannot be imputed to our Dan, because he could not foresee the circumstance. I hope you have before now received his letter which I forwarded you from here, and I beseech you to relieve him from the anxiety he feels lest he might have incurred your displeasure."[1] The Count was equally anxious that

---

[1] *Personal Recollections*, i. 157.

O'Connell should have an adequate allowance. He wrote on March 14th, 1795, " I really spoke from conviction when I told you our nephew could not possibly live in London under £130 or £140 per annum. Every article has risen in price very considerably, and in the line he lives in a certain appearance must be kept up. You know as well as I do that professional abilities, however transcendent, require to be supported by genteel manners and gentlemanly education. Mixing in good company is the only way of acquiring them, and if a young man is obliged, for want of means, to live as a recluse, it cannot be expected that he will appear in the world with all the advantages which the habit of living in good company can alone confer, a consciousness of which is, in my opinion, likely to beget a diffidence and timidity which the world is apt to construe in an uncharitable light. I submit to your better judgment, and believe me, etc." [1]

O'Connell's memorial to be admitted a student of the King's Inns, Dublin, was received on March 4th, 1795, and is signed by J. (probably Jeremiah) Keller. The bond required from all students was executed by John Franks, York Street, Dublin, barrister-at-law, Matthew Franks, of the same street, attorney-at-law, and Henry Wade, of the same street, attorney-at-law. The actual date of his admission as a student is not recorded, but it

---

[1] *The Last Colonel of the Irish Brigade*, ii. 161.

would be the " Grand Day " of Easter term, 1795, which is the second Thursday in that term. Eight gentlemen were admitted students on April 29th, 1795, and no doubt O'Connell was one of them. He did not keep any of his terms at the King's Inns until he returned to Dublin, some time before December 3rd, 1796.

A scrape that O'Connell got into on April 26th, 1795, will be found duly described in the entry in the Journal under date February 18th, 1796.

O'Connell paid a visit to Darrynane in 1795. He set out on June 7th, travelling by way of Milford Haven and Waterford, and returned to London in October of the same year.[1] He gave O'Neill Daunt an account of the return journey: " My first day's journey was to Carhen, my second to Killorglin, my third to Tralee, my fourth to Limerick; two days thence to Dublin. I sailed from Dublin in the evening. My passage to Holyhead was performed in twenty-four hours. From Holyhead to Chester took six-and-thirty hours, from Chester to London three days." [2] The journey, therefore, occupied eleven days and a half. It can now be done in twenty-four hours or less. O'Connell mentions in the Journal below (p. 157) his having been in Iveragh in the summer of 1795, and having hunted there. The following letter from his uncle

[1] Letter from Count O'Connell to Hunting-cap printed in *The Last Colonel of the Irish Brigade*, ii. 168. See below, p. 158.
[2] *Personal Recollections*, i. 136.

Maurice to his mother tells about his doings at this time : " Your son left this ten days ago, and took with him my favourite horse. Had it not been for that, I might have dispensed with his company. He is, I am told, employed ın visiting the seats of hares at Kularig, the earths of foxes at Tarmons, the caves of otters at Bolus, and the celebration of Miss Burke's wedding at Direen—useful avocations, laudable pursuits, for a nominal student of the law ! The many indications he has given of a liberal mind in the expenditure of money has left a vacuum in my purse, as well as an impression on my mind not easily eradicated." This letter is printed in *The Last Colonel of the Irish Brigade* (vol. ii. p. 272). The writer of that work obtained it from the lady known in the family as Miss Julianna, who in her youth had gone to keep house for her aged kinsman. She could not fix the date of the letter ; but as O'Connell never appears to have visited Darrynane while he was a law student but this once, it must have been written during the summer or autumn of 1795.

Having now brought the record of O'Connell's life down to this period, we leave his Journal, which begins towards the close of 1795, to continue the narrative down to June 4th, 1802, when it ends with a statement of the hours of retiring and rising and of the legal work of the day.

The foregoing sketch of O'Connell's life up to the time when he began to keep his Journal will, it is hoped, enable the reader to form a clearer appreciation of the contents of this remarkable record of the pursuits and the studies, the failings and the virtues, the fears and the hopes, the resolutions and the aspirations, of the illustrious man who therein reveals his inmost thoughts, without the smallest idea that one day his written confessions would be read by the public, and would prove to the world that the life which he devoted to the service of his country had been consecrated to that glorious object from the time when he was but a stripling.

The reader will perhaps desire to have some idea what manner of man the Liberator was. The Editor of his Journal saw him once, but it was in the dusk of the evening, and as he was walking between two small men, one of them being Thomas Francis Meagher, and this may have given to a child an exaggerated notion of his size, which seemed immense. O'Connell's cotemporaries have left a full-length portrait of him, and this is what they tell us. His frame was vigorous; his figure was tall and erect. He was broad-shouldered and deep-chested; he had a well-set head. In face he was extremely comely. The features were at once soft and manly; the countenance was national in outline, the expression open and confiding. He had bright and sweet blue eyes, the most kindly and honest-looking. To these natural gifts was added that priceless one a marvellous voice, powerful

—leonine, as Sir Charles Gavan Duffy calls it—
sonorous, penetrating, melodious, capable of expressing every shade of human feeling, " capable of all
modulations in the gamut of passion or persuasion,"
of speaking in the smallest assembly, in the smallest
room, in tones adapted to surroundings so limited,
or of reaching the farthest extremity of an open-
air meeting of hundreds of thousands of people.[1]
Sir Edward Bulwer Lytton finely depicts one of
these scenes :—

> " Once to my sight the giant thus was given,
>   Walled by wide air and roofed by boundless heaven ;
>   Beneath his feet the human ocean lay,
>   And wave on wave flowed into space away.
>   Methought no clarion could have sent the sound
>   E'en to the centre of the hosts around ;
>   And as I thought rose the sonorous swell,
>   As from some church-tower swings the silvery bell,
>   Aloft and clear, from airy tide to tide ;
>   It glided easy, as a bird may glide,
>   To the last verge of that vast audience sent ;
>   It played with each wild passion as it went."

But a voice is nothing without a command of
words, and words are nothing where ideas are lack-
ing. O'Connell had an abundance of both. Poetic
fancy and homely wit, delicate humour and deep
pathos, subtle flattery and bitter sarcasm,· gentle

---

[1] At the " monster " meetings held in 1843 the attendance
ranged from 150,000 at Drogheda and Tullamore, for example,
to 700,000 at Clare and Tara (O'Flanagan, *Life and Times of
Daniel O'Connell*, pp. 679, 680).

persuasion and fierce denunciation, each, as the occasion required, flowed in an inexhaustible stream from those eloquent lips, to charm or to amuse, to persuade or to dismay. Nor was it the masses alone that fell under the spell of his eloquence. Judges and juries bowed to its influence. During the last hour of his practice at the bar he kept the court alternately in tears and in roars of laughter, as he tells us himself.[1] The effect he produced in Parliament may be gathered from the following extracts from a letter addressed to Mr. Edward Dwyer :—

" London, *November 3rd*, 1830.

" My dear Friend,—The scene last night in the House was a most extraordinary one. There never was yet any man so beset as I was when I went into the House, and during the first speeches every allusion to me of an unkind nature was cheered. Although Peel attacked me directly, he sat down amid rapturous applause. I got up at once. They at first were disposed to slight me, but I rebuked them with indignation, and certainly took my wicked will of them fully and to my heart's content. I cannot be a judge of my own speaking, but I know that I threw out in my old Association style. I also know that the result was most cheering for me, for the men who had been standing off from me before, and were not only cool, but hostile, became of a sudden most cordial in their manner and confidential in their declarations. One perceives a change of this description better than they can describe it, and the change was complete. . . . There has been a respectable tradesman in here this moment. He says he belongs to a society who read the newspapers in Paternoster Row, and he came to know whether my speech in the *Morning*

[1] *Life of O'Connell*, by J. A. Hamilton, p. 12.

Chronicle was genuine, because if it were they had entered into a subscription to get it printed and distributed gratis. I of course assented, so, you see, the thing works. Every moment convinces me more and more of the certainty of our repealing the Union. Last night was, in my judgment, almost decisive of it. The House *will* yield to the unanimous petitions of the people."

Such was O'Connell in public. In private life he was the most delightful of companions. His gaiety was exuberant. "When he laughed," said a prelate of the Catholic Church in Ireland to Miss Cusack, who edited the Liberator's public letters and speeches, "he laughed in every inch of his body."

Yet this was the man whom the poets of the *Times* newspaper described as "the long-tailed Irish baboon," and as "a foul creature of the sun and slime," the slime, be it observed, being "slime condensed of Irish bog"! But every Irishman who takes a prominent part in the struggle for the legislative independence of his country must be prepared to see himself made the butt of the clumsy wit and coarse invective of those who deem the Union a thing so precious as to be worth the heavy price that has been paid for it, in the brutalities and the corruption by which it was carried, and the misery and discontent which have followed in its train.

JOURNAL [a]

[a] This word is written, in letters resembling print, on the cover, which is of cardboard, with a marbled pattern upon it.

D.C.   G

A JOURNAL

FOR THE YEARS 1795 AND 1796

AND 1797 AND 1798

AND 1799

KEPT BY D. O'CONNELL

MEMBER OF LINCOLN'S INN

Containing Remarks on the Events of the Day;
Thoughts on Various Subjects; Anecdotes;
Speeches; Quotations, &c., &c., &c.

LONDON, AT MR. TRACEY'S, FROM NO. 1 TO NO. 3.

CHYSWICK, AT MRS. RIGBY'S, FROM NO. 3 TO NO. 25.

DUBLIN, AT MRS. JONES'S, FROM NO. 25 TO NO. 70.

DUBLIN, AT NO. 14, TRINITY PLACE, FROM NO. 70 TO (*b*).

(*b*) This forms the title-page to the Journal. The word
"years" was originally "year," the "s" being added when

the Journal was continued in the year 1796. The word and figures "and 1799" are placed below a horizontal line, as shown above. "And 1797" was added on January 5th of that year, as appears from entry No. 39. After a break from February 4th, 1799, the Journal is resumed on June 1st, 1802, but only for three days.

"Remarks on the Events of the Day"—so far, at any rate, as public events are concerned—are but few, and are very far between. Occurrences of great moment, both to O'Connell himself and to Ireland, happened in the period covered by the Journal, but no reference to them is to be found in it. His call to the bar, which took place on May 19th, 1798, is not recorded, though it must have been a great relief to him to find that the doubt he felt whether, having regard to "the complexion of affairs," as he writes under date January 13th, 1798, he would be called, was set at rest. A discreet silence, too, is observed with respect to the rebellion that took place the same year. The only mention of that event in the Journal is a conversation with his friend Bennett, recorded on January 2nd, 1799, in the course of which they "talked much of the late unhappy rebellion." Even the Union finds no place in the Journal. Not that O'Connell did not feel deeply on the subject, for his first public speech, made at the Royal Exchange, Dublin, on January 13th, 1800, was against that measure. He was in Dublin when the Act of Union was passed, and how deeply he felt at the time can be judged from what he said to O'Neill Daunt : " I was maddened when I heard the bells of St. Patrick's ringing out a joyful peal for Ireland's degradation, as if it were a glorious national festival. My blood boiled, and I vowed on that morning that the foul national dishonour should not last, if ever I could put an end to it " (*Personal Recollections of O'Connell*, by O'Neill Daunt, i. p. 202). As O'Connell was not married until June 23rd, 1802, and the Journal ceases on the 4th of that month, there could, of course, be no reference in it to the actual celebration of the marriage ; but it is somewhat remarkable that the approaching event is not hinted at in any way : there are no apostrophes to Mary, as, five years before, there were to "sweet Eliza." Two events of the day were chronicled in the Journal. One was the attack made in 1795 on George III. in St. James's Park, during which O'Connell had a narrow escape from being cut down by a dragoon. From the "number," to use O'Connell's own term, under date January 5th, 1797, it appears that this occurrence was recorded in the first entry in the Journal, which, with the second and part of the third, has been torn out. The incident will be found fully described in a note to entry No. 39. As it occurred on October 29th, 1795, the Journal must have been commenced on or after that date. The other of the public "events of the day" recorded in the Journal is the change which commenced with the dismissal of the Duke of Leinster from his place in the Hanaper Office, referred to under date May 1st, 1797. The rest of this entry and the whole of the following entry are torn out.

If the Journal is poor in remarks on the events of the day, it is rich in "Thoughts on Various Subjects." The principal subjects, and O'Connell's thoughts upon them, will be found collected in the Introduction, to which the reader is therefore referred.

Anecdotes or speeches are not to be found in the Journal. Quotations are few. Among them there are one from Akenside, on December 31st, 1795, one from Shakespeare, on December 24th, 1796, and one from Adam Smith, on December 3rd, 1796. The Journal abounds, however, in passages giving the substance of what O'Connell read from day to day.

The Journal refers to an incident that occurred before its commencement, namely the scrape that O'Connell got into on April 26th, 1795, which is recorded in the entry numbered 24, under date February 18th, 1796.

[3] (c) I met De Vignier to-day. He is about to go off to St. Domingo. He told me that the emancipated French negroes were tired of liberty ;

that they wished for, nay, called for, their ancient slavery. I will not detail the causes which, according to him, have stirred up this unnatural hatred of freedom in the bosoms of men who certainly experienced few of the *sweets* of despotism. I have enough of nonsense of my own (*d*). I have entirely lost this day owing to my being in town. I believe it will be better for me [to] attend the Society (*e*) no longer. It is true I there acquire a great fluency of speech, but the loss of time and money which my attendance occasions makes me conceive it preferable to go there no more.

(*c*) This figure and subsequent figures placed within brackets, show the pages of the Journal. The first two pages, containing two entries and part of a third, are missing. On the fragment of the missing sheet that remains " Revo- " and "Liberty" appear in what was p. 2. It is probable that O'Connell tore out the entry in 1797 or 1798, when he was in danger of being arrested in connection with the insurrectionary movement at that time in operation (see note to No. 27). In the first entry there seems to have been recorded the incident alluded to in the entry under date January 5th, 1797, namely the attack on the King in St. James's Park in 1795, already referred to. The Editor has been unable to ascertain who De Vignier, mentioned in this entry, was ; but he was probably an *emigré*, who served in one of the West India regiments formed when the Irish Brigade was disbanded. He is referred to again in entry No. 24.

(*d*) By a decree of the Legislative Assembly of May 15th, 1791, it was enacted that the " people of colour " in the French colonies born of free parents were entitled as of right to the enjoyment of all the privileges of French citizens, including those of having votes in the choice of representatives and being eligible to seats in the parochial and colonial assemblies. The plantation slaves rose in rebellion in August, 1791. The decree of May was annulled by one of September 24th, 1791, and thereupon the " people of colour " united with the slaves against the whites. On April 4th, 1792, another decree was passed by which people of colour and free negroes were given votes and made eligible to the Legislature and all places of trust. Meantime the civil war in the island raged with unabated fury. The French Government sent out commissioners, who, in 1793, proclaimed the freedom of the slaves, and the Government ratified their act. In the same year, when the war with France had begun, the English Government were induced by the representations of the planters to send out an expedition to conquer and annex St. Domingo. The island was invaded in September, 1793. Toussaint Louverture, the famous leader of the negroes, united with the French in resisting the invaders. The war lasted till towards the end of 1798, when General Maitland concluded negotiations with Toussaint, giving up all the places of which the English had taken possession, and entering into commercial stipulations which recognised St. Domingo as an independent and neutral Power. The climate played sad havoc with the British troops, which consisted largely of the (English) Irish Brigade, formed after the foreign troops in the service of France had been disbanded. Maurice O'Connell, the Liberator's younger brother, was one of its latest victims. See entry No. 71.

The contempt which O'Connell displays in this entry for the suggestion that the negroes were enamoured of slavery is in harmony with the ardent love of liberty that he expresses in entry No. 36, and his apostrophe to liberty in No. 47. He made a most powerful speech in Parliament in favour of the emancipation of the slaves in the colonies. " Let us," he said, " hear no more of breeding farms for slaves on the one hand, with their consignment to early graves on the other ; but let us pour across the wide Atlantic into the ear of the miscreant slave-owner that we scorn his hypocritical example, and will not debase ourselves by countenancing this foul crime against man and against the Almighty." A friend once suggested that he might at least be silent on slavery at the Repeal Association, as he injured their question by mixing it up with the slavery question. "No," replied O'Connell, "virtues are gregarious, and I assure you that, so far from being weakened, these measures will gain strength by being combined." Some advocates of slavery in Cincinnati addressed to the Association a document in which they defended the institution on the ground that "the very odour of the negro is almost insufferable to the white." O'Connell's reply was scathing. It wound up with the words "The negroes would certainly smell, at least, as sweet when free as they do now, being slaves" (*Personal Recollections*, i. 287—288).

(e) This no doubt refers to "The Honourable Society of Cogers," now commonly called "Ye Antient Society of Cogers," of which O'Connell was a member in the years 1794—1796. At the time this entry was made he was living at Chiswick. In 1831 the Cogers subscribed £10 towards the expenses of defending his seat in Dublin, and in 1844 they celebrated the decision of the House of Lords quashing the conviction of O'Connell and his associates by a packed jury of the city of Dublin. Lord Denman, who, in delivering judgment in the case, declared that "if such practices as have taken place in the present instance in Ireland should continue, trial by jury would become a mockery, a delusion, and a snare," was a Coger. So were Jack Wilkes, John Philpot Curran, Lord Russell of Killowen, and Charles Stewart Parnell. The Society, which was founded by Daniel Mason in 1755, flourishes still (see Peter Rayleigh's *History of ye Antient Society of Cogers*, pp. 35, 36). It originally met at the White Bear, Bride Lane, and continued to do so until about 1856, when it removed to what was formerly No. 10 Shoe Lane, Fleet Street, in a hall adjoining the "Blue Posts" tavern. Those who wish to form an idea of the proceedings at a meeting of the Society will find a graphic description in a quotation given in *Old and New London* from a work by Mr. J. C. Parkinson, where, from the solemn opening of the discussion by "my Grand"—

the President—down to the silent removal by the attendants of
the empty glasses of the audience and their replenishment, they
are duly chronicled, as are also the witty and sarcastic speeches
of some of the orators that took part in the debates.   The hall
in Shoe Lane continued to be the place of meeting until 1870,
when it was bought by the Corporation of London.   The
Society removed to the " Barley Mow," Salisbury Square, in
January, 1871, and subsequently to the " Rainbow " tavern in
Fleet Street, where its meetings continue to be held.   It is the
sole survivor of a number of similar societies that flourished in
London in the seventeenth and eighteenth centuries.   The
constitution and objects of the Society appear from the following entry in a minute-book of 1793, quoted by Mr. Rayleigh
in the interesting work to which reference has been already
made : — " The Society originally consisted of citizens of
London, who met to watch the course of political events and the
conduct of their representatives in Parliament.   The objects
of the Society were the promotion of the Liberty of the Subject
and the Freedom of the Press, the maintenance of Loyalty to
the Laws, the rights and claims of Humanity, and the practice
of public and private virtue."   These were objects dear to the
heart of O'Connell, and he must have found himself in a congenial atmosphere among his fellow-Cogers of the years immediately following the date of this minute.   The name " Coger,"
the second letter of which is to be pronounced long, seems to
come from *cogito*, " I think."

" Irish questions," says Mr. Rayleigh (p. 209), "have always
been popular in Cogers' Hall, and Irish advocates prominent.
During the great Home Rule struggle Cogers' Hall was full,
even though the meetings were held every night of the week,
as was the case up to recent years.   Throughout all modern
press notices of the Society—and these are the impartial
recorders we rely upon—we find that Irishmen were always
foremost in the debates.   It was so in Curran's and O'Connell's
days, so also in the Shoe Lane period ; and it must be regarded
as significant that the persistence of Irish affairs in our national
politics has always been reflected in the Cogerian debates."

During the Fenian agitation Tynan—" No. 1 "—dropped in. The knives intended for the assassination of Lord Frederick Cavendish, Mr. Rayleigh tells us (p. 254), were deposited in a bag at the bar while the owner was within at the debate. Mr. Arthur J. Balfour is one of the existing members.

I sent off a letter to my father by this day's post, and am now going to finish one I have already commenced to John (*f*).

(*f*) His brother, to whom he was greatly attached (see entry No. 43). The despatch of this letter is recorded in the next entry.

No. 4 (*g*), *Friday, December* 11*th,* 1795.—I went to bed last night at a quarter after twelve, and did not get up this morning until five minutes after eleven. I remain in general too long in bed. This I must endeavour to correct. It is a custom equally detrimental to the constitution and to the mind. It destroys the vigour and energy of the one ; and prevents, by its consumption of time, the other from acquiring that strength which information infuses (*h*).

(*g*) When this entry was made O'Connell, as appears from the entries on the title-page prefixed to the Journal, had left Mrs. Tracey's and gone to Mrs. Rigby's at Chiswick. Indeed, it would seem that when the entry No. 3 was written he was already staying at Chiswick, for otherwise the reference to his losing a day by being in town is not intelligible. From the description he gave O'Neill Daunt, Mrs. Tracey's seems to have been situated in a court or *cul de sac* on the north side of Coventry Street. A description of Mrs. Rigby's will be found in entry No. 10. He remained there till about December 3rd, 1796, and during his stay indulged in the pleasure of boating on the river, which, as he told O'Neill Daunt, made serious inroads on his purse (*Personal Recollections*, i. 277).

(*h*) This is the first of many entries in which O'Connell reproaches himself with the habit of lying too long in bed. The very last entry in the Journal, made on June 4th, 1802, records the hours of going to bed and of getting up. This may have been one of the " bad habits " which, as appears from a letter of December 10th, 1795, his uncle Maurice had pointed out to him. How completely he overcame the habit in after-life will appear from the following article, believed to be by Sheil, contributed in 1823 to the *National Review*.

The writer supposes a visitor to Dublin, while returning from a ball, to pass through Merrion Square between five and six o'clock on a winter's morning, and to peer through the parlour windows of one of the splendid mansions of that fashionable quarter. "The half-opened shutters," he writes, " and the light within announce that someone dwells there whose time is too precious to regulate his rising with the sun's. Should your curiosity tempt you to ascend the steps, and under cover of the dark to reconnoitre the interior, you will see a tall able-bodied man standing at a desk immersed in solitary occupation. Upon the wall in front of him hangs a crucifix. From this and the calm attitude of the person within, and from a certain monastic rotundity about his neck and shoulders, your first impression will be that he must be some pious dignitary of the Church of Rome, absorbed in his matin devotions. But this conjecture will be dismissed almost as soon as formed. No sooner can the eye take in the other furniture of the apartment—the bookcases stocked with tomes in plain calfskin, and blue-covered octavos strewing the tables and floor, the reams of manuscript in oblong folds and begirt with crimson tape—than it becomes evident that the party meditating amidst such objects must be thinking far more of the law than of the prophets." This, the writer explains, is but the prelude to a day of incessant exertion in court, at public meetings, and at a public dinner, " from which, after having acted a conspicuous part in the turbulent festivity of the evening and thrown off half a dozen speeches in praise of Ireland, he retires at a late hour to repair the wear and tear of the day by a short interval of repose, and is sure to be found before dawn-break the next morning at his solitary post, recommencing the routine of his restless existence." O'Connell himself in his letter to the Earl of Shrewsbury in defence of his claim to the repeal rent, speaking of this period of his life, says that his sleep was "restricted to the narrowest hours before dawn." The habit of early rising thus acquired he retained till late in life. He tells us himself that in 1841, when he was sixty-five years of age, he rose by candle-light, and often went to mass before breakfast (*Personal Recollections*, i. 225). Even in youth there was one thing that made him get up betimes, hare-hunting. His son John says, "Often has the writer of these pages heard him describe in his own graphic manner his going out before dawn to ensure that his few hounds should have the help of the scent still lying." Fishing as well as coursing was a favourite sport of O'Connell.

Bower, the attorney, got me served with a copy of a writ for the amount of Eugene McCarthy's bill. I owe this to my own negligence. I have the bill for near six weeks, always resolved to send it off without delay; and still it remains as yet unsent. I remark a great deal of neglect, or at least a certain dilatoriness of disposition, which seems a constitutional failing of mine. I must endeavour to be more than usually active for some time to come in order to get rid of this bad habit. I have another observation to make on Bower's business. It is that I have no right to charge E. McCarthy with the expense of the writ (*i*). I read this day thirteen chapters of the Bible, six pages of Espinasse's *Nisi Prius*, and thirty-five pages

of Gibbon's *Decline and Fall of the Roman Empire.*
I have this day begun the Bible. I have never read
it through. I did not read law enough. I will
—at least, I intend for the future to—read twelve
pages, if not more, a day. When I have occasion
to mention Espinasse in future I will do it thus,
viz., " E. N. P."; Blackstone's *Commentaries* thus,
" B. C."; *Coke on Littleton* thus, " C. L." I mean
to study until I go to bed. It wants five minutes to
ten, so this is not the whole work of the day. " Sed
dum loquimur fugit invida ætas " (*k*).

(*i*) The failing here described abode with him to the end of
his days. He was especially careless in money matters. His
brother James said of him that he was in pecuniary difficulties
since the age of fourteen (*Four Years of Irish History*, p. 399, n.).
He mentions another example of it himself in No. 6 below
(p. 77). Eugene McCarthy was, no doubt, his cousin, the son
of his aunt Elizabeth, who married Timothy McCarthy, of
Ochtermony, county Kerry. Eugene, " the wild handsome
boy that sister Betty got so many lectures about," as Mrs.
Morgan John O'Connell describes him, went to France to his
uncle, Count O'Connell, when he was about ten years old.
His wildness gave the Count " a surfeit of bringing over any
others," but nevertheless he rose to be a colonel in the French
service, and was lieutenant-colonel in " O'Connell's " regiment
in the (English) Irish Brigade. Count O'Connell got him a
commission in Walsh's regiment in the Irish Brigade in 1776,
and having distinguished himself in an engagement in which
he was wounded, the Count got him a captaincy and a " gratification " in 1780. The Count also got him, in 1785, a captaincy in the Dutch service, which brought him in an income
of £150, while at the same time his place in Walsh's regiment
was kept open for him. He is mentioned in the Count's letter

of January 26th, 1794, quoted above (p. 47), and in his letter of May 9th, 1801, quoted hereafter, in which he tells Dan of Eugene's death (*The Last Colonel of the Irish Brigade*, i. 9, 194 ; ii. 38, 46, 190, 235, 256).

(*k*) We here obtain for the first time an idea of the works that, at this important period of his life, were the subject of his study. There are only two other references to the Bible in the Journal, namely in entries Nos. 5 and 28.

Espinasse's *Nisi Prius* is a collection of reports of decisions given by judges in the years from 1793 to 1799, inclusive, on points of law raised in the course of trials by jury. In the letter referred to in the next entry he says to his uncle Maurice : " The only law books I have bought as yet are the works of Espinasse on the trials at *Nisi Prius*. They cost me £1 10*s.*, and contain more information on the practical part of the law than any other books I have ever met." O'Connell's keen sense of justice soon led him to feel a profound dislike to the quirks and quibbles by which, at that time, cases were decided (see his observations on this subject in entry No. 20). The other law books mentioned here, Sir William Blackstone's *Commentaries on the Laws of England* and Lord Coke's edition of *Littleton on Land Tenures*, are still standard works, though of course the law has undergone many changes since they were written. Of Gibbon, O'Connell was a most diligent student and a most enthusiastic admirer. By January 13th, 1798, he tells us, he had read five volumes and a half of *The Decline and Fall*, and in a few days would have the whole concluded. He adds, " It is an extraordinary, it is an admirable, work. The genius, the critical acumen, the laborious research, of the author are unrivalled. He has mended my style. He has improved my thoughts. He has enriched my memory."

In the Introduction will be found a classified list of the books mentioned by O'Connell during the period covered by the Journal. He read others not mentioned (see No. 5 below, p. 74). The Latin quotation is from Horace, Od. i. 11. It should have run—" Dum loquimur, *fugerit* invida ætas."

I sent off a letter to John.

No. 5, Saturday, December 12th, 1795.—I went to bed last night a few minutes after twelve, and got up this morning at nine. This is giving too much time to sleep. However, we hope we shall improve as we go on.

I have written part of a letter to my uncle Maurice (*l*). My reading consisted of fifteen chapters of the Bible, fifteen pages of " E. N. P. C.," and thirty-four pages of Gibbon, to p. 132. I have likewise written a page of a book equal in size of extracts from the last-mentioned author.

(*l*) Maurice O'Connell, known as " Hunting-cap," by whom O'Connell was brought up. The letter was not finished until the 14th, as the entry under that date records. It is as follows :—

" CHISWICK, NEAR LONDON,
" *December* 10th, 1795.

" MY DEAR UNCLE,—I delayed answering your letter until I should have it in my power to inform you that I had changed my place of residence in conformity to your desire.

" On calculating the expenses of retiring to a cheaper spot, and returning to keep my term on January 1st, I found it would not answer, so I dropped the scheme. I am now only four miles from town, yet perfectly retired. I pay the same price for board and lodging as I should in London ; but I enjoy many advantages here, besides air and retirement. The society in this house is mixed, I mean composed of men and women, all of whom are people of rank and knowledge of the world, so that their conversation and manners are well adapted to rub off the rust of scholastic education, nor is there any danger of riot or dissipation, as they are all advanced in life, another student of law and I being the only other young persons in the house.

This young man is my most intimate acquaintance, and the only friend I have found amongst my acquaintances. His name is Bennett. He is an Irish young man of good family connections and fortune. He has good sense, ability, and application. I knew him before my journey to Ireland. It was before that period our friendship commenced, so that on the whole I spend my time here not only pleasantly, but, I hope, usefully.

"The only law books I have bought as yet are the works of Espinasse on the trials at *Nisi Prius*. They cost me £1 10s., and contain more information on the practical part of the law than any I have ever met. When in Dublin I saw that carrying any more books than were absolutely necessary would be incurring expense, so I deferred buying a complete set of reports until my return thither.

"I have now two objects to pursue, the one the attainment of knowledge, the other the acquisition of all those qualities that constitute the polite gentleman. I am convinced that the former, besides the immediate pleasure that it yields, is calculated to raise me to honours, rank, and fortune; and I know that the latter serves as a first passport or general recommendation ; and as for the motives of ambition which you suggest, I assure you that no man possesses more of it than I do. I have indeed a glowing and—if I may use the expression—an enthusiastic ambition, which converts every toil into a pleasure and every study into amusement.

"Though nature may have given me subordinate talents, I never will be satisfied with a subordinate position in my profession. No man is able, I am aware, to supply the total deficiency of abilities ; but everybody is capable of improving and enlarging a stock however small, and, in its beginning, contemptible. It is this reflection that affords me most consolation. It is not because I assert these things now that I should consider myself entitled to call on you to believe them. I refer that conviction that I wish to inspire to your experience. I hope, may I flatter myself, that when we meet again the success of my efforts to correct those bad habits that you pointed out to me will be apparent. Indeed, as for my knowledge in the professional line, that cannot be discovered for some years to come, but I have time in the interim to prepare myself to appear with greater *éclat* on the grand theatre of the world.

"You have heard of the capture of Mannheim. The Austrians continue to advance rapidly on the French side of the Rhine. They are said to be marching towards Luxemburg. In the meantime the French are evacuating Holland. Whether this event will be favourable to the Stadtholder is as yet uncertain. The Ministry, who have been unpopular by reason of the two Bills of which you must have heard, and in general [owing] to the ill success of the war, already tottered in their seats; but the brilliant victories of the Austrians have secured them at least for some time. That we shall soon have peace is no longer in question. Everybody believes it, and the King's messages to Parliament confirm the belief.

"I am, dear Uncle,
"Your affectionate and dutiful nephew,
"DANIEL O'CONNELL"

(Fitzpatrick, *Correspondence of Daniel O'Connell*, i. 9).

This diplomatic epistle must have mightily pleased his uncle. Its display of thrift, the deference to his wishes and the submission to his censures which it expresses, must have flattered his vanity; the resolution to spare no effort to shine in the profession which he had chosen for his nephew must have been gratifying to his ambition. Dan had already begun to practise those arts of conciliation in which he afterwards became a past-master. Some account of his fellow-boarders is given by O'Connell in subsequent entries (see pp. 104, 105, 108).

I may here remark that I do not intend to mention everything I read. I conceive the trifling productions of the day unworthy my notice. It is true time is lost in reading, but it would be adding to the loss to write down their names.

I am now at a loss for materials to swell out this number to the size of the others. I shall therefore descant a little on style (*m*). My letters and writings in general have the appearance more of a jumbled mass than of a united train of ideas. This defect has, I believe, two sources, the one an inherent shallowness of conception, [5] the other frequent interruption. The first can be remedied one [*sic*] by the attainment of a more enlarged stock of ideas; the latter, being only a bad custom, may be laid aside with the assistance of care.

(*m*) O'Connell recurs to the subject of his style in the next entry and in No. 23. In No. 70, written on January 30th, 1798, he tells us that the perusal of Gibbon's *Decline and Fall of the Roman Empire* had mended his style. He was in the habit of making extracts from this work, as he mentions above.

No. 6, Sunday, December 13th, 1795.—I went to bed last night at about half after eleven, and got up this morning at half after nine. Since I wrote yesterday's number, which was at a late hour last night, I have read from the 132nd to the 248th page of Gibbon's *Decline and Fall.* The number of pages were consequently two hundred and sixteen. Let me observe that it is the second volume which is mentioned as having afforded the subject of my reading a part of the last days. The extracts mentioned in p. 4 were taken from the first volume. When I change either I will set the alteration down.

In concluding last night I made a few remarks on my style. That subject I shall now take up again. In my letters I perceive that I am too fond of commencing my sentences with " I do this," or " I do that." Thus disuniting the phrases, they cannot run into one another as they should. I remember having read a remark on Cæsar['s] *Commentaries* that in them he shows his modesty by never using the word " Ego." If the contrary is a proof of vanity, I am well aware that it would be hard for me to acquit myself of the charge.

I should have finished my letter to my uncle this day, and have not done it. This [is] another instance of that neglect with which I have taxed myself so justly (*n*). The fact is, I did intend to terminate the letter, but I put off executing my intention from hour to hour. And so while I was resolving to act the day stole away. So true it is that procrastination is the thief of time.

(*n*) See above, No. 4.

Bennett (*o*) is to be married to-morrow. Within a short period that event is to befal him which, at least to one of my way of thinking, is the source of pure happiness or unmixed sorrow. For it is my opinion that there is no medium in the marriage state. To it I look forward for my felicity in this life (*p*). Indeed, I believe we are generally looking forward [6]. I should express my meaning better by saying that, in my opinion, men always look forward to some future period of their lives, to some future event, for their happiness. "When I have done this thing or that, then I will be happy." Such is the usual language of men. But, lo! the period of the completion of their wishes arrives. With one man it is an advantageous marriage ; with another it is the acquisition of a fortune, with a third the restoration of health, etc., etc. The much-desired object once enjoyed, happiness, not found in it, is placed in some other unattained desire, which when come at is found as vain and empty as the former. Happiness again removes, and is again sought for in vain. This pursuit has been well compared by the poet Goldsmith to the endeavour at reaching the circle which bounds the horizon (*q*).

I read two chapters in the Bible.

(*o*) Richard Newton Bennett. He was a fellow-boarder of O'Connell at Chyswick, as appears from the letter to Hunting-cap of December 10th, 1795, above quoted. He was the son of Mr. Richard Bennett, a county Wexford gentleman, and was a student of Gray's Inn (*The Register of Admissions to Gray's Inn*, 1521—1889, by Joseph Foster, p. 398). The friend-ship between them was lasting. Mr. Bennett accompanied O'Connell on his journey to Clare at the famous election. He lent and loaded the pistols, still preserved at Darrynane, which O'Connell used in his duel with D'Esterre. He afterwards became a colonial Chief Justice. In a letter to the Knight of

Kerry dated June 24th, 1827, O'Connell writes, " There is a most particular friend of mine—a Mr. Bennett, of this bar—in London, looking for a judicial seat in the colonies. He has hopes of being made Chief Justice of Ceylon. I got Blake to write warmly to Philip Horton for him. Doherty wrote at my instance to Canning. I wrote in the strongest terms I could venture upon to Brougham. I most anxiously wish you could speak to Lord Lansdowne for him. If there be nothing inconsistent with your present relations with the Marquis, to do it will be conferring another obligation upon me. I could not be more anxious for my brother than I am for Mr. Bennett. He has been at all times the decided friend of civil and religious liberty, and his promotion would give the greatest satisfaction to all that part of the Catholic party in Dublin who have been working for emancipation—that is, the really influential portion of the Catholic community " (Fitzpatrick, *Correspondence of Daniel O'Connell*, i. 147).

(*p*) O'Connell's own marriage was a very happy one. He was married to his cousin, Mary O'Connell, on June 23rd, 1802. She was descended from *Sheara-na-mo-Mor*, or Geoffrey of the Vast Herds. Her father was a medical man practising in Tralee. The ceremony was performed privately by the Rev. Mr. Finn, parish priest of Irishtown, at the residence of Mr. James Connor, brother-in-law of the bride. For many months the marriage was kept a secret. " On one of our repeal journeys," says O'Neill Daunt—" namely, to Waterford—he adverted, as he frequently did, to the memory of the late Mrs. O'Connell. ' I never,' said he, ' proposed marriage to any woman but one—my Mary. I said to her, " Are you engaged, Miss O'Connell ? " She answered, " I am not." " Then," said I, " will you engage yourself to me ? " " I will," was her reply. And I said I would devote my life to make her happy. She deserved that I should : she gave me thirty-four years of the purest happiness that man ever enjoyed. My uncle was desirous I should obtain a much larger fortune, and I thought he would disinherit me. But I did not care for that.' ' Did your wife live in Tralee ? ' O'Neill

Daunt asks. 'She did, with her aunt,' replied O'Connell, 'and it was my delight to quiz the old lady by pretending to complain of her granddaughter's want of temper. "Madam," said I, "Mary would do very well, only she is so cross." "Cross, sir ? My Mary cross ? Sir, you must have provoked her very much ! Sir, my little girl was always the gentlest, sweetest creature born." And so she was,' he added, after a pause. 'She had the sweetest, most heavenly temper, and the sweetest breath'" (*Personal Recollections*, i. 133). If ever a great political leader and a true patriot found a help meet for him, O'Connell found one in his wife. His life was precious to her—she saved him from the risk of being killed or wounded in a duel with Peel—but his honour was more precious still. How many men have through the influence of their wives and children been induced to accept some office or some title which has blasted their career and destroyed their reputation for independence ! O'Connell was happily saved from such a temptation. The following letter was written by Mrs. O'Connell on the occasion of his having declined the offer of the Government of the day. It is dated " Merrion Square, Wednesday." The postmark is December 3rd, 1830.

" MY DEAREST LOVE,—Thank God, you have acted like yourself, and your wife and children have more reason to be proud of you than they ever were. Had you acted differently from what you have done, it would have broken my heart. You can't abandon the people, who have always stood by you, and for whom you have sacrificed so much. You will, darling, be rewarded for all : you will have the prayers and blessings of your country to cheer and console you for what you have given up. Had you been betrayed into acceptance of the terms offered by Government, you would die of a broken heart before six months expired. You now stand firmly in the affections and in the love of your countrymen, and when that country is aware of the splendid sacrifice you have now made for them, depend upon it, they will strain every nerve to reward you. I shall hold up my head higher than ever I did. I shan't be afraid to look at the people, as I certainly should if you were a titled pensioner of the Government. I shan't say a word, as they give you their sentiments, their respective signatures attached. I never saw anything like [the] pleasure that danced in their eyes when assured of your refusal. May God bless you, my own love. Words are inadequate to tell you how much I love and respect you for this late act, so like and so worthy of yourself. My heart overflows with gratitude and pride for being the wife of such a man, and the mother of such grateful children. The report through town yesterday and to-day is that you are to be the new Master of the Rolls. You may rely on our discretion, though we long to have the great news public. What a welcome you will get from the people of Ireland! May God bless and protect you. You will carry the repeal of the Union without bloodshed, as you did the emancipation. I put my trust in that God who sees and knows the purity of your heart. I can't write more here, there are so many in and out. With love from your children, believe me always with truth,

" Your fondest and most grateful

" MARY O'CONNELL."

The letter is addressed to 14, Manchester Buildings, Westminster, London. On the envelope containing the copy of the letter from which the above is printed is written, " When the Liberator was offered a peerage."

The match was very displeasing to his uncle Maurice, who wished him to marry Miss Healy, of Cork, a lady of wealth, but of homely features (*Personal Recollections*, i. 194). It must have been some time before his uncle forgave him, for we find the Count, who was the good genius of the family, interceding for Dan in a letter of August 1st, 1804: " His fate must be truly deplorable, if you irrevocably cast him off. The bare perquisites of his profession are probably very inadequate to the support of a wife and family, besides his personal expenses." He adds, speaking of Dan's brother John, " I sincerely wish the unfavourable change in the expectations of his brother, to which no sense of his demerits, whatever they may be, is likely to reconcile his mind, may not make a dislike, or at least a *froideur*, between them " (*The Last Colonel of the Irish Brigade*, ii. 243).

O'Connell had a very high opinion of the influence of a mother on the character of her children. His son-in-law, Charles Bianconi, asked his advice about sending his daughter, a lovely child, to school. "Oh! no, no, no," replied O'Connell eagerly, "never take her from her mother. Get a governess to assist her mother in little Kate's education, but never take the child from the mother's care. The tender affection of the mother educates the daughter's heart " (*Personal Recollections*, i. 136).

> (*q*) " Impelled, with steps unceasing, to pursue
> Some fleeting good, that mocks me with the view,
> That, like the circle bounding earth and skies,
> Allures from far, yet, as I follow, flies."

These lines, extracted from *The Traveller*, follow immediately those in which Goldsmith describes so beautifully his brother's home :—

> " Blest that abode where want and pain repair,
> And every stranger finds a ready chair ;
> Blest be those feasts, with simple plenty crowned,
> Where all the ruddy family around
> Laugh at the jests or pranks that never fail,
> Or sigh with pity at some mournful tale,
> Or press the bashful stranger to his food,
> And learn the luxury of doing good."

Probably O'Connell had such a domestic circle in his mind when he moralised on the felicity that flows from a happy married life. If so, the prospect was realised. In a speech that he made in January, 1841, at a temperance soirée given in Belfast by four hundred and fifty ladies of different religious opinions, he said, after a glowing eulogy upon his mother, " I am a father, and I know what it is to respect as well as to love those whom, in parental language, I call my angel daughters. They have never given breath to a word of offence against

me. . . . I am a grandfather, and the chirping of my darling
granddaughters sounds sweetly in my ears. . . . I think within
myself, ' How happy the man will be that obtains them ! ' But
that subject brings me back to a being of whom I dare not
speak in the profanation of words. No, I will not mention
that name. The man who is happiest in his domestic circle
may have some idea of what my happiness was. Yes, I was
her husband then. Did I say I *was ?* Oh ! yes, I am her
husband still. The grave may separate us for a time, but we
shall meet beyond it, never, I trust, to be separated more."
O'Connell does not mention his sons in this speech because
it was made in praise of womankind. But it is well known
that his sons were equally as dutiful and attached to their
father as his daughters were.

Nowhere did a more generous or genial hospitality abound
than at Darrynane. There indeed every stranger found a ready
chair, and jests and pranks never failed, though it is not many
mournful tales were told in that delightful circle.

No. 7, Monday, December 14*th,* 1795.—I went to
bed last night at a quarter before twelve, and got
up this morning at a quarter before nine. I have
finished my letter to my uncle, and read thirty-two
pages in Gibbon—164.

I am just going off to London, so that the
transactions of this will afford subject for part of
to-morrow's number (*r*).

(*r*) There is no " to-morrow's number," for reasons explained
in that of the 16th. The only transaction recorded is his visit
to the play at Drury Lane.

No. 8, Wednesday, December 16*th,* 1795.—I would
have written something yesterday but for the reason

which I am going to mention. After returning from town I put it off for a while, then deferred it till after supper. I found it oppress me as a disagreeable task. It in fact occasioned the same sensations which I used to feel when, formerly, I intended on a [particular] day to go to confession. Now I mean that this Journal should give me only pleasure and profit. Therefore I resolved not to write anything last night, as I felt writing a burthen.

In the foregoing paragraph I have expressed myself very ill. I have not said what I meant. Tha⁺ I shall do the same now seems to me scarce doubtful. There is a kind of cold hanging about me these two days which dulls [7] my faculties. Besides, my trip to town has put me very much out of sorts. It has damaged my plans of study, and I do not yet feel myself quite at home again. I will go to town as seldom as possible, since I feel the pernicious effects attending my journeys thither. They are productive of no benefit; yet they make me spend a great deal of money.

I went to the play on Monday night at Drury Lane Theatre. The tragedy of *Alexander the Great* was acted, with the farce of *The Devil to Pay*. I did not on the whole admire the acting. Kemble, who played Alexander, does not give many of the lines the smoothness for which, and for which alone, many of them are remarkable. Let me instance the lines beginning with

" When Glory like the dazzling eagle stood,"

lines which contain a tissue of false, unmeaning, or exaggerated images. There is, indeed, a smooth flow of numbers in them pleasing to the ear. To render them palatable, they should receive from the speaker this the only beauty they possess. Now Kemble, on the contrary, pronounces them as if they consisted of a number of disjointed half-sentences. In the mad scene he was too tame. In the cold fit which the poison occasions he puff[ed] and blew, and swelled his cheeks to puff and blow, in a manner that was truly pantomimic, and highly ridiculous.

Mrs. Siddons, I find, is not much admired in the character of Roxana. It is not, in my opinion, because the part ill suits her style of playing. The strength and modulation of her voice render any character doubly interesting in her hands. With our modern actors it is no small difficulty to understand the dialogue of a tragedy. But Mrs. Siddons has the faculty of making herself clearly understood in every part. And to this faculty, I conceive, she owes no small share of her high estimation. Binsley in Clytus was more chaste than he usually is. The character seems adapted to his manner of acting. That stern gravity of the veteran Greek was happily displayed. As for Charles Kemble, I believe he possesses no other requisite for a theatrical hero than a large stock of impudence. And impudence unaccompanied by merit is [8] not very captivating in any condition. Miss Miller will, in my opinion, be a good actress (s).

(s) The tragedy of *Alexander the Great* is by Nathaniel Lee. *The Devil to Pay; or, The Wives Metamorphosed*, is by Colley Cibber in collaboration with others. The lines commencing

" When Glory like the dazzling eagle stood "

are as follows :—

" When Glory like the dazzling eagle stood,
Perched on my beaver in the Granick flood,
When Fortune's self my standard trembling bore,
And the pale fates stood frighted on the shore,
When each immortal on the billows rode,
And I myself appeared the leading god."

" The Granick flood " was, of course, the water of the river Granicus.

O'Connell's criticism of Kemble's elocution is all the more curious and interesting as Kemble is generally reputed to have excelled in declamation, and to have had a fine sense of rhythm, but to have been deficient in fire and passion. The embryo orator was not likely to have erred in his judgment, and the contrast which he draws between the elocution of Mrs. Siddons and that of her brother shows that he was well able to discriminate between the excellence of the one and the faultiness of the other. Charles Kemble was a younger brother of John Philip Kemble, mentioned above. He was born in the same year as O'Connell, and was therefore only in his twenty-first year when O'Connell saw him play on this occasion. He too had been at Douay, but on his return to England obtained a situation in the Post Office, which, however, he soon resigned to go on the stage. The defects which O'Connell observed were probably due to his youth and inexperience, for he ultimately became a very finished actor, playing such parts as Doricourt, Charles Surface, Antony, and Henry V. with considerable success. It was during John Philip Kemble's management of Drury Lane that *Vortigern*, mentioned in No. 40, was produced. Miss Miller, whose name O'Connell mentions here with approval, played Rowena on that memorable occasion.

The plot of *The Devil to Pay* turns on the transformation by a magician of the shrewish lady of Sir John Loverule into the good-natured but ill-used wife of Jobson, the village cobbler, and the retransformation of both into their original forms, after a short experience of their novel surroundings, resulting in the reformation of the lady and the cobbler, and the happiness of their households. The play, though rather coarse in parts, is amusing enough. It went through several editions, one of which was printed in Dublin.

I read this day and last night eighty-five pages of Ossian's *Poems* (*t*), one hundred and eight pages of Godwin's *Political Justice* (*u*), and two hundred and thirty-four of Pindar's *Poems* (*v*).

(*t*) Further references to Macpherson's Ossian will be found in Nos. 27 and 40, from the former of which it appears that O'Connell was familiar from infancy with the names of the heroes mentioned in the poems, and from the latter that he disbelieved in the authenticity of the poems.

(*u*) This work, the full title of which is *The Inquiry concerning Political Justice and its Influence on General Virtue and Happiness*, was published in 1793. It was written by William Godwin, who was the son of a Nonconformist minister, a man of the strictest Calvinistic principles and practice. William Godwin at first followed his father's profession, and joined the Sandemanians, the straitest sect of the Calvinists. While officiating at Stowmarket, however, the writings of the French reformers were brought under his notice, and these undermined his religious opinions. In 1782 he published six sermons under the title *Sketches of History*, in one of which he laid down the proposition that " God Himself has no right to be a tyrant." His work on *Political Justice* had a profound influence on the thought of his own and the succeeding generation. By political justice he meant " the adoption of any principle of morality and truth into the practice of the community." His doctrines were of the most far-reaching character. Monarchy he considered a species of government unavoidably corrupt. All control of man by man he considered more or less intolerable. He looked forward to the time when each man, doing what seemed right in his own eyes, would also be doing what was best for the community, because all would be guided by the principles of pure reason. He was opposed to all punishments, to accumulated property, and to marriage. It was with difficulty that he was induced to go through the ceremony when, in 1796, he was married to Mary Wolstone-craft, whose work on *The Rights of Woman* was one of those read by O'Connell, and of whom some particulars will be found below (p. 101). Godwin wrote her memoirs, under the title of *Memoirs of the Rights of Woman*, published in 1794. As a novelist he will be best remembered as the author of *Caleb Williams ; or, Things as they are*, mentioned below (p. 122). The Government of Earl Grey conferred on him the office of Yeoman of the Usher of the Exchequer. He died in 1836 in the residence in Palace Yard attached to that office.

(*v*) Pindar, a lyric poet of ancient Greece, born about 522 B.C. His versatility was so great as to be recorded by Horace (*Carm*. iv. 2). Numerous fragments of his compositions have been preserved, but the only complete work of his that has come down to us is *The Epinicia*, or Odes of Victory, com-memorating successes in the great games. From the fact that O'Connell seldom quoted poetry in his speeches it has been inferred that he had no appreciation of it (Macdonagh, p. 373). But men of his abounding eloquence have little need of such adventitious ornament, and one who could at one sitting read two hundred and thirty-four pages of Pindar or six hundred lines of *Paradise Lost*, as he tells us he did on June 1st, 1802, could not have been quite dead to the beauties of poetic composition. That the verses he wrote himself " hardly entitle him to a place even among the very minor bards " (*ib.*) may be admitted ; but those which **Mr.** Macdonagh quotes had a personal and a patriotic interest which made them suitable both to the occasions upon which they were quoted and the audiences for whom they were intended. The lines which Mr. Macdonagh refers to as having been often repeated in O'Connell's repeal speeches, and as having been quoted against him in the speech of the Attorney-General during the State trials of 1844, were calculated to strike a responsive chord in the breasts of his hearers : —

> " O Erin, shall it e'er be mine
> To right thy wrongs in battle line,
> To raise my victor hand and see
> Thy hills, thy dales, thy people, free ?
> That glance of bliss is all I crave
> Between my labours and my grave."

It is easy to understand Mr. Macdonagh's estimate of O'Connell's taste for literature when we read the following passage, which occurs on p. 23. Speaking of the Journal, he says, " His reading consisted of Blackstone's *Commentaries*, *Coke on Littleton*, and Espinasse's *Nisi Prius*, and outside these law books the Bible and Gibbon's *Decline and Fall of the Roman Empire*." The list of works mentioned in the Journal which is given in the Introduction (*supra*, ˜p. vi.) shows that this statement is a serious error. Moreover, we know from the entry under date December 12th, 1795, that all the works O'Connell read were not recorded in his Journal, and no doubt he read much in the intervals during which the keeping of the Journal was suspended. That he was not deficient in the poetic sentiment is evident from a beautiful letter to Walter Savage Landor describing the romantic scenery in the midst of which his childhood was passed, which contains an exquisite passage in prose that rises to the height of poetry. That letter, like several others, contains a poetic quotation, and he not only admired, but knew by heart, and often recited, Moore's melodies (*Personal Recollections*, i. 150), which he considered to have done good service to the cause of Ireland. His criticism on Cowley, that " he never wrote to the heart," shows that he understood wherein lay the essence of real poetry, as opposed to lines merely composed in metre, and ending in rhyme.

No. 9, Tuesday, December 29th, 1795.—Near a fortnight has elapsed since the last number was written. A transaction took place during the interval which prevented me from continuing this Journal with regularity. I allude to my quarrel with Douglas Thompson, the son of a porter-brewer of Chyswick. The circumstances of the quarrel I am going to relate.

On Thursday, the 17th instant, I made one of a large party which was entertained by General Morrison at his house in Hammersmith. I went thither early in the evening, accompanied by a Mrs. Atkinson and Miss King. At about half after eleven Mrs. A. sent me from the dining-room to call Miss K. She took my hand, when D. Thompson, who sat next to her, seized the hand of hers that was disengaged and led her out of the room. So soon as he returned I went up to him and told him in an undertone, " You have behaved in a rascally manner to me, and you shall hear about it." He replied, " I tell you what, sir : if we were not at General Morrison's, I would see which of us should quit the room first." While I was at breakfast on Friday morning I received a most impertinent letter, requiring my reason for calling him a rascal (*w*). As Bennett was married so lately, I had no one to send ; I therefore went myself. We canvassed the subject standing at the street door of his father's house. After some conversation he rushed in for a cane, with which he struck me three times. I seized him, and though I had a heavy cane in my hand, I did not return the blow. On Saturday morning I sent Bennett with a message. Thompson, under pretence of agreeing to a meeting, detained him until the father [9] had procured a constable, who took Bennett up. I went to the magistrate, and was then obliged to give security that I would keep the peace. The General came down the next day, and became my bondsman.

(*w*) The letter is in the following terms :—

" To Danl. O'Connell.

" CHISWICK, *December* 18*th*, 1795.

" SIR,—Unless you make a point of disclosing to me the reason of your expressions last night, I shall most certainly look upon and treat you as everyone deserves who deviates so much from the character and manners of a gentleman. Depend upon it, nothing but the idea of the mortification it would have been to General Morrison prevented me from treating you at that moment as you justly deserved.

" I am, etc.,

" DOUGLAS THOMPSON."

Thompson was one of the party at the Pack Horse mentioned in No. 24. The sequel to this quarrel will be found described in subsequent numbers. Macdonagh (*Life of Daniel O'Connell*, p. 26) speaks of the dispute with Douglas Thompson as having arisen at a tavern bar in the village. He is very severe on O'Connell for involving himself in such vulgar brawls, and wasting his money, while he was writing dutiful letters to his uncle. But the imbroglio after the wine party at

D.C.   I

the Pack Horse was not of O'Connell's making; he merely
stood by his friend. Thompson's letter is given by Fitzpatrick (*Correspondence*, vol. i.). Chiswick knoweth the name
of Thompson—as brewing there—no more. The General
referred to in this entry is, no doubt, Count O'Connell, and
not General Morrison.

No. 10, *Wednesday, December* 30*th*, 1795.—
D. Thompson is much my inferior in stature (x) and
in strength. I did not, however, return his blow
when he struck me. My conduct in this instance
was guided by two considerations. First, I apprehended putting a period to his existence. This
apprehension was founded on the consciousness of
my superior strength and of the weight of my cane.
Secondly, I bore in mind the transaction with
De Faria's servant and its consequent expences,
troubles, and inconveniencies (y). In other words,
having no witnesses, I was afraid of the law.

(x) According to the prison register at Richmond Peniten-
tiary, reproduced in *The Liberator: his Life and Times* (p. 724),
O'Connell was five feet eleven inches and three-quarters in
height.
(y) De Faria was Mrs. Rigby's landlord (see No. 12). The
incident is described in No. 24 (p. 120).

I reflect with pleasure on the courage which I *felt*
on this occasion. All I have to fear is precipitation
in plunging myself in future quarrels. I know that
duelling is a vice; yet there is a certain charm
in the independence which it bestows on a man
that endears it even to many thinking minds. I

have, however, made a resolution not to fight a duel from the time that I become *independent* of the world.

The General has vouchsafed to become one of my securities ; Bennett (*z*) is the other. The message and consequent actions of Messrs. Thompson took place on Saturday. The General did not come down until the next day. In the interval I received a great deal of civility from Mr. Reed, the justice of peace, and a butcher of Hammersmith, with whose name I am not acquainted. This butcher is one of the headboroughs. He liberated me, first on the security of Mrs. Rigby, and afterwards on my own word. The General scolded me very much. He divided his sermon into many parts. He commented on my impropriety of returning to Chyswick [10] after having been once before engaged in a scrape there (*a*), as if my once having been unlucky in a certain place portended future evils to attend me in that place. He spoke of my folly in being a democrat, of my absurdity in displaying my political opinions. He railed at me for not having returned the blow. Now, if I had struck Thompson, he certainly would have blamed me as much, if not more. He then would say with justice that there was a more gentlemanlike method of revenging an injury than that of fighting with cudgels like common porters, etc., etc., etc.

(*z*) The General is Count O'Connell. Bennett is Richard Newton Bennett, so often mentioned in the Journal.

(*a*) The Middleton affair (see No. 24, p. 120).

A sketch of the character of some of my fellow-lodgers and some of my acquaintance may perhaps at a future period be amusing. The drawing, or attempt at drawing, it must be of present utility. These arguments justify in my mind the enter-prize. I shall preface the characters with a description of the situation, etc., of the house.

This house fronts the Thames, and commands a view of Barnes at the one side, and of the Margrave of Ansbach's house and improvements at the other (b). An island covered with reeds and osiers lies opposite the door, and extends to some length both ways. Nothing can be better calculated for a lodging-house than this is. The apartments are extensive and unconnected. Each inmate is as much alone as if in possession of a separate house.

(b) The house is still standing, and is called Walpole House. It is a handsome edifice. A description of the interior is given in O'Connell's letter to his uncle of December 10th, 1795, quoted above (p. 72). It is said to have been the house in which Miss Pinkerton kept the academy in which Becky Sharp taught. If so, the " enamelled iron gates " are still there. Walpole House is now the residence of Mr. Beerbohm Tree, the well-known actor.

Mrs. Rigby, who rents the house, at first kept a school in it. But about five years ago, on the death of a sister who assisted, she commenced taking in lodgers. All those who lodge in the house board there likewise. At least an instance to the contrary never reached my knowledge. Mrs. Rigby is about forty-five years of age. * * * Nature, so penurious in the gifts of form and feature, has given her a strong mind, a clear com- prehension [11], and a tenacious memory. Her faculties are cultivated by an almost universal study. She speaks French. She understands and speaks Italian. She speaks French correctly, though without a great fluency or a proper accent. She has some acquaintance with the Latin tongue. Many branches of history are familiar to her. Her knowledge of players, ancient and modern, of the dramatic and poetic works in the English language, and of the private lives of their authors, is extensive. Of the peerage of England her mind is a register. The profession of her father, a coach-painter, enabled her without difficulty to acquire skill in heraldry.

Mrs. Hunter desired me insert in my Journal an observation of her daughter. It is "that in fifty years I would doubt whether I was a man or a cabbage-stump, so much was I inclined to scepticism " (c).

(c) Mrs. Hunter was a boarder at Mrs. Rigby's (see No. 15). It is noticeable that O'Connell does not repudiate the charge of scepticism. In the extracts from the Journal printed in the *Irish Monthly* the word "suspicion" is substituted for "scepti- cism." But there is no doubt but that the word is not "suspicion," which would be meaningless, but "scepticism." The asterisks replace a passage in which poor Mrs. Rigby's personal appearance is very unflatteringly described.

No. 11, *Thursday, December* 31*st,* 1795.—With this day the year closes. How fleet has it been in its progress, how rapid in its course ! It seemed to commence but yesterday, and, behold, it already is no more. A few more such years, and the scene will close on me. I, who now write, who now think, who now move with strength and velocity, shall be stretched, pale, motionless, inanimate. My mind now can grasp in its comprehension the million of

> " . . . adamantine spheres
> Rolling unshaken through the void immense "
> (Akenside, *Pleasures of Imagination*).

It can descend from this elevation either gradually or with one bold stride to the minute insect that escapes the eye of the microscope. What is to become of this comprehensive mind ? The body placed in a solitary corner, a prey to worms and vermin, soon will restore to the elements the portions of each which it has absorbed, I should rather say of which it is composed. But the mind, the mind ! Through what variety of untried being is that to roam ? What changes is it to suffer ? Does it perish as a dependant on the corporal system ? Such are the questions to the solution of which the light of reason cannot direct the inquirer. Reason faintly glimmers [12] on futurity, or perhaps, did not prejudice vitiate our senses, we should perceive that reason affords no light to enable us to discover whether the mind is immortal or not. Of things not arrived we can only guess. Our best surmises are founded on an analogy. Now, what analogy can there be between any part of corporal existence and the state of the mind when separated from the body, supposing separation actually takes place ? This subject may afford matter for further speculation.

I read this day twelve pages of " E. N. P.," about forty pages of Godwin and as many of Gibbon, and five pages of Para's *Physique Experimentale*. For some days past I have not inserted what I read. It was *not* because I was idle these days.

No. 12, *Friday, January 1st*, 1796.—The closing year yesterday put me in mind of the close of life, and made me reflect on the consequences. This day gives me an opportunity of speculating on the prospects of youth, but particularly the prospects which my situation and, much more, my imagination present [to] me. I am not, however, in a fit humour for descanting on such topics. In a future number, perhaps, I may engage in some attempts to analyse my opinions on these subjects.

I read this day twelve pages of " E. N. P.," about forty pages of Godwin, fifty of Gibbon, and sixteen of Para. (In continuation, see p. [11].) Mrs. Rigby is a most violent and inveterate democrat, as well as a deist. Her own misfortunes make [her] peevish on these subjects. But, with all her information, she has not a grain of common prudence. The servants neglect their business, plunder and cheat her. De Faria has served her with notice to quit this house on the twenty-fifth of March. This will inevitably be her ruin. Yet while she should be exerting herself to procure another house she is talking of Beaumont and Fletcher's plays, descanting [13] on Paine's *Age of Reason* (*d*), or arguing on the politics of the day. She seems in general to study the ease and convenience of servants rather than of her lodgers. Her authority is therefore gone. In her attachment for cats she becomes foolish and absurd. But she has a greater failing than any yet mentioned. It is a fondness for liquor. She gets drunk sometimes, and would in all probability do it oftener were she unrestrained by the fear of her lodgers forsaking the house. She is at all times familiar, but when heated with drinking she is rude in her familiarities.

(*d*) O'Connell became himself a student of this work. His opinion upon it will be found in No. 20.

No. 13, *Saturday*, *January 2nd*, 1796.—I shall now conclude my character of Mrs. Rigby with observing that, though possessed of a comprehensive and cultivated mind, she is deficient, in many respects, in common decorum and cleanliness.

I this day received a letter from Maurice, dated at Carhen on the 21st ulto. He is extremely irritated against the General (*e*). It would be extremely improper in me to inform the latter of the opinion on his conduct which the letter contains. However, I will behave with prudence and firmness on the occasion. I will not deny having the letter, nor will I show it. It would be well for me if I could follow the same method of conducting myself at all times. And why should I not? It is necessary for this purpose only to weigh well each action before I commence it.

(*e*) Maurice was O'Connell's brother, whose death is recorded below (p. 233). The General is Count O'Connell. Carhen was the residence of O'Connell's father. The letter was not asked for (see below, p. 104).

I am not *en train* for deep speculation, neither am I fit for gaiety or vivacity. What I write must be dull and lifeless, void of sense as of wit.

I this day read the usual quantity of " E. N. P.," sixteen pages of Godwin, about ninety pages of Gibbon, 3rd volume, and thirty of Boote's *Historical Account of a Suit at Law*. This work will in future be mention[ed] under the title " B. S. L." I read likewise some passages of *The Manual of Liberty* (to be contracted in future numbers to "M. L.") and 122 pages of *Hugh Trevor* to Miss Hunter (*f*) [14]. *The Memorial of Liberty* is composed of quotations from different authors, which quotations contain arguments to demonstrate the folly, or ridicule, to show the absurdities, of many of the existing political institutions. The confused, exaggerated, or false representations which crafty tyranny invents in support of these institutions, and blind prejudice receives, are dangerous to the liberty—that is, to the happiness—of mankind. The book in question supplies arguments to combat and convince even prejudice, and must therefore be useful in propagating the cause of truth (*g*).

(*f*) Miss Hunter was blind (see below, p. 105). The work here referred to is *The Adventures of Hugh Trevor*, by Thomas Holcroft. They are supposed to be told by Hugh Trevor himself. It is well written. The characters are vigorously drawn. There is a parson who entertains an inordinate opinion of the dignity of his cloth, and is eaten up with family pride. There is a squire who detests him, and upon one occasion shows his dislike by insisting that he shall receive payment of tithe of *rats*, as well as other produce of the estate, an incident which leads to a scuffle in which the Church is not only militant, but, with the assistance of Hugh, triumphant also. There is Hugh's father, a gentleman farmer, who is a capital judge of a horse, and hunts with the county magnates. There is a college tutor, who is treated with contumely by the young squire, and so on through several volumes of not unentertaining matter.

(*g*) *The Manual of Liberty ; or, Testimonies in behalf of the Rights of Mankind*, published in 1795. It is later on referred to erroneously as *The* Memorial *of Liberty*. The compiler quotes from Godwin, Burke, Rousseau, Voltaire, Bolingbroke, Machiavelli, Swift, Bacon, Shakespeare, Sterne, Goldsmith, and a number of other authors.

No. 14, *Sunday, January* 3*rd*, 1796.—I wrote this day a letter to Mr. Hobson about a proposal, or rather a request, he made me about twelve days ago. He wanted that I should join him in a *post obit* bond for twelve hundred pounds. A young man of the name of Fullarton, who boarded with Hobson, was to be the third security. At least so the latter asserted. He asserted likewise that Fullarton was bequeathed by an uncle thirty thousand pounds. Now, Fullarton is only seventeen. He may die before he comes of age. After he comes of age he may refuse to pay on a plea of *nonage*. Hobson may, and I suppose he will, become a bankrupt; so thus I would possibly be saddled with the debt. Add to this, the chance of this transaction coming to my uncle's knowledge would (had I been concerned in it) be a source of continual anxiety and apprehension. Of course I have declined in the most unqualified manner having anything to do with the business.

Let me now make a few observations on this affair. In the first place, Hobson must, in all probability, be either a fool or a knave, or perhaps both. He must be a fool to engage to pay twelve hundred pounds by a deed on which he could not possibly, as far as I can judge of the matter, get above three or four hundred, that is if he meant to discharge the engagement; and if he did not, he must be a knave. As for my own part, I blame myself for not giving an unequivocal denial to the proposal the moment it was made. I have given Hobson expectation of doing that which I never had any intention of doing. As for Hobson, he has neither information [15] nor worth to induce me to continue his acquaintance. The line of conduct which this fact bids me follow is obvious. Felix McCarthy(*h*) now lives entirely at Hobson's. An intimacy with this man may be dangerous. I must therefore shun him.

(*h*) Felix McCarthy was probably O'Connell's cousin.

I read to-day eighty pages of Gibbon, third volume, and sixty-three pages of *The Rights of Women* (Wolstonecraft). This work may, if perused with attention, be very useful. It is calculated to open the road to truth by clearing away prejudice. That the present system of female education is miserably erroneous, that mind has no sex, and that women are unjustly enslaved, are opinions I have long entertained. What portion of power in the government of the world ought to be entrusted to the female sex is a question which I cannot decide. However, Godwin has in some measure made up [my] mind on the subject by proving that government to be best which laid fewest restraints on private judgment. Surely the judgment of the one sex ought to be as unshackled as that of the other (*i*).

(*i*) The work here referred to is *A Vindication of the Rights of Woman*, which appeared in 1792. In it the authoress argued in favour of equality of education, and united education for boys and girls. The main argument of the work, as she states herself in the dedication to Talleyrand, was built on the simple principle that if woman were not prepared by education to become the companion of man, she would stop the progress of knowledge, for truth must be common to all, or it will be inefficacious with respect to its influence on general practice. She held up to scorn the educationists of the school of

Rousseau and Dr. Gregory, who taught that the whole duty of woman was to make herself agreeable to man, and be his willing slave; that for the purpose of captivating him she should cultivate a high degree of sensibility. Mary Wolstonecraft, who had been a governess, and had at one time kept a school in conjunction with her sisters, held the very opposite view. Girls should be brought up to be strong and healthy, should have plenty of outdoor exercise, and not merely the formal walk in procession to which the schoolgirl was generally confined. She anticipated the kindergarten system in her suggestions for the education of the very young, and she advocated women's suffrage and their admission into the medical profession. Her views naturally excited strong opposition, more especially as they were those of a woman who had answered Burke's *Reflections on the French Revolution*. Horace Walpole, in a letter to Hannah More, refers to her as "that hyæna in petticoats." Her views on marriage were lax, and she was in favour of greater facilities for divorce. She unfortunately formed an intimacy with a Captain Imlay, who deserted her after the birth of a daughter, Fanny, who after her mother's death poisoned herself, at the age of twenty-two. As mentioned above (p. 87), Mary Wolstonecraft afterwards married Godwin. They had one child, Mary, who married Percy Bysshe Shelley. Mrs. Godwin died a short time after her confinement, on September 10th, 1797, and was buried in the churchyard of Old St. Pancras; but her remains were afterwards removed by Sir Peter Shelley to the churchyard of St. Peter's, Bournemouth. Shelley, in his dedication of *The Revolt of Islam* to his wife, refers to her mother, and her father also, in the following stanza :—

> "They say that thou wert lovely from thy birth,
> Of glorious parents thou aspiring child :
> I wonder not, for one then left this earth
> Whose life was like a setting planet mild,
> Which clothed thee in the radiance undefiled
> Of its departing glory; still her fame
> Shines on thee through the tempests dark and wild
> Which shake these latter days; and thou canst claim
> The shelter from thy sire of an immortal name."

The Vindication of the Rights of Woman was finished in six weeks. As might be expected, it exhibits marks of this haste. O'Connell criticises the work in No. 23 below (p. 120). But the authoress thought little of the graces of style in comparison with the matter of her essay. "I shall disdain to cull my phrases or polish my style," she says in the introductory chapter. "I aim at being useful, and sincerity will render me unaffected." As Kegan Paul remarks in his collected edition of her letters, "her opinions have become in many particulars the commonplaces of our own day, while she who first proclaimed what is now held innocently was forgotten or assailed." Some of her maxims deserve to be remembered, such, for example, as these: "Make the heart clean, and give the head employment"; "A slavish bondage to parents cramps every faculty of the mind"; "If children are to be educated to understand the true principles of patriotism, the mother must be a patriot." Those who are interested in the life and work of this remarkable woman will derive a vast amount of information from Emma Rauschenbusch-Clough's *Study of Mary Wolstonecraft and the Rights of Women.*

No. 15, *Tuesday, January* 5*th,* 1796.—I was in town yesterday, and did not return until late in the evening. The General did not ask for Maurice's letter (*j*).

(*j*) See No. 13, p. 78.

I went to bed last night at one o'clock, and got up this morning at eight. My watch was at the maker's this some days past. This [is] the reason of my omitting the insertion of the hours of going to bed and rising. I will no longer insert the number of pages which I read each day; I shall content myself with setting down the day I begin and the day I end each book. From this rule I will except my law study. I have already resolved to read twelve pages a day of "E. N. P." Should I fail in this article, I will remark it in order that the insertion of one fault may serve to admonish me and prevent a repetition.

I shall for the future draw at least one *character* each week. Unless I thus limited myself to some fixed period, I should be putting off the execution of the project from day to day until it was no longer time.

MRS. HUNTER is the widow of a gentleman who resided in Rhode Island, on the coast of North America. She came to England about five [16] years since. Three daughters and a son, the whole of her family, accompanied her. The journey to Europe was undertaken for the purpose of consulting oculists on a disorder which had deprived the eldest daughter of sight. I do not now recollect whether this was pointed out to me by some person as the object of the journey, or whether I drew the conclusion myself from circumstances with which I have become acquainted. The son entered in the Temple, kept terms there, and is now practising at the American bar. He bears a very good, I should say excellent, character. Application and ability are its leading features. The two younger daughters are married, and, I believe, to advantage. The elder certainly has got a capital match. They are both fine women ; but the younger of them is truly beautiful. I never was so struck by female beauty as by hers. (To be continued.)

I last night begun the *Life of Dr. Johnson* by Arthur Murphy (*k*). This is reckoned the best Life of Johnson extant. He neither fatigues by the recital of trifles into which Boswell, Mrs. Piozzi, etc., descend ; and still it is so managed as not to disgust by a mere list of dates. Mr. Murphy is now sitting at tea with Mrs. Hunter in the room beneath that in which I write. He is a very agreeable, lively old man ; and looks extremely well, though at the age of seventy-five. He was attentive to me when I was here last year. He once attempted to argue me out of my democratic opinions. But he handled the subject very ill ; and, indeed, gave me several arguments against the propositions which he endeavoured to establish. However, I was not permitted to make use of any arguments. He kept the *debate* entirely to himself, and so of course had it all his own way.

(*k*) *An Essay on the Life and Genius of Samuel Johnson*, published in 1792. Murphy, as he states himself, " enjoyed the conversation and friendship of that excellent man more than thirty years." That partiality which he shows to the subject of his essay (see below, p. 114) may be accounted for by this long acquaintance.

I got the second volume of Godwin's *Political Justice* from Cawthorne's Library last night. I have this day read some chapters of it. I admire this work more, beyond comparison more, than any I ever met with. It has enlarged and strengthened my understanding, and infused into my mind a serenity never before enjoyed. In other words, it has made me a happier, and, I think, a better, man. I probably shall at another period give my sentiments concerning the book more at large (*l*).

(*l*) See p. 119.

I forgot to add to the paragraph in which I mentioned Mr. Murphy that his civility did not put on an air of coldness towards me until after my quarrel with D. Thompson (*m*). To the Thompson family Murphy is extremely attached. To me he is still very civil.

(*m*) See No. 9 above, p. 90.

No. 16, *Wednesday, January 6th,* 1796.—I went to bed last night at one o'clock, and got up this morning at half after nine. While I was yet in bed Thadee Sughrue called (*n*) [17]. The servant took him for a bailiff, and brought up his name, which he pronounced " Shrew." This occasioned a puzzle, during which T. S. went away, probably offended. I apprehended lest Thompson the father might wish to prosecute me in the court of King's Bench, and had employed the sheriff's officers to arrest me. This opinion it was that occasioned me to hesitate.

However, I was not long before I determined on meeting the man, let him be what he would.

(*n*) Probably a cousin of O'Connell. His aunt, Honora O'Connell, was the second wife of Charles Sughrue, of Fermoyle (*Last Colonel of the Irish Brigade*, i. 9 ; ii. 53).

I called on Mr. Murphy this morning about the affair with D. Thompson. We had some conversation on the subject, by which I found it was his opinion that a reconciliation should take place. To effect this reconciliation he and General Morrison were to be appointed arbiters. They were not to enter into the merits of the business, but, contenting themselves with the knowledge they already possessed, to cause us to *shake hands* after each asserted his sorrow for what had passed. I begged leave to say " that I could not agree to any such determination ; that I had been struck and could not therefore consent to meet on equal terms the person who, having injured me, had made no reparation ; however, that, rather than be bound to the peace a second time, I would pledge myself not to resent what was past either by action or word." Mr. Murphy coincided with me in the propriety of such sentiments. He, moreover, avowed his sense of *their* having acted in a blackguard manner. He has since been at Thompson's. I shall know something more about the business this evening.

No. 17, *Wednesday, January* 13*th*, 1796.—A week has elapsed since the last number was written. A soreness in my eyes—a trifling one indeed—and negligence were the causes of the interruption. I now reassume my pen, having formed a resolution to write something every day. The time of sitting down to begin the number for the day shall not, I intend, be later than half-past three. In mentioning the studies of the *day*—a practice I mean to reassume—the term *day* must be understood to mean the time that elapsed since a similar entry was made on the preceding day.

I went to bed last night at half after twelve, and got up this morning at ten.

Since I commenced this Journal at Chyswick I have felt many salutary effects from the thus taking a retrospective view of my conduct. I study much more than I did before. Indeed, while at home I read or write almost continually. But in the article of sleep I am as culpable as ever. Instead of going to bed early and getting up early, I do the reverse. Many resolutions have I formed on this head. No beneficial effect has [18] ensued. The resolution of the present moment may not be as futile as its predecessors.

(In continuation see p. [16]) Mrs. Hunter is about fifty-three years old if I form my judgment from circumstances, if from appearance not within six years of that age. She is tall and well made. Her eyes still retain a youthful lustre. When young her beauty must have been uncommonly striking. Her manners are agreeable and genteel, and she possesses a fund of good sense, knowledge of the world, and politeness. She has one foible. Even that is never carried to a troublesome length. She is fond of telling of the rank she very probably did in reality possess in her native country. But to perceive even this foible one must be a considerable time acquainted with her ; nay, must almost have gained her confidence. She is said to be attached to Mr. Brady. I did not discover this circumstance myself, though since I was [told (*o*)] it I have seen many things that confirm the information.

(*o*) The portion of the page where this word occurred is torn off; but there can be little doubt what the missing word was.

I have lately read the first part of Paine's *Age of Reason*. This work gave me a great deal of pleasure. In treating of the Christian system he is clear and concise. He has presented many things to my sight in a point of view in which I never before beheld them. Both the commencement and conclusion of *The Age of Reason* are well executed. The part in which the planetary system is treated does not please me in the same degree as the rest of the work (*p*).

(*p*) *The Age of Reason, being an Investigation of True and Fabulous Theology*, was published in Paris in 1794. Paine, who was the son of a Quaker staymaker, emigrated in 1774 to

America, where he took an active part in the War of Independence. He wrote a pamphlet, entitled *Common Sense*, in favour of separation, which had an electrical effect. While serving under Washington as a private soldier, he wrote by the light of camp fires a stirring tract called *The Crisis*. Fortune was at that time turning against the colonists. The tract opened with the words " These are the times that try men's souls." It was read to the army, and had an immense influence in restoring their courage. He returned to England after the republic was established, and wrote *The Rights of Man*, in reply to Burke's *Reflections on the Revolutions in France*. For this he was prosecuted on a charge of high treason, but allowed to escape to France, where he had been elected a deputy for Calais. Having excited the suspicions of Robespierre, he was thrown into prison. On his way there he put into the hands of his friend Joel Barlow the first part of *The Age of Reason*, which he had composed in the interval between his accusation and his arrest, and had only completed seven hours before the latter took place. The work excited the greatest indignation in America as well as in England. Washington, to whom *The Rights of Man* was dedicated, showed his disapproval by refusing to interfere to obtain his release. He lay in prison several months after the fall of Robespierre, which took place on July 28th, 1794. The second part of *The Age of Reason* was published after his release. O'Connell's opinion of it will be found below (p. 116). Paine believed in one God, and hoped for happiness in a future state. He disbelieved in all Churches. " My mind," he said, " is my own Church." In another place he says, " I believe in the equality of men, and I believe that religious duties consist in doing justice, loving mercy, and endeavouring to make our fellow-creatures happy." While denying the Divinity of Christ, Paine spoke of His life and doctrines with the utmost respect. " The morality which he preached and practised was of the most benevolent kind. Though similar systems of morality have been preached by Confucius and by some of the Greek philosophers many years before, by the Quakers since, and by many good men in all ages, it has not been exceeded by any." " Jesus Christ founded no new religion. He called men to the practice of moral virtues, and the belief in one God. The great trait in his character is philanthropy." One passage in *The Age of Reason* was, unconsciously no doubt, plagiarised or imitated by O'Connell in his speech in defence of Magee, the editor of the *Dublin Evening Post*. Paine writes, " Infidelity does not consist in believing or disbelieving ; it consists in professing to believe what he "— man—" does not believe himself." O'Connell said, " Every religion is good, every religion is true, to him who in his due caution and conscience sincerely believes it. There is only one bad religion : that of a man who professes a faith in which he does not believe." *The Age of Reason* has been translated into Japanese by Viscount Hayashi.

Were this Journal to fall into the hands of any of my acquaintance, how ridiculous would it appear ! But it would be the *devil itself* if it was by any accident met with by one of those persons whose characters I have endeavoured to sketch.

Bennett (*q*) set off for Ireland on Monday evening. He was not married a month at the time of his departure. How happy or how miserable would not his condition render me ! I mean not his absence from his wife ; I mean his connection with her. But I will not now speculate on this subject.

(*q*) Richard Newton Bennett (see above, p. 78).

No. 18, *Thursday, January* 14*th*, 1796.—I went to bed last night about one, and got up this morning at nine. I read this day fifteen pages of " E. N. P.," twenty-two pages of Para, and thirty of Godwin.

I have likewise read two volumes and a half of a

novel called *The Ring* (*r*), the most stupid, insipid work I ever met with. Yet I mean to finish it before I go to bed.

(*r*) The Editor has been unable to trace this work; but having regard to O'Connell's estimate of it, perhaps it is no great matter.

I received [a letter] from Anny this morning. It mentions the conduct of Maurice while at home, which I shall treat of in a future number (*s*).

(*s*) There is no further reference to this matter in the Journal. Maurice is, of course, his brother. O'Connell had an aunt Anne, who married Maurice Geoffrey O'Connell. She may be the Anny mentioned here.

No. 19, *Monday, January* 18*th*, 1796.—I went to town on Friday, and did not return until Saturday evening. On Friday I attended at the Old Bailey. Two highwaymen were tried and found guilty. Now, if these unfortunate individuals are hanged, will one more virtue be infused into the bosom of any individual ? Will one crime less be committed than would be had they escaped ? Certainly not. The experience of ages has shown the inefficacy of punishment. The reasoning of the speculatist shows its immorality. Yet men continue to inflict punishment on their fellow - beings. Driven to despair by the wants of nature and the contempt of his acquaintance, the man whose most strenuous efforts are insufficient to procure him subsistence

takes the road and forcibly deprives the luxurious
or the unfeeling of a portion of their superfluities.
The sacred rights of property, thus violated, devote
the head of the *unwilling* spoliator to destruction.
And this is what we are thought to call justice.
O, Justice, what horrors are committed in thy
name! (*t*).

(*t*) We can in this passage trace the influence of the
teachings of Godwin, who was opposed to all punishments.
The criminal law of England was at this period a barbarous
and sanguinary code, the most trifling offences being punished
with death. The unfortunate victims of the law were, in some
instances, not merely hung, but disembowelled before death.
Women were, from motives of delicacy, spared this cruelty;
they were, as an indulgence, burned alive instead!

I read this day fifty-eight pages of Para, about
sixty of Godwin, and about one hundred and three
pages of *An Essay on the Life and Genius of
Johnson*, by Arthur Murphy.

I believe that I have already remarked that Mr.
Murphy's style is clear, easy, and not inelegant.
But he is nothing less than a philosopher. He
seems to defend not truth, but Johnson. He runs
out in [to] many unnecessary declamations on
modern reformers or *metaphysical theorists*.

I wrote and dispatched a letter this day to my
uncle Maurice for money. The style of this letter
satisfied me more than that of many other letters
of mine had done.

I dined with . . . (*u*) on Friday, and spent the

night with him. The lady of the house is a fine young woman. She seemed to be partial to me, and I endeavoured to improve this partiality. She is a most debauched woman. She pretended before we parted to have taken a great liking to me. Nay, she acted the part of an *inamorata*. My vanity has *not* frequently suggested the flattering idea that it may in reality be so. But when I recollect the side of her character which her conversation showed me, I must imagine that she is only an artful woman who meant to take me in. However, I have little [20] chance of ever being able to profit of her good graces, did I possess them, for want of an opportunity.

(*u*) For obvious reasons the name of O'Connell's host is omitted.

No. 20, Tuesday, January 19th, 1796.—I read this day 110 pages of Gibbon, Vol. 4, thirty-two pages of Godwin, and thirty-three pages of Para. I read likewise part of the treatise on aerology in Hall's *Encyclopædia.*

I read but five pages of " E. N. P." The artificial, unnatural distinctions of the law disgust, while the iniquity of punishing ignorance shocks. To understand the second branch of the foregoing sentence, it is necessary to recollect that in new cases the probability is that the losing party was prompted by the doubtful terms of the Acts of Parliament to undertake or defend the suit. Ignorance is punished in another manner by the English courts of *justice*. Men not unfrequently lose considerable interests through the ignorance of their special pleaders. The omission of a word in a declaration is sufficient to set aside the best-founded judgment. And this case is peculiarly cruel, as the individual who suffers is innocent of the mistake or neglect which proved fatal to his interests.

I this day finished the second part of *The Age of Reason* (v). This part has given me more satisfaction than the former. It has put the foundation of the religious question of the Christians in a point of view in which a judgement is easily formed on its solidity. I now have no doubts on this head. I may certainly be mistaken. But I am not wilfully mistaken, if the expression has any meaning. My mistakes I refer to the mercy of that Being who is wise by excellence. To the God of nature do I turn my heart; to the meditation of His works I turn my thoughts. In Him do I find my soul saturated. He will not, justice tells me, punish for a darkness, if such it be, that cannot be removed ; He will not punish for the unbiassed conviction of the soul. To affirm the contrary would, in my apprehension, be to calumniate.

(v) O'Connell's views as to the first part will be found above (p. 110).

Mrs. Hunter got a letter this morning from

Mr. Murphy (*w*), who is now at Streatham, the residence of Mrs. Piozzi and Mrs. MacNamara. With the latter, I believe, he now resides. Murphy says that he got a letter from Douglas Thompson informing him that he was content to submit our quarrel to his decision. Mrs. Hunter was requested to prevent my taking any steps in the business until Mr. Murphy's arrival, which is to be on Thursday. I have not yet determined on the line of conduct which I ought to pursue steadily. I wish Bennett was here to assist me with his advice.

(*w*) Arthur Murphy, the biographer of Dr. Johnson (see above, p. 106).

[21] In the sixteenth number I have concluded by expressing my expectation of hearing something concerning the affair. I did not speak with Murphy until the next day on the subject. He then told me that Thompson the father said he would drop the legal prosecution, as it was his request; that he replied that it was not his request, for I had my remedy at law as well as my antagonist. Thompson refused to have any *sort of reconciliation* take place. Mr. Murphy was not a little irritated against him. He went so far as to advise me in pretty plain terms to revenge myself by violence.

I read a sermon by Blair of 24 pages (*x*).

(*x*) Dr. Blair, a Scottish divine, pastor of the High Church, Edinburgh. He published five volumes of sermons, the first of which appeared in 1777. Dr. Johnson admired them greatly, and George III., to mark his approval, conferred a pension of £200 a year upon Blair. He wrote a dissertation on Macpherson's Ossian, which is referred to below (p. 132).

No. 21, *Wednesday, January* 20*th,* 1796.—Religious subjects engross much of my attention. The prejudices of childhood and youth at times frighten and shake the firmness of my soul. These fears, these doubts, perhaps imply a libel on the First Cause, the Great Spirit who created the planetary systems that roll around. It is impossible that He whose justice is *perfect* should punish with eternal torments the belief which is founded on conviction. It appears impossible because the conviction of the mind does not depend on us. We cannot prevent, we cannot change, the belief that our souls form on the perceptions of the senses. Again, these perceptions are not in our power. We receive impressions from the surrounding objects notwithstanding all our efforts to the contrary. It would in fact be as absurd and criminal to say that the Great Spirit would punish me for not believing that it is *now* noon as to affirm that He would inflict tortures for not believing another proposition the belief of which is equally impossible.

I went to bed last night at about one, and got up this morning at half after eight. I read this day thirteen pages of " E. N. P." and sixty-eight of Gibbon, twenty of Godwin, eleven of Para, and a *novel* called *The Man of Feeling* (*y*), in one volume. I was very much entertained with this work. There is cast of melancholy in it that pleases and sympathises with my soul. Besides, the goodness of heart, the kind benevolent love for his fellow-creatures, which the hero of the tale is made to display, have charms for every mind that preserves any portion of the purity [22] of nature. Whether the idea I have just expressed is or is not philosophical I have not *leisure* or *means* now to determine.

(*y*) By Mackenzie. It was published anonymously in 1771, and obtained great popularity. A man named Eccles laid claim to the authorship. He transcribed the whole in his own handwriting, with interlineations and corrections! The author published *The Man of the World* a few years later. He died in 1831, at the age of eighty-six.

No. 22, Saturday, January 30th, 1796.—Since I wrote my last number the train of my usual occupations has been much disturbed. I went to town several times to endeavour to conclude Middleton's affair (*z*). I went to town likewise to keep my term. A detail of the events of the last would be uninteresting. I wanted time and resolution to put my thoughts to paper.

(*z*) See below, p. 121.

I have finished Godwin (*a*). His work cannot be too highly praised. All mankind are indebted to the author. The cause of despotism never met a more formidable adversary. He goes to the root of every evil that now plagues man and degrades him almost beneath the savage beast. He shows the source whence all the misfortunes of mankind flow. That source he demonstrates to be political government.

(*a*) See above, p. 87.

No. 23, *Sunday, January* 31*st,* 1796.—I did not get up this morning until ten o'clock, notwithstanding the many resolutions which I have made on the subject of lying in bed. I do not know when I shall be able to cure myself of laziness. I lose to it the most precious part of the day.

Were I to make a few remarks on my style, I should find much to blame. My sentences do not flow into each other with natural ease. They are unconnectedly jumbled together. It is not necessary to quote anything I have written to illustrate these assertions. Even while I mention my faults I give a specimen of them. Yet I cannot help observing that since I treated this subject in a former number my style seems to me to have improved.

[23] I read this day 148 pages of *The Rights of Women,* by Mary Wolstonecraft ; 124 pages of Gibbon, Vol. 4.

In *The Rights of Women* there are many truths mixed with several errors. The authoress certainly possesses a strong mind. Her style is not good, though the language is correct. She is too fond of metaphor. Images crowd too fast on the reader.

And in the decoration we lost [sic] sight of the substance. I have this [day] finished the first volume. I am told a second has lately appeared (b).

(b) See above, p. 102.

No. 24, *Thursday, February* 18*th*, 1796.——Since I wrote the last number I have been much occupied by the trial of the affair with George Middleton. To retain the recollection of this transaction, I will make mention of its commencement. I will give a sketch of the entire.

On Sunday, the 26th of April last, I invited Bennett and De Vignier to take a bottle with me at the *Packhorse* tavern in Turnham Green. Douglas Thompson (c) joined us. We remained drinking until about ten o'clock. As we returned home, and after Thompson had quitted us, De Vignier, heated with wine, amused himself by rapping at several doors. Arrived at *this house*, we unfortunately agreed to take a turn before we came in. During our walk Bennett and I rescued De V. from a scrape he had got into by frightening a woman. As we advanced towards home De V. rapped repeatedly (twice) and loudly at the door of a Mr. de Faria, a Portuguese (d). The servant rushed out. De V. had joined us. The servant, after using abusive language, challenged any (or, I believe, *all*) of us to fight. I stept forward to accept the challenge. We made some blows at each other without effect, when

De V. rushed at my antagonist and gave him a kick in the belly.   A moment after Bennett, interposing, received a blow from the servant on the face. Bennett had a small cane in one hand.   He seized the boy with the other and beat him severely.   The boy received a wound on the head.   The neighbour-hood was alarmed.   The Misses de Faria rushed forth, as did their father, etc.   One of the former began to pummel Bennett [24].   We had almost effected our retreat, when the watchman stopped us. De Faria charged him with Bennett.   We set off for the watchhouse accompanied by one half of the inhabitants of the village.   Arrived at the watch-house, De V. and I were told that [we] may depart. But we remained there all night.   I would not quit Bennett, and De V. did not know that he could quit him.   In our way to the watchhouse I abused De Faria grossly.   (To be continued) (*d*).

(*c*) Middleton was no doubt De Faria's servant. Bennett is Richard Newton Bennett, so often mentioned in the Journal. De Vignier is the gentleman mentioned above (p. 63). Thompson is Douglas Thompson, with whom O'Connell had the quarrel described above.   The " Packhorse " still exists. It is called " The ' Old Packhorse ' Inn," and has undergone some changes since that bottle was drunk ; but the fabric of the original building, to a large extent, has been preserved. The inn lies on the high-road which is now traversed by the electric trams that ply between Shepherd's Bush and Kew. It is only a short distance from the Mall, Chyswick.

(*d*) De Faria seems to have been Mrs. Rigby's landlord (see above, p. 98).

There is no continuation of the account of this incident.

I this day finished the fifth volume of Gibbon.
I have, since I wrote the last number, [read] *Caleb
Williams*, 3 vols. by Godwin; the 1st, 2nd, and
4th volumes of Voltaire's works: these volumes
contain some of his tragedies; *Confessions of
J. J. Rousseau*, 1st volume; *Recueil Nécessaire*, 1 vol.
I finished *The Manual of Liberty*. I have begun
yesterday a translation of Zapata's *Questions* from
the *Recueil Nécessaire* (*e*). I have likewise begun a
novel which I probably never shall finish (*f*).

(*e*) Godwin is the same person as the author of *Political
Justice* (see above, p. 87). *Caleb Williams* is a political, or
rather a social, novel, illustrating the oppression practised by
the British aristocracy upon their tenants and dependants.
Voltaire's works and Rousseau's *Confessions* are too well
known to need further reference. *The Manual of Liberty* is the
subject of a brief note above (p. 100). The *Recueil Nécessaire* was
published at Leipsic in 1765. It consists of a series of pieces
written by Freethinkers, for example *Analyse de la Religion
Chrétienne*, par Dumarsais; *Le Vicaire Savoyard*, tiré de *L'Emile*
de J. J. Rousseau; *Catéchisme de l'Honnête Homme ; ou, Dialogue
entre un Caloyer et un Homme de Bien: Dialogue du Douteur et de
l'Adorateur*. The *Questions*, by Domenico Zapata, were translated from the French "by a Lady." The French original is by
Voltaire, who wrote, on this occasion, under the *nom de plume*
of Domenico Zapata. It professes to be itself a translation by
Le Sieur Tamponnet, Doctor of the Sorbonne, and was
published at Leipsic—or more probably at Geneva—in 1766.
The following account of the origin of the work is given as a
sort of preface: The Licentiate Zapata, being appointed
Professor of Theology in the university of Salamanca, presented these questions to the junta of doctors in 1629. They
were suppressed. A Spanish copy is preserved in the Brunswick Library." The *Questions* are pointed to the difficulties

presented by the Old and New Testament Scriptures, an explanation of which Zapata asks the doctors to give him for the purpose of assisting him in the discharge of his duties as professor. The work winds up thus :—" Zapata, not having got any answer, proceeded to preach God simply. He proclaimed to men the Father of men, who rewards, punishes, and pardons. . . . He was gentle, kind, and modest, and he was roasted at Valladolid in the year of grace 1631."

(*f*) It is doubtful whether O'Connell means that he has begun the reading, or the writing, of a novel. He undoubtedly was at one time going to write one, for he told O'Neill Daunt so. " We spoke," says the author of *The Personal Recollections*, " of a story I meant to weave into a novel. ' I think,' said I, '*you* would be somewhat out of your element assisting a novelist in his compositions.' 'Not in the least,' he answered. ' I was once going to write a novel myself.' ' Indeed ! And what was your story to have been ? ' 'Why, as to the story, I had 'not that fully determined on. But my hero was to have been a natural son of George III. by Hannah Lightfoot. The youth was to have been early taken from his mother, and I meant to make him a student at Douay, and thence to bring him through various adventures to the West Indies. He was to be a soldier of fortune, to take part in the American war, and to come back finally to England imbued with republican ideas.' " Needless to say, O'Connell was right in the forecast, if such it were, recorded in his Journal. The novel never was finished.

This is the last entry made in the Journal while O'Connell was living at Chiswick. He was entered as a student at Gray's Inn on April 16th, 1796, and kept one term there. He came to Dublin and there kept his terms at the King's Inns preparatory to his call to the Irish bar. The only compulsory training then undergone by a candidate for the higher branch of the legal profession was the eating of a certain number of dinners—so many legs of mutton, as O'Connell described it—in the common hall of one of the English Inns of Court and of the King's Inns, Dublin. Neither attendance

at lectures nor passing a qualifying examination was necessary.
The association with other students while consuming the prescribed number of meals was, and apparently still is, supposed
in some mysterious way to operate as a kind of legal education,
probably on the erroneous assumption that law students discuss
jurisprudence over their wine, of which, as well as of beer,
they get an adequate allowance from the cellar of the Inn,
English or Irish, to which they happen to belong. When the
Inns of Court in London formed a sort of legal university, in
which the students and barristers lived, there was much to be
said in favour of the custom of dining together. It is only
since May, 1885, that the Irish law student has been relieved
of the necessity of paying periodical visits to London for the
purpose of consuming the number of dinners supposed to be
requisite to complete his legal education. The origin of this
rule was a statute passed in the reign of Henry VIII. by the
Irish Parliament, 33 Hen. VIII., sess. 2, chap. 3, sec. 3, which
enacts that "no person . . . shall be admitted or allowed as a
pleader in any of the King's principal courts . . . but such
person hath or shall be by the space of   [*sic*] years complete demurrant and resiant in one of the Inns of Court within
the realm of England, studying, practising, and endeavouring
themselves the best they can to the true knowledge and judgment of the said laws, upon pain of c. s." This Act was to
continue only till the last day of the next Parliament, but was
made perpetual by the eleventh, of Elizabeth, sess. 1, chap. 5.
In time the provisions of the Act came to be considered as
sufficiently complied with by eating three dinners in each of
the four law terms for a period of one and a half years.
O'Connell, as we have seen, kept one term at Gray's Inn, as
well as keeping seven terms at Lincoln's Inn. Thus, when he
had kept terms at the King's Inns, Ireland, he served, as he said,
"a threefold apprenticeship to the law." A curious regulation
existed until very recently as regards the bill of fare at dinner
at the King's Inns. It probably existed in O'Connell's time.
It was this. The bill of fare was a fixed thing for every day in
every term. Thus in Michaelmas and Hilary terms the student

or the barrister, if he chose to dine, was regaled with boiled beef, mashed parsnip, and boiled fowl or turkey, on every Monday ; while on the same day in Easter and Trinity terms he dined off boiled chicken, pig's cheek, or bacon, spinach, parsley, or plain sauce, and roast mutton. The *menu* varied each day in the week, vegetable soup and fish, as well as flesh meat, being provided on Fridays and some other days, to meet the wants of Catholics.

In the correspondence between Count O'Connell and Hunting-cap during the year 1796 there is one reference to O'Connell. On March 7th the Count writes, " I have received £20 sterling British, which I shall deposit here in Captain Fagan's hands, for the use of our nephew Dan, in case you should wish it to be so employed, or to be remitted to you by bill on Dublin, if you prefer the latter method. . . . Dan is well."

No. 25, Saturday, December 3rd, 1796.—I now resume my Journal, after almost a year of neglect, with the resolution of continuing it with punctuality for the future. I know not how long this resolution will last. But this I know : that to persevere in it would be of the utmost utility to me. Did I regularly record the reading of the day, shame would prevent me from being negligent. The perusal of my Journal would be the best reward of diligence, the surest punishment of idleness.

I read this day 130 pages of Gibbon, Vol. 1, p. 324—454. I read, and read with attention, the first chapter of Smith's *Wealth of Nations* (p. 14). Dr. Smith in this chapter proves that the product of labour is increased by division, so that ten men can make more of a given work in one day than one man can in two hundred days and upwards. He supports his position by the example of pinmen, nailors, etc., by reasoning : (1) argument, improvement of dexterity ; (2) no time lost in passing from one branch to another, more ready [25] invention of machinery. " It is the great multiplication of the productions of all the arts, in consequence of the division of labour, which occasions in a well-governed society that universal opulence which extends itself to the lowest rank of the society " (p. 11). Each workman has to spare a great quantity of the produce of his labour. Each can therefore easily procure the necessaries of life in great quantities.

The division of labour cannot take place in agriculture. . . . The corn of the rich country therefore will not always in the same degree of goodness come cheaper to market than that of the poor. The corn of Poland is as cheap as that of France, etc.

I wrote a letter to John Hayes and part of one to Henry Baldwin (g).

(g) John Hayes was probably one of the family of that name who lived at Kinneigh, between Cahirciveen and Waterville. Henry Baldwin was the Liberator's first cousin, being son of his aunt Mary, who is described by Mrs. Morgan John O'Connell as " the flower of the flock, blue-eyed and golden-haired." She captivated an elegant young Englishman named Herbert, a near relative of the Earl of Powis, who came over to visit some Irish estates, and was wrecked on the rocks at Darrynane, but rescued and hospitably entertained there. He proposed for Mary O'Connell, but her mother, Maur-ni-Dhuiv, was too proud to allow her daughter to enter any family on sufferance, and, as he had not obtained the consent of his parents, gave him a very bad reception when he addressed himself to her. He departed, and nothing was heard of him for several months. Meantime Maur-ni-Dhuiv arranged a marriage with Mr. James Baldwin, of Clohina, county Cork, whom the fair Mary married in 1762. At the wedding breakfast a letter came from Mr. Herbert announcing that he had obtained the consent of his parents and Earl Powis (*Last Colonel of the Irish Brigade*, i. 162). Henry Baldwin is referred to again below (pp. 136 and 142).

No. 26, *Monday, December* 5*th*, 1796.—I yesterday read 145 pages of Gibbon, p. 454—599, to the end of the first volume. The edition was printed for Luke White, in Dame Street, 1789 (*h*).

(*h*) The ancestor of Lord Annally.

I this day extracted from Gibbon a chronological list of the emperors from Gallus, successor to Decius, A.D. 252, to the year 324, when Constantine, falsely called the *Great*, was sole emperor. I read and noted eight pages of *Coke on Littleton*, Vol. 1. I read Blackstone's *Commentaries* to p. 38, Vol. 1. It is the small Dublin edition which I read at present. I mean to peruse it with the most accurate care, the most searching attention. I will afterwards read Christian's edition of the same work, in order to imprint on my mind more strongly the doctrines of my author. Blackstone possesses one very singular advantage for a law-writer : he is clear and not uninteresting. As for Coke's *Institutes*, were it not for the happy absurdities with which they abound, the pedantry of style, the obscurity of matter, and the loathsome tediousness of trifling would create unsurmountable disgust (*i*).

(*i*) *The Commentaries on the Laws of England* consisted of the substance of a series of lectures delivered in the university of Oxford. They commenced in 1753. The Preface to the work as published is dated November 2nd, 1765. How great was the demand for it may be judged from the fact that the eighth edition appeared in 1778. No English law book ever passed through so many editions. That by Christian is still, with the necessary alterations resulting from statute-made and judge-made law, a text-book for the students of our jurisprudence. *The Commentaries* have been translated into Chinese.

[26] *No. 27, Wednesday, December 7th, 1796.*— I yesterday subscribed to the Dublin Library, in Eustace Street. I paid two guineas—a great sum of money for me. But I think I shall have very ample value for it. I mean to spend four days in the week in it (*j*). I am at present engaged in reading Whitaker's *History of Manchester* (*k*) and Henry's *History of England* (*l*). The former, I find, has an implicit belief in the genuineness of Ossian's poems. On this subject I must read Blair's critical essay. I must remark that the names of Ossian's heroes were familiar to my

infancy, and long before I had heard of Macpherson or his translation the characters of the poem[s] were mostly known to me (*m*).

(*j*) O'Connell, as he tells us in No. 29, made great use of this library, remaining there until it closed at ten o'clock, and then leaving with reluctance.   The Dublin Library Society, Eustace Street, was founded in 1790.   The library was afterwards removed to D'Olier Street, where it remained until it was closed some years ago.   It must have been a great boon to a man in O'Connell's position.   There was then no free library in Dublin, except Marsh's, the contents of which were not suited to O'Connell's requirements, and he would not have access to the library of Trinity College, not being a student of the university.   O'Connell's constant visits to the Dublin Library brought some suspicion upon him.   Macdonagh in his *Life of O'Connell* (p. 34) quotes a report, dated March 7th, 1798, made by Francis Higgins, better known as "the Sham Squire," for Edward Cooke, the Under-Secretary, stating that James Tandy, the son of Napper Tandy, an agent of the United Irishmen in France, waited on a Mr. Connell with a letter. "Connell," says the report, "holds a commission from France (a colonel's).   He was to be called to the bar to please a rich old uncle, but he is one of the most abominable and bloodthirsty Republicans I ever heard.   The place of rendezvous is the public library in Eustace Street, where a private room is devoted to the leaders of the United Irish Society."   The statement as to O'Connell being a Republican, bloodthirsty or otherwise, at that time was, we know from the Journal, utterly false.   But that he attended meetings of the Reformers in Eustace Street, though not at the Dublin Library, we know from his own lips.   "In my young days," he told O'Neill Daunt once when passing Eustace Street, "there used to be a celebrated tavern in that street where the Reformers of the period held several of their meetings.   I was at one of these meetings in 1797; it was a meeting of lawyers.   John Sheares and the present Judge Burton attended it. . . . I was not then a lawyer; I only went as a spectator. It was fortunate for me that I could not then participate in the proceedings. I felt warmly, and a young Catholic student stepping prominently forth in opposition to the Government would have been in all probability hanged. I learned much by being a *looker-on* at that time. I had many opportunities of acquiring valuable information, upon which I soon formed my own judgment. The political leaders of the period could not conceive such a thing as a perfectly open and aboveboard political machinery. My friend Richard Newton Bennett was an adjunct to the Directory of United Irishmen. I was myself a United Irishman. As I saw how matters worked, I soon learned the lesson to have no secrets in politics. Other leaders made their *workings* secret, and only intended to bring out the results. They were therefore in perpetual peril of treachery. You saw men on whose fidelity you would have staked your existence playing false when tempted by the magnitude of the bribe on one side, and on the other the danger of hanging " (*Personal Recollections*, ii. p. 98). O'Connell himself, though he knew nothing of the Sham Squire's report, felt that, despite his wariness, he ran some risk. In entry No. 67 he writes, " It is impossible for any young man at the present day to guess with probable success at the mode in which his existence will terminate. This opinion has been in my mind these two days past. I have in consequence been accustoming myself to consider death without shrinking. . . . I must avoid disclosing my political opinions so frequently as I do at present. It would be a devilish unpleasant thing to get caged! Nonsense! Liberality can never become dangerous." He writes in No. 70, under date January 30th, 1798, " Such is the complexion of affairs that it must appear extremely doubtful whether I shall be called to the bar." No action appears to have been taken on the report made by Francis Higgins, and as O'Connell was called on May 19th, 1798, the inaccuracy of Higgins's suggestion that the intention to get called had been abandoned probably convinced the authorities that the rest of his disclosures were equally unfounded. The premises occupied by the Dublin Library in D'Olier Street became the offices of the Alliance and Dublin Consumers' Gas Company.

(*k*) The Rev. John Whitaker's *History of Manchester* appeared in 1731. The plan of it was to divide the work into four books, containing as many periods, namely, (1) British and Roman-British; (2) Saxon; (3) Danish and Norman-Danish; (4) Modern. The first and second only were finished. The work was not confined to the history of Manchester, but extended to whatever curious particulars could, with any propriety, be connected with it, including anything that served to illustrate the general antiquities of the country or the county.

(*l*) *History of Britain Written on a New Plan*, by Robert Henry. The novel feature consisted in combining with the narrative of events occurring in each era an account of the domestic state and social progress of the people during the same period. The first volume appeared in 1771. Henry died in 1790, before the tenth volume was ready for the press. A continuation by J. Petit Andrews, bringing the narrative down to James I., was published in 1796.

(*m*) *A Critical Dissertation on the Poems of Ossian, the Son of Fingal*, by Hugh Blair, D.D., the author of the volume of sermons mentioned above (p. 117). The first of the poems is called "Fingal," after the hero of the tale. He hails from the land of *Morven*, and falls in love with Agandecea. She is the daughter of his enemy, Swaran, whom he defeats, but spares for her sake. The poems are dedicated to the Earl of Bute, and are preceded by a dissertation on their antiquity, in which Macpherson gravely fixed the date, *from internal evidence*, at the end of the third century A.D. Blair was Professor of Rhetoric and *Belles-lettres* in the university of Edinburgh. He was a friend of Macpherson, and lectured on his Ossian. The *Dissertation* consisted of the substance of his lectures. Blair was enthusiastic in praise of the poems. They were the composition of an eye-witness of the events they chronicle. They unconsciously conformed to the rules prescribed by the *Ars Poetica* of Horace, and the canons laid down by Aristotle.

Ossian was equal, if not superior, to Virgil, and did not suffer by comparison with Homer, whom he excelled in the matter of ghosts. After the publication of the *Dissertation* the authenticity of the poems was questioned. Blair was greatly shocked, and appended to a new edition of the *Dissertation* the testimony of a number of Scots, clergymen, officers in the army, and others, who vouched for having heard the poems recited in the original Gaelic or Erse. This, with the assenting silence of the whole nation of Scotland, was enough to convince the Doctor. But it did not convince the public, who wanted to see the original manuscripts, but never could, though Macpherson, in the second edition of the work, inserted what purported to be a copy of that of the seventh book of "Temora," one of the poems. Johnson was among the unbelievers. Blair, for whose sermons he had, as we have seen, a great admiration, was introduced to him, and asked him whether any man of the present day could have written the poems. Johnson, who was not aware that Blair had written the *Dissertation*, replied, "Yes, sir, many men, many women, and *many children*" (Boswell's *Life*). This was, of course, only a specimen of Johnson's usual exaggeration, for *Ossian* is far from being without literary merit of a kind. Johnson based his disbelief in the authenticity of the poems on the fact that, unlike the more cultivated Irish and Welsh, the Scotch did not commit their poetry to writing. Macpherson sent a threatening letter to Johnson, who "answered it in the rough phrase of stern defiance" (Murphy's *Essay on the Life and Genius of Samuel Johnson*). O'Connell's familiarity with the names of Macpherson's heroes was quite natural, as they were *Irish* heroes. Those who are interested in the Ossianic controversy will find the subject fully discussed in the recent work by Mr. J. S. Smart.

I yesterday read the article "Gladiator" in the *Encyclopédie* and in the *Encyclopædia Britannica*. The latter seems, if I may judge by *this* article, to be the work of compilers, the former that of

philosophers (*n*).   They both agree in deducing the
savage custom of gladiators' shows from the perhaps
less savage one of sacrificing prisoners at the
funeral of deceased kings and heroes.   The first
show of gladiators at Rome was exhibited by M.
and D. Brutus on the death of their father in
the year of the city 490.   It is possible that there
were but three pair of gladiators.   The Romans
became so fond of this sanguinary diversion that
candidates for the different offices found it necessary to gratify them in it.   But the eloquent, the
patriotic Cicero, Cicero, on whose fame my heart
delights to dwell, Cicero, who deserved to be born
in a better age—he got a law passed prohibiting
any person from exhibiting gladiators within two
years before he appeared candidate for any office.
The gladiators were commonly slaves brought up
to this profession by the *lanistæ*.   The gladiators
seem to have been almost as fond of fighting as the
people were of seeing them fight.   The passion for
this *amusement* is a strong proof of the malevolence
of the human disposition.

(*n*) O'Connell's criticism of the *Encyclopédie* was just.   It was
he work of some of the best intellects of France.   Diderot, the
moving spirit in the undertaking, secured the co-operation of
such men as D'Alembert, Montesquieu, Turgot, Voltaire,
Rousseau, Condorcet, and Bernouilli.   The special department
assigned to Condorcet as a contributor included arts and trades.
He spent whole days in workshops.   He learned to work the
machines himself, first having examined them carefully, and
having them taken to pieces and put together again.   The

Encyclopédie was, however, very unequal in quality. D'Alembert compared it to a harlequin's coat, containing some good material, but too many rags. It was produced, moreover, under great difficulties. The Church denounced it ; the Government suppressed it ; and, worst of all, the printer, in a panic, mutilated it by leaving out whatever was too daring or was likely to give offence. The first edition of the *Encyclopædia Britannica* was completed in 1771. The publication of the third edition, which is probably that which O'Connell read, was commenced in 1787, and completed in 1797.

The Gladiators' war, under Spartacus, commenced [27] in the year of the city 630, and was terminated by Licinius Crassus in the year 632.

I read yesterday fourteen pages in folio of the Preface to Bayle's *Dictionnaire Philosophique et Critique.* I likewise read fifteen pages of the Preface to Dr. Henry's *History of England.*

I this day read eighteen pages of Whitaker's *History of Manchester*, to p. 18, and 79 pages of Henry's *History of England*, to p. 80.

No. 28, Thursday, December 8th, 1796.—To what I wrote yesterday concerning gladiators I must add that I know not where this barbarous custom first was established. I believe that the first fact in the history of gladiatorship well authenticated is that mentioned in the foregoing page. It was not introduced into Greece until the reign of Antiochus Epiphanes. The Athenians never would receive it in their city. It was once proposed by some person that some gladiators should be exhibited in Athens. " Let us first," cried an old Athenian quickly—" Let us first pull down the altar which our forefathers erected to mercy a thousand years ago."

I wrote this day a letter to Jerry McCartie (*o*), another to my mother, and finished one that I had partly written to Henry Baldwin (*p*). I read the bible for some time, and finished O'Brien's pamphlet against the Ministry entitled *Utrum Horum* (*q*). I have likewise inserted my notes on the eighteen first pages in Whitaker's *History of Manchester*.

(*o*) The Liberator's brother-in-law, Jeremiah McCartie, of Woodview, near Millstreet, county Cork, who married his sister Mary. Burke (*Landed Gentry*) describes Woodview as being in Kerry. Jerrie McCarthie, mentioned in No. 38 below (p. 166), is probably the same person. The name appears to have been spelt sometimes with, and sometimes without, an " h," and sometimes with " y," and sometimes with " ie," at the end. Denis McCartie, of Headfort, county Kerry, a descendant of the younger branch of the McCarthys of Muskerry, married Catherine O'Connell, daughter of Daniel O'Connell, of Tralee, and Ellen, sister of the Liberator (*The Last Colonel of the Irish Brigade*, i. 233).

(*p*) See above, p. 128.

(*q*) The Editor has not been able to obtain a copy of this pamphlet.

No. 29, Saturday, December 10*th,* 1796.—I yesterday received a letter from my father. I must answer it by the next post.

I have very little to say in my Journal at present of my private life and opinions. Perhaps it would now be more useful to me to write on them than on the subjects of my late speculations. Certainly it would be more entertaining if at a future and distant period I should read the contents of this book. But [28] unfortunately I have nothing to write on. My life, though it is not in any degree insipid, is monotonous and unchequered. I spend the greater part of the day in the library (r). In the perusal of a favorite author I feel not the time slip away. Was the library to remain open till one o'clock, I am sure I should frequently be there at that hour. As it shuts at ten, I am forced very reluctantly to leave it at that hour. I supped with Marshall, Bland, and Fuller, and Hickson, of the Brigade, last night (s). We remained up until about two. I was not by any means intoxicated, nor was I much amused. Marshall paid the bill.

(r) The Dublin Library, Eustace Street (see p. 129).

(s) Marshall, one of the Marshalls of Callinapercy, county Kerry; Bland, one of the Blands of Derriquin, county Kerry; Fuller, also of a Kerry family; Hickson, probably one of the Hicksons of Fermoyle, county Kerry. Marshall is mentioned again in entry No. 31 below (p. 142). None of these names appear in the lists of officers in the (English) Irish Brigade; and as these lists contain the commissions down to July, 1796, probably these gentlemen belonged to some of the disbanded regiments of the Irish Brigade, and did not take service under the British crown. Marshall and Hickson may be the same gentlemen who are mentioned in the account given by O'Connell to Daunt of his ride from Carhen to Tarbert, inserted below (p. 225); and Hickson may be the hero of an anecdote told by O'Connell of the amateur who, having, in private theatricals, a part which only required him to say, "Put the horses to the coach," said, "Put the horses *into* the coach."

I like Marshall very much, as everybody must who knows his character. He *knows* me not; yet he wishes to be acquainted with my heart, my disposition. I will not hurry his knowledge of it. Let time unfold by degrees that which it would not be easy to show at once. A man, I believe, meets with many difficulties in playing even his own character. I am anxious for the friendship of Marshall and Bland. I think we will make a valuable triumvirate. I can here indulge what elsewhere would be deemed vanity. I am now thinking on paper. That is all.

I yesterday read thirty pages of Henry's *England*. I read within these two days the seventeenth chapter of Gibbon. I now read much slower, though I write much faster, than I was accustomed to do. I read slower, but I read with more reflection and profit.

I inserted some notes taken from Henry's *England*.

No. 30, Tuesday, December 13*th*, 1796.—I have let two days slip without adding a word to my Journal. But they were two days in which little was added to my knowledge. After having heard mass on Sunday I went to Bennett's (*t*) [29]. We walked out together to view the volunteers (*u*). In the evening I read a play. Yesterday I read a few pages of the 18th chapter of Gibbon and 48 pages of *La Cour de Berlin*, par M. de Mirabeau (*v*).

(*t*) See above, p. 78.
(*u*) O'Connell afterwards became a volunteer himself (see below, p. 166).

(v) *Histoire Secrète de la Cour de Berlin,* an account of a secret mission upon which Mirabeau was sent to Prussia in June, 1786, and from which he returned in January, 1787. It consists of a series of eighty-six letters commencing on July 5th, 1786, and ending on January 19th, 1787. The second letter, written on July 12th, mentions the serious illness of Frederick the Great, who died on August 17th. Mirabeau addressed a remarkable memorial to his successor, Frederick William II., on his accession.

I have been much more diligent this day. I read 70 pages of Henry's *England,* 100—171 ; Boswell's *Life of Dr. Johnson,* p. 44 to p. 54 ; and the article " Dog " in Buffon's *Natural History,* 1—49. I likewise wrote a letter to my father in answer to one I received from him on Saturday.

I have little to speculate on at present. I have been looking out for a subject, but could find none to please my fancy. Many present themselves on a distant view. When I endeavour to contemplate any one nearer I find that I am not able to say anything satisfactory on it. These remarks put me in mind of a man who makes a long discourse in praise of silence.

John Segerson is arrived in town, and has outbid my father for one of his own farms that has been set up to sale under a decree of the Court of Exchequer. This farm was sold under a mortgage which Segerson had granted to a Mrs. Chute. It was on the subject of this farm that I wrote to my father (w).

(w) The Kerry Segersons, or Sigersons, are a branch of an

ancient family whose name is a corruption of the Norse. They are descendants of Sigurd, Jarl of the Orkneys, who fell at the battle of Clontarf, raven banner in hand. Alice, daughter of Christopher Sigerson, married Daniel O'Connell, of Darrynane and Ahavore. Their son John was the father of Daniel O'Connell, the Liberator's grandfather. Alice O'Connell, an aunt of the Liberator, married John Sigerson, of Ballinskelligs Abbey, county Kerry, about the year 1750 (*The Last Colonel of the Irish Brigade*, i. 9). Possibly he is the gentleman mentioned in this entry; but from the suggestion of a duel contained in the next entry, it is more likely to have been a son of his. In Burke's *Landed Gentry*, the christian name of Alice O'Connell's husband is given as Thomas. The present interest in the family centres round the fact that Dora, the gifted wife of Mr. Clement Shorter, is a Sigerson, daughter of Dr. Sigerson, of Dublin. One of the Sigersons is the hero of a somewhat comical incident that happened during the career of O'Connell at the bar. This gentleman made a charge against a Captain Butler. A commission, which sat in Kerry, was appointed to investigate its truth. O'Connell was engaged in the case, and handled Mr. Sigerson so severely in the course of his speech, that he lost his temper, jumped up, and called O'Connell a purse-proud blockhead. O'Connell replied, " In the first place, I have no purse to be proud of ; and secondly, if I be a blockhead, it is better for you, as I am counsel against you. However, to save you the trouble of saying so again, I'll administer a slight rebuke." Whereupon O'Connell whacked him soundly with the President's cane. The result was a challenge ; but soon after it was received Mr. Sigerson wrote to O'Connell to say that he could not proceed in the affair, as he had ascertained that O'Connell was one of the lives in a valuable lease. " Under these circumstances," he wrote, " I cannot afford to shoot you, unless you first insure your life for my benefit. If you do, then I'm your man ! " O'Connell did not adopt this cool suggestion (*Personal Recollections*, ii. 113). The entry in O'Connell's fee-book as to this case is as follows : " August 23rd to Nov. 12th, 1800.—John Segerson, memorialist *v.* Whitwell Butler and Captain Winder. Brief for Captain Butler before three sub-commissioners, Collector Frizell and Day, on charges exhibited by Segerson. Grand Jury Room, Tralee. 52 days at £2 5s. 6d.''

A further reference to the Mr. Sigerson mentioned in this entry will be found below (p. 142).

The Chutes are an old Kerry family. The mention of the name will recall Anne Chute, of *The Collegians.*

My life is very easy at present ; and if I can contrive to raise twelve pounds or thereabouts on my note payable next November I shall this winter enjoy more happiness than ever I tasted. The dark clouds which have frequently overshaded my youthful horizon are withdrawn, or are, I hope, about to withdraw. I am of a sanguine disposition. I have a relish for happiness, and have often reflected on that subject. I feel no present inconvenience ; and the sum I have already mentioned would take away all apprehension of future difficulties. I enjoy the use of a moderate collection of well-chosen books, of which I am growing daily fonder and more fond. Add to all this, I live in a most pleasant family (*x*). Why should I not therefore be happy ? I feel that I am so. The recollection of this [30] winter will during the course of my life bring with it pleasure. Yet perhaps danger, difficulty, and distress are nearer me than I am aware. This world of ours is so badly organised that the most penetrating judgment cannot assure the permanency of any blessing.

(*x*) The family of Mrs. Jones.

I received a letter from Henry Baldwin yesterday advising me to go to confession to Mr. Beattie, a Jesuit, etc., etc. (*y*).

(*y*) Henry Baldwin is referred to above (p. 128). Father Beattie was probably Father Betagh (see *The Irish Monthly*, vol. x. p. 452).

No. 31, *Friday, December* 16*th*, 1796.—I found on Wednesday that John Segerson (*z*) had made use of some declamatory and virulent language against me in a letter or letters addressed to Colonel McCarthy (*a*). I immediately left a note at Marshall's (*b*) lodgings requesting that he would not lend his pistols to any person until he saw me. When I met Marshall yesterday he gave me to understand that he would not lend his pistols to *any* person. Yet I imagine that, were I to apply for them to-morrow, I should get them. My belief is founded on the intimacy which has commenced between us. We dined together yesterday and spent a great part of this evening in conversation. (C'est mal exprimé !)

(*z*) See No. 30 above, p. 139.
(*a*) Probably Lieutenant-Colonel Sir Charles McCarthy. His real name was Guéroult, but being adopted by a childless uncle, Colonel Charles Thadeus McCarthy, he took the name of McCarthy. He was a captain in Berwick's regiment, in which he served with distinction until its dissolution in 1792. He entered the (English) Irish Brigade, in 1794, as ensign in Count Conway's regiment; became Lieutenant-Governor of Sierra Leone and Governor-in-Chief of Senegal in 1812, and brigadier-general on the west coast of Africa in 1821. He was

killed by the Ashantees in 1824 (*The Last Colonel of the Irish Brigade*, ii. p. 129 *et seq.*).

(*b*) See above, p. 137.

I have read since Tuesday Boswell's *Johnson*, 122 pages, 54—176, Vol. 1st ; Adams's *History of Republics* (*c*), Preface and 28 pages of account of author's life ; Watson's *Chemical Essay* to p. 48, the end of the first essay. I have learnt but little from this essay. It contains a kind of history of chemistry. The author, with a prejudice which *his* profession will scarce excuse, derives the commencement of this science from Tubal-Cain—nay, from Cain himself, who built a city. " Tantum religio potest."

(*c*) The author of this work was the future President of the United States. He succeeded Washington in May, 1797, having previously been Vice-President. He had been ambassador to England, and while in London published his *Defence of the American Constitution*, in which he combated the views of Turgot and others in favour of a single legislative chamber. In this Adams differed from Godwin, who laid down that " the institution of two Houses of Assembly is the direct method to divide a nation against itself" (*Political Justice*, Book V. chap. 21).

Diocletian towards the end of the third century caused [31] the books on alchemy in Egypt to be burnt. This is the first *fact* established in the history of this science (see Gibbon's *Decline and Fall*). Roger Bacon in England and Albertus Magnus in Germany, both monks, flourished in the thirteenth century. Paracelsus flourished in the beginning of the sixteenth century. He was, I believe, the first who cured the venereal disorder systematically. It was reckoned incurable a short time before him. He died at the age of forty, even whilst he boasted that he had found out an *universal* medicine which would prolong the life of man to a wonderful length.

I this day read and took notes on the article "Gladiateur" in the *Encyclopédie* (*d*). There were gladiators for the morning and gladiators for the afternoon. About the time of Nero even women fought on the arena.

(*d*) See above, p. 133.

Gladiators were frequently exhibited at the funerals of women.

I have read some pages of Plutarch's *Life* prefixed to the translation of his works by the Langhorns.

Mr. Adams (see the last page) was born at Massachussetts October 29th, 1735. He is by profession a lawyer.

I have likewise read the Prefaces and three chapters of Godwin to p. 25, Vol. 1, and 57 pages of Gibbon's *Miscellaneous Works*, 313—370. They include part of his answer to Mr. Davis, etc.

No. 32, *Saturday, December* 17*th*, 1796.—I read this day 100 pages of Boswell's *Johnson*, Vol. 1st, p. 176—276. I do not admire this work. Yet I will read it through (*e*).

(*e*) See below, p. 146.

I read 59 pages of Watson's *Chemistry*, Vol. 1st,
p. 46—107, to the end of the second essay. In this
essay the author explains many words made use of
by chemists, such as " crystallisation," "distillation,"
" sublimation," etc. His manner is very simple and
very entertaining. From this essay I have learnt
that boiled water will not communicate its own heat
to a body immersed in it. For instance [*sic*]

[32] I read this day 65 pages of Henry's
England, Vol. 1st, 171—206, to the end of the
second chapter. What I read this day treats of
the introduction of Christianity into Britain, and
the history of religion until the arrival of the
Saxons. It is not *probable* by any means that any
of the *Apostles* were ever in Britain. Dr. Henry
imagines that he has done a great deal in *proving
that* St. Paul might have been there. The stories
related of Joseph of Arimathea, King Lucius, etc.,
are too ridiculously false to merit attention. They
may, and they do, serve as a specimen of the
ignorant impudence of monkish fictions. Pelagius,
author of a *dangerous, damnable,* and *absurd* heresy,
was a native of Britain. He asserted *that* " man
by the constitution of his nature must have died
although Adam had not sinned," that " the punishment of Adam's crime was limited to himself," and
a third opinion which I do not now recollect. (I
will insert it to-morrow) (*f*).

(*f*) No entry was made on the following day, and there is
no further reference to Pelagius.

The closing of the library at ten o'clock prevented me from finishing the 18th chapter of Gibbon, Vol. 2nd. Two pages remain unread.

No. 33, *Friday, December* 23*rd,* 1796.—I am sorry that so much time has elapsed since I wrote the last number. It would be advantageous to me for the present, and amusing in future, was I each day to put on paper the *mode of thinking that rules the hour.* I do not express myself accurately ; I meant to say, the thoughts—*thoughts of the day.*

I have read the remaining part of the first volume, 276—536, of Boswell's *Johnson,* and the second volume, 1—605, and 14 pages of the third volume. I dislike Boswell very much (*g*). Yet why should I ? He was not a man of genius. He ought not to have obtruded himself on the public notice. His *Life of Johnson,* however, will long be read with pleasure. Boswell should have remembered that the public were not curious about his affairs, his family transactions, opinions, etc. He says that he differed with Dr. Johnson on the right of the British Parliament to tax the colonies. The affirmative was argued with vehemence by the Doctor in some pamphlets. Dr. Johnson said if he was a country gentleman [33] he would punish any tenant of his who voted for any but the candidate of his master's choice. Johnson hated the name of a Whig. He complained that our *Government* was too *weak ;* that the King had too little power ! Boswell too boasts of his Toryism !

At the end of the eighteenth century, as it is pompously exclaimed, such things still continue.

(g) O'Connell altered his opinion. See p. 153.

We are still barbarians. We have just civilisation enough to perceive that we are barbarians; that is all.

I took my seat on Wednesday night in the Historical Society (h), now metamorphosed into a law society. The admission fee is a guinea and a half. The question was a comparison between biennial and septennial parliaments. I had prepared myself to speak in favour of the former. I did not do it, as there was no debate.

(h) See No. 36, p. 156.

Boswell's wife remarked on his partiality to Johnson "that she had often seen a man lead a bear, but that she never before saw a bear lead a man." The jealousy was truely feminine. She wished, I suppose, that nobody should lead her husband but herself.

No. 34, Saturday, December 24th, 1796.—I read in Boswell's *Johnson* 184 pages, Vol. 3, p. 14—198. I read the Introduction to the " Pagan " and that to the " Monastic Antiquities of Ireland " in Grose's *Antiquities of Ireland.*

Dr. Johnson doubted of the appearance of ghosts. Murphy (in his *Life of Johnson*) says that the Doctor wished to believe it. Johnson said it was a point which at the end of five thousand years was

yet unsettled in the world.   All belief was for it, all
argument against it.   That is to say, men believed
it they knew not why.   Yet this universal belief is
seized, I think, by Johnson in the *Rambler* in favor
of the opinion believed.   Addison, or one of the
writers in the *Spectator*, has expressed that thought.
With regard to myself, though I am perfectly
convinced of the non-existence of ghosts—I mean,
when I reason, when I make use of my faculties, I
am convinced of it—yet I have preserved a strong
superstitious dread of them.   Let me employ my
judgement on this subject.   Let me controvert the
existence of ghosts [34] whenever it is mentioned
in conversation.   I have often declared that I
would wish to see a ghost.   I did not tell truth.
But the assertion made an improper impression on
my mind.   I grant to my mind that there are such
things when I make any supposition concerning
their appearance.   Yet if there really were ghosts
it would be *extremely useful* for me to see one.
There are none.   Philosophy teaches me there can
be none.

> " Hence, horrible shadow !
> Unreal mockery, hence ! "

Dr. Goldsmith died on April 4th, 1774.

I have formed the resolution to go in the night tc
the abbey below Darrinane (*i*).   I can by doing it
give a practical proof of my disbelief in ghosts.   I
would be ashamed that anyone thought I believed
in them.

(*i*) A small ruined church on the abbey island was a dependency of a great abbey in the county of Waterford, whose possessions were granted to Sir Walter Raleigh. At his fall Darrynane passed into the hands of Boyle, first Earl of Cork, whose descendants let it on very favourable terms to the O'Connells (*The Last Colonel of the Irish Brigade*, i. p. 5). No doubt this church is the abbey O'Connell refers to. There is no record of O'Connell's having undergone the test he proposed to himself. Grattan went through the ordeal of repairing nightly to a churchyard to conquer the fear of ghosts which he had imbibed from his nurse.

Mr. Grose (*j*) or Mr. Ledgwick (*k*) (whom I believe I knew in London in the affair of Denis *Kain* Mahony's robbery), the editor, says that there were two religions in the northern regions, the Celtick and the Scythian. The Scythian got the upper hand in Britain about 300 years before Christ. Whitaker has partly the same opinion (see *Hist. Manchester*). The groves were druidical, Celtick ; the circle of stones Scythian.

(*j*) Grose, while in Dublin, was seized with an apoplectic fit at the table of his friend Hone, on June 12th, 1791, a short time after his arrival in Ireland, and died immediately. *The Antiquities of Ireland*, published in the same year, though bearing his name, was partly written, as well as edited, by Ledwich. Grose wrote *The Antiquities of England and Wales*, published in 1773—1787, and *The Antiquities of Scotland*, published in 1789—1791. While in Scotland in 1790 he met Burns, who told him of the ruined church of Alloway, on the banks of Doon, which was the traditional scene of strange witch and warlock stories. Grose promised to give Alloway Kirk special prominence in his book if Burns would furnish a witch story. To this offer the world owes *Tam O'Shanter*, first published in *The Antiquities of Scotland.* The two became "unco pack and thick thegither." Grose was a boon companion after the whole heart of Burns, who has celebrated his convivial qualities in appropriate verse, and handed him down to posterity in the lines in which he tells his "brither Scots" that

and that

> " A chield's amang you taking notes,"

> " If in your bounds ye chance to light
> Upon a fine fat fodgel wight,
> O' stature short, but genius bright,
> That's he, mark weel."

O'Connell told O'Neill Daunt the following anecdote of this "fine fat fodgel wight," whose figure was said to be "the title-page of a joke " : "Grose came to Ireland full of strong prejudices against the people, but they gave way beneath the influence of Irish drollery. He was very much teased while walking through the Dublin markets by the people hustling him for his custom. At last he got angry, and told them to go about their business, when a sly, waggish butcher, deliberately surveying Grose's fat, ruddy face and corpulent person, said to him, ' Well, please your honour, I won't ax you to buy, since it puts your honour in a passion. But I'll tell you how you'll sarve me : *just tell all your friends that it's I that supply you with your mate, and, never fear, I'll have custom enough.'* "

(*k*) Ledwich, the part author and the editor of *The Antiquities of Ireland.*

Our cromleachs were sepulchral monuments. The cromleachs were erected by placing a large oblong square stone on three or four supporters. They are in the shape of altars. There is one of them not far from the top of Comb, a kistih near Darrinane, and another near Currane. I will examine both next summer.

The cairns were heaps of stones raised in the

figure of a cone. They were likewise monuments.
It is still a custom, though almost worn out, to raise
a pile of stones on the spot where any person met
with an unexpected death. In Ivreagh, I mean, this
custom is just expiring. There [are] two large heaps
of stones near Drung Hill of which tradition tells
us a monstrous story. They are at the distance of
from twenty to thirty paces one from the other. Yet
it is said that they were [35] erected in order to
facilitate, by supporting its sides, the stripping of
an ox. This ox was killed on this spot by Bran, a
greyhound belonging to Fion MacCoul, after a
course that commenced in Ulster. As I have got
so far, I will finish the story. The ox swam
across the bay from the opposite mountains. The
greyhound, unwilling through delicacy to wet its
skin, galloped round and arrived at this side so
soon as the ox had landed.

No. 35, Monday, December 26th, 1796.—I read
nothing this day but Boswell's *Life of Dr. Johnson,*
280 pages, Vol. 1, p. 198—478. I went to bed
last night at one, and got up this morning at
ten—eleven hours' sleep. This is too much.
This indulgence must be corrected.

" I would be a philosopher but that gaiety
breaks in upon me," said Edwards, a schoolfellow
of Dr. Johnson, to him. So should I be, too. But
in the gaiety of my heart I forget that sacred love
of what is fact, that noble spirit of rectitude that
enlivens my retired moments. I hope that, in spite

of the allurements and falsehood of the world, I shall yet find means to practice the lessons of wisdom. I know that I have not sufficient recollection to enable me to avoid entangling myself in the opinions of a misjudging world. When I think by myself, my notions are in general very correct.

I dined yesterday at Bennett's (*l*). He seems to enjoy as much happiness as most men I know.

(*l*) See above, p. 78.

I received this day a letter from my father, containing a draft on Mr. Franks for forty pounds. This money I am to pay to the college (*m*).

(*m*) Trinity College, Dublin, from which his father held land. Mr. Franks is mentioned below (p. 198). He was an attorney, and acted for the O'Connell family. The firm exist still, and are solicitors to the Irish Land Commission. O'Connell's memorial for admission as a student of King's Inns is signed by a Mr. Franks, a barrister, and a Mr. Franks, an attorney. In *The Last Colonel of the Irish Brigade* (i. 139) there is given a bill of costs furnished by Thomas Francks, jun., in a case of *Samuel Windes* v. *Maurice Connell and others*. It is debited to Hugh Falvey, Esq., and dated Easter and Trinity, 1775. The suit was a friendly bill of discovery brought against Hunting-cap, in order to protect him against the forfeiture of his property, to which his faith exposed him in those evil days. Hugh Falvey performed this friendly office many times, until in extreme old age he felt a scruple on the point, oaths that were not strictly in accordance with truth having to be taken.

Boswell states a curious incident that happened in Scotland about the year 1780. The attorneys of Edinburgh, having got a new charter, called themselves solicitors. They had been hitherto called procurators. On this change of denomination a squib appeared in the newspaper called *The Caledonian Mercury*. It said that the *cunning stationers* (I know not what is meant by this term. They were likewise styled Chaldeans or Chaldees) were [36] to get a charter in imitation of their respectable brethren, etc., etc. It was a poor attempt at wit, and the rascal that wrote it deserved to be laughed at or ducked in a horse-pond. The wise *solicitors* did not think that would be sufficient. They brought an action, and actually recovered five pounds damages. Thus we see that to joke is in Scotland a crime.

Boswell thought the Parliament wrong in the affair of the Middlesex election.

No. 36, Thursday, December 29th, 1796.—I read on Tuesday ninety-seven pages of Boswell's *Johnson*, to the end of the third and last volume, 478—575.

On the whole I am better satisfied with this work of Boswell than I expected I should have been. Indeed, I entered upon it with a very unfavourable impression of the merit of the performance. For a long time, nay, until I was concluding the book, I considered it through the clouded medium of prejudice. But the candid criticism of the reviewers has made me regard it in a new point of view. Boswell was certainly a well-disposed man. Johnson I admire and I pity. I love him one moment, and almost hate him the next. He must indeed have been a great man, as his minutest actions and expressions are very well worth the relation. His mind was powerfully strong. His intellectual view was most acute and distinct. Yet his mind was clouded with many prejudices. He was intolerant of any opposition to his own orthodox opinions in [*sic*] Church and State. I do not assent that his opinions were strictly conformable to the doctrines of the Church of England. On the contrary, he fostered notions received by the Church of Rome, such as praying for the dead.

I believe it was Johnson that said that he did not love a man who was jealous for nothing. Whoever said it, the sentiment is quite in unison with my opinion. The man whose mind is not forcibly excited by some object is not capable of receiving any strong impression. He is incapable of love or friendship. Give me the man whose generous mind is inflamed now with an ardent enthusiasm, is now chilled with causeless apprehensions. I mean not the apprehension for self, which degrades the man [37], but the apprehension that arises from excess of desire and anxiety for success. The man who conceives strongly is the man of genius. He is the friend and the patriot.

The French fleet is arrived in Bantry Bay (*n*). One whom chance had cast on shore was this day examined before the Privy Council. The French will perhaps meet with a greater resistance than they have been in all probability led to believe. I know not what conjecture to make with respect to the future. I love, from my heart I love, liberty. I do not express myself properly. Liberty is in my bosom less a principle than a passion. But I know that the victories of the French would be attended with bad consequences. The Irish people are not yet sufficiently enlightened to be able to bear the sun of freedom. Freedom would soon dwindle into licentiousness. They would rob; they would murder. The altar of liberty totters when it is cemented only with blood, when it is supported only with carcases. The liberty which I look for is that which would increase the happiness of mankind. In the service of this liberty I have devoted my life and whatever portion of talents I may have or acquire.

(*n*) It arrived on December 22nd, but, after having lain in the bay for six days, had to return to France. The fact of its arrival was communicated by letter of December 24th to Hunting-cap by his nephew Daniel O'Sullivan, who lived on the shores of the Kenmare river, quite close to Bantry Bay. Hunting-cap immediately sent the letter to Lord Kenmare's agent, Mr. Thomas Gallwey, and Lord Kenmare on receiving it sent an express to Bantry to obtain information. From Daniel O'Sullivan's letter it appears that the fleet consisted of thirty-six or thirty-eight sail, of which twenty-eight were ships of the line. The people in the country remained quiet. For the correspondence see *The Last Colonel of the Irish Brigade,* ii. 197.

D.C.   N

I attended the *Historical* Society last night (*o*). I spoke twice against the partition of Greece into small portions. I spoke pretty well, better, indeed, than I expected. I knew the part of Blackstone in which we were examined, I may safely say, better than any individual (*p*).

(*o*) See above, n. (*h*), p. 147.

(*p*) Efforts have been made by the Editor to ascertain this allusion to an examination, but without result. There was at this time no examination preparatory to a call to the bar, and as O'Connell was not a student in Dublin University, any legal examination in that institution to which he would be admissible is out of the question. As the society referred to was a legal debating society, it may have been part of the system pursued there to have periodical examinations in tandard law books.

No. 37, *Saturday, December* 31*st*, 1796.—With this day there closes the year. Twelve months have fled with rapid and eager course since I wrote the same sentence in my Journal. During this period I have advanced somewhat, though not much, in science. The summer was almost entirely thrown away. I have had many happy moments during the year 1796; I have had many miserable ones. I have declined, or rather suddenly fallen off, in the opinion of my uncle. Indeed, I knew not what [38] it is to be economical in London. I spent foolishly what I bitterly regretted since. During this year there has been no action of mine which ought to bring regret to my conscience or shame to my cheek. I have done nothing which should exalt the self-love of my heart into approving joy. The only things I have acquired are something more knowledge of, and firmness in, the ways of life, somewhat more of prudence in the conduct of my opinions. This, indeed, is a late acquirement; I had it not in the country. I have added to the stock of my miscellaneous knowledge. My acquaintance with the law has not been much, if at all, improved.

I was yesterday informed that Darby Mahony (*q*) was dead. I heard it with real concern. I remember with delight the commencement of our intimacy. When infants, or a little older, we were kept asunder by family dissensions. When we became acquainted our former distance rendered the change more pleasing. I remember as the happiest days of my life a couple of Sundays on which he was allowed to join us at Carhen. Our intimacy increased. We hunted together; we were at school together; we barred out *Linahan, our master,* together. Darby on this occasion did signal service. Armed with a sword, he attacked in the rear Linahan, who was forcing open with a rafter a door filled with stones. This was at Bahaclis (*r*); the difference of the school's breaking up was only one day! The Passion week of the year 1790 we had the unfortunate quarrel which caused a total coldness until our departure for Harrington's in the summer of the same year. I

saw not him until the year 1793. In February
we met in London. I was come from Douay, he
from the campaign with Brunswick. As we walked
down the Haymarket together I shewed him some
caricatures. We were to have come with him and
Marquis Sullivan to Ireland (*s*). The General
interposed (*t*) and sent us to Fegan's (*u*). I met
Darby in Ivreagh in the summer of 1795. We
were together at our hunting match at Therboy.
He shot a hare the first evening at Canuge.
His conversation [39] was always agreeable to
me ; but he was in general very silent. He sang
pretty well. I have frequently heard him sing
Wolf's song, " *Why, soldiers, why?* " and " Immortal was his soul," etc. Nay, there are a few
words which he used frequently to repeat, and
which I now insert because they appear to me
the sacred reliques of my friend :—

> " ' *Hanminun Daul*,' says Darby ;
> ' I'll dislocate your jiggling bone ' " (*v*).

He had a great deal of natural drollery. He
followed me the day I left Carhen for London in
October, 1795. He did not overtake me, though
he came as far as the top of Drung. His brother
Dan did overtake me, and we stopped from a
violent shower in a forge in Glanbeak. I have
nothing more to say, or the rest is in general not
distinguished by any remarkable features. I was
told by John (*w*) that he went out in despondency

for the West Indies. Too well, alas! have been the forebodings of his heart justified. Oh, Darby, oh, my friend, accept this tribute from him that loved you. But already are the particles that composed his frame dissolved in their union; already have they been absorbed by the elements to which they belonged. How soon will this be the case with me. And who will then strew a tear of sorrow over my grave? Oh that I were remembered by some soft, sympathetic heart; that the gay and thoughtless may sigh over my tomb; that the sedate and grave may mournfully bend over the spot that contains my ashes! (x).

But as life is short, let us acquire what knowledge we can. For my part, I will endeavour to be as happy as I can. I will make my heart a heart of love; that, and [that] alone, is the way to be happy.

(q) Probably one of the Mahonys of Castlequin. O'Connell's great-aunt, the eldest daughter of John O'Connell, of Darrynane, was married to Myles Mahony, of Castlequin (*The Last Colonel of the Irish Brigade*, i. 52). Darby Mahony was a lieutenant in the "Second Walsh's" regiment of the (English) Irish Brigade (*ib.* ii. 191).

(r) This word is hard to decipher in the original manuscript. It, however, probably refers to Bahaglis, which is about three miles from Carhen, the residence of O'Connell's father. As to O'Connell's doings during the visit to Ivreagh in 1795 mentioned in the next sentence of the Journal, some information will be found above (p. 54).

(s) *Marcus* Sullivan, "Captain Mark," the "wild son" of O'Connell's aunt Honora, "Nonny," as she was called in the

family, wife of Morty O'Sullivan, or Sullivan, of Couliagh.
He was a captain in " O'Connell's " regiment of the (English)
Irish Brigade, and was brought out by Count O'Connell, who
obtained for him a bourse in the college at St. Martin's, Isle
of Rhé, and to whom he appears to have been somewhat of a
trouble; but he became a colonel in the French, and died a
captain in the British, service (*The Last Colonel of the Irish
Brigade*, i. 9, 28, 52 ; ii. 23, 28, 30, 33, 55, 56, 68).   Burke
(*Landed Gentry*) states that Honora married Charles Sugrue, of
Fermoyle ; but this is a mistake.   It was Joan, whose name
he does not mention among the sisters of Hunting-cap, that
married Charles Sugrue.   " Miss Julianna," who, at the time
that *The Last Colonel of the Irish Brigade* was written, was the
eldest surviving member of the O'Connell *gens*, gave Mrs.
Morgan John O'Connell the particulars of the names of the
eight ladies, and of their husbands, which are set out on p. 8
of vol. i.   Marcus O'Sullivan was the leader of the bull hunt
mentioned above (p. 20).

(*t*) Count O'Connell.

(*u*) This word looks in the original like *Sejan's*, but there can
be very little doubt that it should read " Fegan's," for we know
that in 1793 O'Connell was at school at a Mr. Fagan's (see
above, p. 46).

(*v*) " Jiggle, to move backwards and forwards with a light,
unsteady motion ; to move in rapid succession of slight jerks ;
to rock or jerk slightly " (English Dictionary) ; " to wriggle "
(Worcester's Dictionary) ; " the jiggle of the screw " (Rudyard
Kipling, *The Seven Seas*).   " Hanminun Daul " is an impreca-
tion in Irish.

(*w*) O'Connell's brother (see pp. 71 and 176).

(*x*) How little did the youth of one-and-twenty summers,
when he penned these halting sentences, anticipate the passionate outburst of grief with which the tidings of his death
would be received in Ireland, and in every home throughout
the world where love of liberty or reverence for the Catholic
faith abode !   There lies at this moment before the Editor of
the Journal of Daniel O'Connell the *Evening Freeman* of Tuesday,

May 25th, 1847, in the deepest mourning, announcing the melancholy event. It chronicles the ordinary occurrences of the day. There are calls to the Irish bar, which had just lost its brightest ornament. There is an account of the funeral of the late Lord Lieutenant, the Earl of Bessborough, "the good and patriotic Viceroy," as he is described in an extract from the *Tipperary Free Press* of the previous Saturday; but it is not in sorrow for his loss that the page bears those heavy lines of black. There is a copy of the notice in the *London Gazette* of the appointment of his successor, the Earl of Clarendon. Then we are reminded that the great struggle for Free Trade had commenced, and learn that the *Standard* and its fellow-labourers had adopted as the battle-cry of their party "Protestantism and Protection," which the *Standard* assures its readers would triumph at the approaching election. Births are announced, and deaths, among the latter being the death, at the age of eighty-three, of Mary Ann Lamb, "sister of the late Charles Lamb, author of *The Essays of Elia*." There are marriages, too, one being celebrated by Dr. O'Connell, P.P., and a divorce, the contemplated divorce of Queen Isabella of Spain. Of course the debates in Parliament are recorded. One is about the effect of poor relief in disfranchising the recipient. These be the commonplaces of journalism, hackneyed, even modern, some of them. But side by side with these are recorded events that are out of the ordinary, strange, portentous, awful. A dark shadow broods over the land. From all quarters come heart-rending descriptions of the ravages of plague, pestilence, and famine throughout the length and breadth of Ireland. The coroners are kept busy. Mary Mooney is found dead "from cold and exhaustion" in the townland of Rynn, Queen's County. Doolan, a ploughman, "once of a stalwart, but now, alas! of a famine-stricken, frame," "suddenly dropped dead from sheer exhaustion and debility," at Nenagh, "while in the act of eating a small piece of bread which he had begged." "The public works are discontinued," writes the *Sligo Champion* in an article which is quoted, "and the people are starving. Their condition beggars description. . . . We are surrounded on all sides by famine and pestilence. Our streets are infested with breathing skeletons." *Anatomies of death*, Spenser would have called them. " Some of these creatures are labouring under dysentery ; more are actually far gone in typhus fever." No part of the unhappy land was free from these dreadful scenes. Even Ulster, where the one Irish industry that had escaped the destroying hand of England furnished some employment outside of agriculture, enjoyed no immunity from them. " More deaths from starvation " is the heading of a paragraph copied from the *Ulster Gazette*, in which is recorded, among others, the case of a man named Tierney, who fell a victim to hardship and destitution, in the county Down, nothing being found in his stomach by the doctors who made the post-mortem examination but *some undigested seaweed*. To crown all, the dead are uncoffined, often unburied.

In the midst of this appalling misery and desolation came, on the morning of that black Tuesday, the agonising news of the death of the great chieftain, the people's only hope on earth, their prudent counsellor, their faithful friend, their fearless champion. A wail of anguish and despair went up from Ireland. " Surely," says the leader in the *Freeman*, " we are an unfortunate and afflicted people. Famine is among us, fever is among us, discord is among us, and O'CONNELL *is dead*."

One consolation there was. Though he died on foreign soil, a letter from Dr. Miley to his son Maurice announced that his remains—all but his heart, which, enclosed in a silver urn, was to repose in Rome, whither his dying footsteps were hastening—were to return to the land he loved so wisely and so well, there to receive the tribute of a nation's sorrow, a nation's affection, a nation's gratitude, and a nation's reverence. In a stately tomb in the beautiful cemetery of Glasnevin, beneath the shadow of a tall and slender shaft, fashioned in the shape of one of those solemn and mysterious towers the secret of whose era and whose use has baffled all research, surrounded by the graves of many of his faithful followers, repose the ashes of the great Tribune. " Tears of sorrow " have flowed abundantly beside his grave. Well is he remembered by many a " soft, sympathetic heart." " The gay and thoughtless," as they gaze upon his tomb, do not withhold the tribute of a sigh. Often have " the grave and sedate " mournfully bent over the spot that contains his ashes.

How beautiful is the sentiment, and how beautiful the resolve, with which he concludes the reflections on his death: " As life is short, let us acquire what knowledge we can. For my part, I will endeavour to be as happy as I can. *I will make my heart a heart of love ;* that, and that alone, is the way to be happy." Truly he made his heart a heart of love for everything worthy of being loved, but before and above all earthly things his afflicted country.

I read Bolingbroke's vindication of his own conduct towards the Jacobite party, which he had joined in his exile in France in the years 1713–14–15, in a letter to Sir William Wyndham in 1717. This letter must have injured the Pretender's party very severely. He was a rigid bigot, a man without talents or virtue. Bolingbroke seems to have been innocent. Read to p. 107, Vol. 1, the edition in quarto by Mallet (*y*).

(*y*) After the accession of George I. Bolingbroke fled in disguise to France, leaving behind him a letter to Lord Lansdowne, in which he accounted for his departure by the fact that he had certain information that a resolution had been taken to pursue him to the scaffold. In the letter to Sir William Wyndham Bolingbroke accounts for his flight by his dislike to Oxford and his resolution not to be associated with him in any way. The letter can hardly have had the effect attributed to it by O'Connell, for it was not published till 1753, two years after Bolingbroke's death, though it may have been circulated to a small extent, in print or manuscript, before that time.

[40] I have read the first section of the third chapter of Henry's *England*, on the British divisions. The Romans divided Britain into four provinces : Flavia Cæsariensis, Brittania Prima, Secunda, Magna Cæsariensis. And afterwards a fifth was added, called Valentia, from the Emperor Valens.

I read the Preface and twenty-four pages of the *Transactions of the R.I.A.* (z) (p. 24), the nineteenth chapter of Gibbon, and Johnson's *Poems of London* and *The Vanity of Human Wishes*. I read the third essay in Watson's *Chemistry on Salts*.

(z) " The Royal Irish Academy of Science, Polite Literature, and Antiquities," commonly known as the Royal Irish Academy, founded by royal charter January 28th, 1785. Among the original members were the Earl of Charlemont, who was President ; the Earl of Moira ; Richard Lovell Edgeworth ; James Gandon, the celebrated architect, designer of several of the public buildings in Dublin ; and Sir Joseph Bankes, the President of the Royal Society. Grattan was among the members earliest elected. The *Transactions* commence with an account of the observatory at Dunsink, near Dublin, belonging to Trinity College, by Dr. Ussher, one of the senior Fellows, who planned the building and arrangements. Among the papers in this volume there is a severe critique by the Rev. Robert Burrowes, on Dr. Johnson's style, " his perpetual affectation of expressing his thoughts by the use of polysyllables of Latin derivation," which must have greatly interested O'Connell. Certainly some of the specimens given by Mr. Burrowes seem to prove his case. The following is one of them : " Experience quickly shows the tortuosities of imaginary rectitude, the complication of simplicity, and the

asperities of smoothness." The Earl of Charlemont contri-
butes a paper on the antiquity of the woollen manufacture in
Ireland, proved from a passage which occurs in a poem called
" Dittamondi," written some time before 1364, by Fazio delle
Uberti, a Florentine poet, in *Terza Rima.* It is a historical
account of all the nations of the world. The author having
travelled through England and Scotland, crosses to Ireland,
saying,—

> "Similamente passamo en Irlanda,
> La qual fra noi e degna di fama
> Per le nobile saie che ci manda,"

which Charlemont translates,—

> "In like manner we pass into Ireland,
> Which among us is worthy of renown
> For the excellent serges that she sends us."

There is much about Ossian and Macpherson in a paper on
ancient Gaelic poems respecting the race of the Fians
collected in the Highlands of Scotland, in the year 1784, by
M. Young, D.D. The collection was made with a view to the
controversy concerning the authenticity of the alleged original
of Macpherson's Ossian, a question in which, as appears from
his Journal above (p. 87), O'Connell took an interest.

No. 38, *Tuesday, January 3rd,* 1797.—I do not
mean to write much ; yet I have much to write. I
have many resolutions to form ; I have many pernicious habits to disclaim. But I must refer [*sic*]
all to another time.

I read since I wrote last forty-one pages in
Bolingbroke's works, to p. 142. They contain
reflexions on exile and the first number of the
Occasional Writer. The reflexions on exile are
elegantly written, as is everything that Bolingbroke
wrote. They are pleasing and philosophic. Works

of this kind are not of much service. The weak-minded are unable to relish them. From them such derive no support. The philosopher they may amuse. He needs not their assistance. The letters of the *Occasional Writer* were written for one occasion, and relate to it. They are now uninteresting. They were written in 1726 against the Minister (*a*).

(*a*) Walpole. As to Bolingbroke see further below, pp. 167, 171, 173.

I have read, since I wrote the last number the second section of the third chapter of Henry's *England*. It treats of the constitution of the British States. The Britons were savages. They were superstitious savages. Consequently their priests had a great deal of power. This is a summary of all that has been written on this head.

I was on Monday admitted in the Lawyers' Artillery (*b*); and I have this day written to my uncle to get leave—that is in fact money—to enter into this corps. I wrote this day to Jerry McCarthie (*c*).

(*b*) His uncle wrote in the severest terms refusing permission. This threw O'Connell into a state of despair. He talked of suicide! (see No. 43). But his uncle, a week after, gave a grudging assent (see No. 48). He seems to have been a regular attendant at drill, for he writes under date February 3rd, 1797, " I read nothing this week. Between the attendance at drill and that at Commons, the days slip away unnoticed." On the 5th he appeared for the first time in uniform, and no doubt was a gallant figure. In No. 59 he records that he was the greater part of the day under arms, and was taught the exercise of the cannon. O'Connell was evidently very keen on this kind of soldiering, proud of being a recruit in a citizen army; though he would have read and written much more if he had not been in any corps, yet in the " number " last referred to he says that the recollection of having been in one would hereafter be pleasant, and adds, " It will be still more pleasant to be always able to say, ' I was a volunteer.' " O'Connell after his call to the bar incurred some personal risk from having joined the yeomanry, as described below (p. 204).

(c) No doubt the same person as mentioned above (p. 136.)

[41] *No. 39, Thursday, January 5th,* 1797.—I read twenty-eight pages of Bolingbroke's works, Vol. 1, p. 142—170, the second letter of the *Occasional Writer*. Had the Allies succeeded in placing the crown of Spain on the head of the brother of the Emperor, the balance of power would be exposed to the same kind of danger to rescue it from which was the avowed purpose of the war.

I have read the third section of the third chapter of the first volume of Henry, thirty pages, 338—368, to the end of the volume. This section contains an account of the Roman government in Britain. The learning of the druids is in a great measure a matter of mere conjecture. They committed nothing to writing—to p. 96.

. I have likewise read *The Travels of Anacharsis the Younger in Greece,* (d) by the Abbé Bartelemi—the Introduction to p. 108. He gives a sketch of the history of Greece in the first volume by way of introduction. This is deservedly esteemed a

masterly production.   He places the expedition of
the Argonauts in the year 1360 before Christ, the
first siege of Thebes 1329, the second 1319.   The
siege of Troy ended 1282.   All that is known of these
remote transactions is that they are very doubtful.

(*d*) *Voyage de Jeune Anacharsis en Grèce dans le Milieu de
Quatrième Sèicle avant l'Ere Vulgaire*, written by M. Jean Jacques
Barthélemy, and published in 1788, in seven volumes.   O'Connell
probably read a translation.   The author supposes a Scythian
to have taken up his residence in Athens, and to have visited
the neighbouring provinces and observed their manners and
customs, of which he made notes.   These he arranged after
his return to Scythia, which took place as soon as Greece was
conquered by Philip of Macedon.   He is represented as having
conversed with the great men who flourished at the time,
Xenophon, Plato, Aristotle, Demosthenes, and others.   He is
described as having, in order not to interrupt his narrative,
prefixed to it an account of what had occurred in Greece
before he arrived there.   This Introduction forms the first
volume.   The work is based upon authorities which are referred
to in notes at the foot of each page.

I dined yesterday with the three Rices in Eustace
Street.   Stephen Rice seems to me to possess more
information than any man in whose company I have
ever been.   How different, how decisively superior,
is his knowledge to mine !   He made me creep into
my ignorance.   Yet I am at times apt to be vain of
what little I know.   Perhaps I may when at his age.
He is by no means obtrusive in his learning (*e*).

(*e*) O'Connell's memorial for call to the bar is signed by
Dominick Rice.

I have just this moment added this year to the two former in the title-page. Had I written every day, according to my first intention, there would be little occasion to insert this remark.

I wish it was in my power to get entirely rid of all propensity to falsehood. I wish I could content myself with simply stating the fact on all occasions. Wilful [42] error is degrading to the mind of the utterer. It lessens him amongst the hearers. I told a lie this night point-blank. I said I had been at the theatre the first night that the King went there after the attack made on him (see No. 1 of the Journal). I now form the resolution of not departing from the truth in any one instance to-morrow (*f*).

(*f*) The incident recorded in the missing entry No. 1 was this. O'Connell and a friend went on October 29th, 1795, to see the King's return from the House of Lords. The royal carriage moved slowly along, surrounded by a noisy and excited mob. Someone in the crowd flung a penny at his Majesty. The guard of dragoons with drawn swords dashed through the crowd and advanced at a gallop in front of the carriage. As the procession approached O'Connell pressed forward to get a sight of the King, when a dragoon made a slash at him, which cut a deep notch in the tree under which he was standing, an inch or two above his head. The King made good his entrance into St. James's Palace, took off his robes, came out of the opposite side next Cleveland Row, got into a coach, and drove to Buckingham House, as Buckingham Palace was then called. Just as he was passing the bottom of Green Park the mob swarmed round the carriage, seized the wheels, and prevented their turning. A man took hold of the handle of the carriage door, and was in the act of turning it when a tall determined man pointed a pistol at him from the opposite window, which caused him and another man who was with him to shrink back. The mob then relaxed their hold on the wheels, the postillions flogged their horses, and the King reached Buckingham House in safety (*Personal Recollections*, vol. i. p. 258).

There is something deliciously naïve in the resolve not to depart once from truth "*to-morrow*"!

No. 40, *Friday, January 6th*, 1797.—I do not mean to write much, as my fire is out.

I read this day the fourth essay in Watson's *Chemistry*, thirty-two pages, Vol. 1, 148—180, on sulphur, fire, and phlogiston. I read Bolingbroke, twenty-nine pages, vol. 1, 171—200. They contain the third and last letter of the *Occasional Writer*, "The Vision of Camellick," an allegory relative to Magna Charta and corruption, and part of a paper entitled *An Answer to the "London Journal"* (*g*). I read Gibbon to the end of chapter 20th, Vol. 2nd, twenty-eight pages, on the conversion of Constantine and the empire to the religion of Christ. The EDICT OF TOLERATION was published at Milan in March, 313, by Constantine and Licinius. Maximin soon after approved of it. The edict empowering the disposal of testamentary property in favour of the Church was published in Rome A.D. 321—pp. 164—192. I likewise read thirty-seven pages of Henry, vol. 1, pp. 96—133, on the arts of the first period. The arts of a barbarous people are few. The Britons were barbarians. I have been surprised at their war-chariots. Henry believes the authority of Ossian's poems (*h*). Yet I think the man must have a strong faith who coincides with his opinion. It seems to me impossible to prove their *antiquity*. Macpherson had the impudence to assert that he had the manuscripts. But he could not be persuaded to show them, though frequently called upon to do so. The other day—I mean during the last year—a man called Ireland [43] had the consummate assurance to endeavour to pass a patched-up piece, styled *Vortigern and Rowena*, as the work of Shakespeare (*i*). The forgery was ill managed. The fellow was not acquainted with the language of the reign of Queen Elizabeth. The play was very bad. That indeed was no argument of its not being Shakespeare's. He wrote a wonderful deal of nonsense, and has been the occasion of much more nonsense, like his own Falstaff with regard to wit (*j*).

(*g*) Bolingbroke contributed to the *Craftsman* in the beginning of 1726—1727 three papers by an "Occasional Writer," bitterly attacking the Walpoles.

"The Vision of Camilick" was supposed to be a translation by "the learned Mr. Solomon Negro" of a Persian manuscript presented to Bolingbroke by his friend Alvarez. The *Answer* is "to the *London Journal* of December 21st, 1728."

(*h*) See No. 27 above, pp. 129, 132.

(*i*) "*Vortigern*," *an Historical Tragedy in Five Acts*, was represented at Drury Lane on April 2nd, 1796. It was the fabrication of William Henry Ireland, who acknowledged the imposition in the same year in his *Authentic Account of the*

Shakespeare Manuscripts.   Pye, the Poet Laureate, Boswell, and others believed in them.   But Malone's inquiry into the authenticity of the manuscripts appeared before *Vortigern* was produced at Drury Lane, and prepared the public for it. Kemble played Vortigern ; Miss Miller, mentioned above (p. 86), played Rowena. The play was duly damned. Ireland's father nevertheless published it in 1799, together with another forgery, "*Henry II.*," *an Historical Drama supposed to be written by the Author of "Vortigern."* In the Preface the editor, that is Ireland's father, speaks of "the ludicrous manner in which the principal character" (in *Vortigern*) "was sustained." Kemble was too well versed in Shakespeare to be taken in by so "ill managed" a forgery.

(*j*) In this harsh criticism O'Connell was anticipated by another diarist, Pepys, who wrote on August 20th, 1666, " To Deptford by water, reading *Othello, Moor of Venice*, which I heretofore esteemed a mighty good play ; but having so lately read *The Adventures of Five Hours*, it seems a mean thing." O'Connell must have studied the great dramatist with some care, for he makes the just remark that in his writings you find his priests and friars good men. From this he concluded that Shakespeare was a Catholic, as a writer who was not a Catholic himself, writing at such a period, would naturally have indulged in abuse of Popery in order to court the ruling powers.

O'Connell mistakes the character of Falstaff in supposing that Shakespeare intended to make *wit* one of his attributes. Falstaft's strong point was not wit, but *humour*, or rather fun, drollery.

No. 41, Saturday, January 7th, 1797.—I read this day eighty-one pages of *The Travels of Anacharsis*, 108—189, Vol. 1.   They contain the laws of Solon, the usurpation of Pisistratus and his sons Hippias and Hipparchus, and the restoration of the Democracy by   (*k*).   I read sixty-one pages of Henry, 133—194, Vol. 2, Chap. 5, on the arts of the first period. The arts of the Britons were like their situation, barbarous. They were further advanced by a good deal than the North American Indians when first visited by Europeans.

(*k*) There is a blank in the Journal here. It was Clisthenes who restored the Democracy.

I have read twenty pages of Bolingbroke, pp. 200—220, the remaining part of the answer to the *London Journal*. I have received no advantage from the perusal of this paper. It was written against the Minister on affairs that were then interesting, but are now forgotten (*l*).

(*l*) See above, n. (*y*), p. 163. The Minister was, of course, Walpole.

I read forty-four pages of a treatise on the police of London by *Patrick Colquhoun*, Esq., acting magistrate for the different quarters of that city, 25—69 (*m*). Various and complicated are the means which man employs in purloining the property of his fellow. The sacred claims of *meum* and *tuum* are not strongly imprinted in our breasts even by the state of society in which we now live. Distinction of property is a great evil; the spirit of self is a great evil; the love of superiority is a great evil. Man is a complication of evils. It is a very doubtful question whether the disposition of man can ever be so much improved as to admit of real liberty. I believe it is capable ; and this belief is founded on the knowledge of what has already been done. Was I born in the wilds of America, I should spend my life in devising the means of destroying the beasts of the field, and principally my fellow-brute man. But, born in Ireland, education has poured the milk of human kindness into my bosom. I would, and I trust I will, serve man. I feel, I really feel, the sacred and mild warmth of true patriotism. I will endeavour to make the narrow circle of my friends happy, I will endeavour to give cheerfulness and ease to the peasantry over whom I may command, I will endeavour to give liberty to my country, and I will endeavour to increase the portion of the knowledge and virtue of humankind. Oh, ETERNAL BEING, Thou seest the purity of my heart, the sincerity of my promises. Should I appear before your august tribunal after having performed them, shall not I be entitled to call for my reward ? Will the omission of a superstitious action, will the disbelief of an unreasonable dogma, that day rise in judgment against me ? Oh, God, how hast Thou been calumniated !

(*m*) *A Treatise on the Police of the Metropolis, containing a Detail of the Various Crimes and Misdemeanours by which Public and Private Property and Security are at present injured and endangered, and suggesting Remedies for their Prevention.* The author estimated the criminal classes in London, including fallen women, at

115,000. The chapter on punishment is exceedingly well written, and contains views much in advance of the time. Colquhoun there points out the true principles on which punishment should proceed, and deprecates the unnecessary severity of the existing penal code, which visited with death no less than one hundred and sixty different offences, from treason to concealing the birth of an illegitimate child or sending a threatening letter.

[44] *No. 42, Saturday, January 14th, 1797.*—How easily are bad habits produced! How difficult is it to overcome them even in trifles! The last week has been a blank in my Journal, and almost the same in my studies. I read but little during [that time]. I attended the drill two days at the King's Inns.

I read this day 100 pages in Henry, Vol. 2nd, 241—341; fifty-eight pages in Bolingbroke, 270—328; eighteen pages of Johnson's works, 100—118. I have read the foregoing pages of Johnson cursorily during the past fortnight. I am not now in a fit mood to continue writing. Sweet Eliza! (*n*).

(*n*) This is the first of four references to this lady. The others are in Nos. 43, 47, and 51. O'Connell evidently fancied himself deeply in love with her. Most men under such a delusion wish to do something heroic, to rescue the adored one from some terrible danger at the risk, and even with the loss, of life. But O'Connell wished he was mad, so that he might rave properly about his sweet Eliza! This at least was original. The fit does not seem to have lasted long. The lady's name is mentioned for the last time on January 28th, 1797, just a fortnight after it first made its appearance. Who she was that lit this transient flame in O'Connell's breast it would be idle to attempt to discover. It could hardly have been Miss Upton, whose reproaches for having deserted her drew from O'Connell only the remark, " How blind are unfortunate mortals to their defects. Miss Upton imagined that she had made an impression upon me!" (see No. 56). Could her name by any chance have been Eliza?

No. 43, Wednesday, January 18th, 1797.—I now firmly resolve to continue my Journal regularly. It will be a proof of weakness if I am not able to keep this resolution.

I received on Monday a letter from my uncle Maurice, refusing in the severest terms to permit me to enter into the Lawyers' Corps of Artillery (*o*). Good God, what a strange world we live in ! How stale, flat, and unprofitable are to me its uses ! Would I was quietly in my grave ! But what is there to prevent me from going to rest ? Unreal mockeries, womanish fears, hence ! Do not shake the firmness of my soul. ETERNAL BEING, in whose presence all things exist, look to the wretch who addresses Thee. Direct as it has been ordered by Thee. Rule as Thy wisdom pleases. But let not the phantoms of disordered imaginations disturb him who reposes on Thee with confidence.

(*o*) See above, p. 166. There is another reference to suicide in No. 60 (see p. 206). O'Connell, who was so much down on Shakespeare (see p. 171), might have quoted from *Hamlet* and *Macbeth* more correctly than he does here.

I was informed by my father in a postscript to my uncle's letter that Miles Mahony (*p*) and John were to fight on Friday last. Would that I knew the event [45] of the duel! John, if you have perished, if you have deserted me so early in life, if you render my path clouded and cheerless, why should I remain here, the sport of contingencies and the victim of regulated events? No, my dear brother, my dear brother, I cannot—indeed, I cannot—afford to part with you. Oh, my cold, unfeeling heart, how can you bear even the thought?

(*p*) Probably Myles Mahony, of Castlequin, grandson of Myles Mahony, who married O'Connell's great-aunt (see above, p. 159, n. (*q*)). Myles the grandson married in 1788 Mary, daughter of Charles Jeffrey O'Connell, of Portmagee (*Last Colonel of the Irish Brigade*, i. 52). The duel never came off (see below, p. 185).

Sweet Eliza (*q*), let my love for thee mingle in the cup of my sorrows. Perhaps the time is near when the infusion of so many ingredients may make it strong enough to overpower my reason. There must, assuredly there must, be an exquisite pleasure in madness. Would I was mad! Then, Eliza, I would rave of thee; then should I forget my uncle's tyranny, the coldness and unfeelingness of his heart, my own aberrations. What more can I write? On what other subject can I speculate? Wherever I should endeavour to lead off my thoughts, hither would they continually return.

(*q*) See above, p. 175.

No. 44, *Thursday, January* 19*th,* 1797.—My mind

is more calm to-day. Study has restored it to tranquillity. I have been reading all day. I finished the second volume of Henry's *Britain.* The history commences with the invasion of Britain by Julius Cæsar 55 years before Christ, and is brought down in the two first volumes only to the year of the Christian æra 449, when the Romans finally departed from Britain. The plan is well executed and very entertaining. Dr. Henry was nothing of a philosopher. He knows not how to enliven his narrative. A steady, calm, but tiresome style remains invariably the same throughout the work. About twenty pages of Whitaker's *History of Manchester,* twenty-five of Dr. Watson's *Chemistry,* being the fifth essay. This essay treats of the causes of subterranean fires. If I have an opportunity during the summer I will make an artificial volcano—p. 180—205. One hundred and seventy-one pages of the Introduction to *The Travels of Anacharsis* I read with delight ; I contemplate [46] with enthusiasm the war with Persia in the years 480 and 479 before Christ. The heroes slumber in peace at Thermopylæ and at Platæa. While the cloud-capt palaces rise in glory and moulder in oblivion, while the mountains rear their heads on high and dwindle by degrees into the plain, their fame continues to increase from age to age—189—360.

Miltiades conquered at Marathon, and a few years after perished in chains even in that Athens which he had saved. The fine which ingratitude loaded was too heavy to be borne.

The Lacedæmonians—I should say the Spartans —were a nobler people than I thought them to be.

"What Themistocles proposes is of the greatest utility to you," cried Aristides to the Athenians, "but it is most unjust." "Let his advice remain then ever concealed," answered the Athenians with one voice.

Themistocles had proposed to burn the fleet of the allies of Athens, in order to give to her the undoubted and indisputable superiority at sea. Such was the event of his proposal.

No. 45, Friday, January 20th, 1797.—I read to-day thirteen pages in Gibbon, to the end of the twenty-first chapter; twenty-three pages of Bolingbroke, 345—368; the first article in the *Memoires de l'Académie des Sciences*, on observations made on the planet Jupiter and its satellites in the year 1691 by M. Cassini. Jupiter performs his revolution round the sun in twelve years, and his situation in the heavens is twice the same at the end of eighty-three years. The spots which Cassini observed *remained visible* for nine hours and about 55 minutes. M. Cassini makes an ingenious comparison between the appearance of these spots and that which the different objects that form the surface of our globe would make if viewed from a great distance. I read to, I believe, p. 32. I read likewise one hundred and two pages of *Anacharsis*, 360—462, the end of the first volume. This volume is called the Introduction, and contains an abstract of the [47] history of Greece from the earliest periods until the restitution of the Democracy at Athens and the downfall of the thirty tyrants.

No speculations this night.

No. 46, Saturday, January 25th, 1797.—I read a few days ago Cowley's Life in Johnson's *Poets*, p. 77, Vol. i. Abraham Cowley was born in 1618, and died at Chertsey, in Surrey, in the forty-ninth year of his age, A.D. 1667. He published a book of poems at thirteen. He was the last of the metaphysical poets. I looked over his poems superficially, and did not meet one that I thought would repay me for the time lost in perusing it. His versification is smooth and musical. His poetry displays a great store of learning, disgraced by the company of puerile conceits without number. Yet the fault was not Cowley's; it was that of his age. This reflection serves to clear his merit as a poet, but it is not sufficient to recommend the poetry. He is now very little read; indeed, he is not calculated by any means to excite the attention of the present day. He is too learned and abstruse for idle readers; he is too trifling and affected for philosophers. In fine, he never wrote to the heart.

This day I read fifteen pages of Bolingbroke, 368—383, part of his remarks on the history of

England. They were written in order to show the
utility of keeping up the spirit of liberty. Sixteen
pages of Whitaker's *Manchester*, 51—67. He differs
from Dr. Henry in the situation of the Roman-British
provinces. Dr. Henry places Flavia Cæsariensis
in the south of Britain, and Brittania Prima in the
east, from the Thames to the mouth of the Umber.
Whitaker reverses this position. Dr. Henry does
not tell us his motives for the deviation. I have
no documents whence to judge of the propriety
of the measure. Whitaker gives a sixth province,
Vespasiana, to which he has not yet assigned a
position. Forty-one pages of Watson's *Chemical
Essays*, the sixth essay on vitriol. Vitriol is composed of an *oxide* and the acid of sulphur. Green
vitriol is composed *or has for its basis* the oxide
of iron, blue vitriol that of copper, white vitriol that
of zinc [48]. The acid of sulphur has a greater
affinity with iron than with copper, with an
alkaline salt, as potash, than with iron—205—246.
I read one hundred and one pages of *Anacharsis*.
I have already accompanied him from Scythia
down the Tanais, through the Palus Mæotis, along
the Tauric Chersonesus, through the Black Sea,
through the Thracian Bosphorus, to Byzantium;
thence through the Propontis, the Hellespont, the
Ægean Sea, to Mytilene, in the island of Lesbos;
thence to Colchis, in Eubea, to Thebes by Aulis,
and to Athens. The Hellespont at the place where
Leander was drowned in attempting to swim from

the coast of Asia to his beloved Hero, priestess of
Venus, is not more than a mile in breadth.   A
little below this spot, and near the towns of Abydos
and Sestus, Xerxes constructed a bridge of boats
in the year before Christ 480.   Pittacus, one of
the Seven Wise Men of Greece, was of Lesbos;
Arion of Mythymona and Terpander of Antissa
do honor to this island.   And the names of
Alceus and Sappho will live for ever to add to
its glory.

The last action during the Peloponesian war
was the naval combat near Ægos Potamos, in the
Hellespont.   The victorious Lacedæmonians soon
after made themselves masters of Athens, in the
year before Christ 404.

Epaminondas was a man of the most brilliant
talents and the most unshaken and endearing
virtue.   The character given to him in this work
is unbounded in praise.   There is one trait which
alone would be sufficient to make me love him.
The day after the victory which he gained over
the Spartans at Leuctra, in Beotia, he exclaimed,
" What gives me most pleasure is that the authors
of my existence live to enjoy my renown."   Amiable
piety !   " He was perhaps more just than Aristides,"
says our author.   This is indeed praise.   I know
that praise is useless to the dead, yet I would not
die unknown.   In spite of reason, the second and
durable existence which fame confers is dear to the
heart and cheering to the expectant soul.

I read *The Plan of a Dictionary*, by Johnson (*r*), eighteen pages—177.

(*r*) *The Plan of a Dictionary of the English Language* was addressed to the Earl of Chesterfield, and published in 1747. The Earl, as is well known, treated Johnson with neglect and indifference until the eve of the publication of the dictionary itself, when, hoping perhaps that the work, as well as the plan of it, would be inscribed to him, he contributed to the *World* two papers containing fulsome praise of Johnson and his dictionary, and proposing to make him an irresponsible dictator and an infallible pope in everything that concerned the language. This elicited from Johnson the famous letter in which he rejects his Lordship's overtures with scorn, and defines a patron as " one who looks with unconcern on a man who is drowning, and when he has reached ground encumbers him with help." The " Plan " was so extensive that Chesterfield may have thought that Johnson would never succeed in carrying it out. Johnson laid down in the "Plan" the principles by which he would be guided in determining what words should be inserted, and as regards orthography, pronunciation, etymology, "analogy of the language" (by which he meant the rules by which the inflection of words was governed), syntax, interpretation, and distribution of words into their proper classes, *i.e.*, for example, whether they are poetic expressions, obsolete, barbarous, or impure. One gathers from some of the illustrations which he gives that in his time *wound* had been generally pronounced like *sound*, that *wind* had been invariably pronounced like *mind*, while *great* could be pronounced either like *state* or *feat*. " Risk " he spells *risque*, " crowded " *crouded*. He classes as barbarous or impure the words *lesser* and *worser*.

[49] *No. 47, Sunday, January 22nd, 1797.*— I should not write now but that I wish to persevere in this practice of writing every day. My Journal differs this season widely from the Journal of the

last. Then I contented myself with recording the
number of 'pages read every day; now I give
remarks on the subject of my studies. Then I
mentioned the actions of the day; now I have
little to mention, and that little I omit. But it
is not well to do so. The purpose of this Journal
would be much better answered was I to write both.

I walked with Dawson and Bennett for a long
time this morning (s). We talked some pure, because
moderate, democracy. Hail, Liberty! How cheering
is thy name! How happy should mankind be if
thou wast universally diffused! Strange it might
appear that thou shouldst be hateful to any. But
thou art calumniated, as thou art disgraced by
the nominal advocates. The interested, those who
grow fat on the miseries of mankind, the tyrant,
and the demagogue condemn thee. The one raises
his voice aloud and is heard in the public places to
declaim against thee ; the other more effectually
damns thee by his support.

(s) It is not known who Dawson was. As to Bennett
see No. 6.

I read sixty-two pages of *Anacharsis* this evening,
102—164, Vol. 2nd, a few pages of Gibbon, 160—,
Vol. 2nd. Julian was elected emperor in 360.

" Satis superque." Oh, sweet Eliza ! (t).

(t) See No. 42. " Satis superque," part of the language
addressed by Anchises to Æneas (Virg., *Æn.*, Book II.
602—603) :—

" Satis una superque
Vidimus excidia et captæ superavimus urbi."

No. 48, Monday, January 23rd, 1797.—I received this day three letters : from my uncle, from my mother, and from John. My uncle gives me leave to enter into the corps (*u*) with almost as [50] [great] harshness as he last week refused to permit me. John informs me that he and Miles Mahony met near Killarney, but did not fight (*v*).

(*u*) See No. 38, p. 166.
(*v*) See No. 43, p. 177.

I read this day to the end of the twenty-third chapter in Gibbon, to p. 194. I believe the portion of the history which I read to-day contains the actions of Julian from the time that the legions declared him emperor in Gaul, in the year 360, till he was ready to set out from that Persian expedition from which he never returned. Julian was a great man. But he too was blind in his religious prejudices. " Tantum religio potest " !

I read two sections of Henry's *Britain*, Vol. 3rd, to, I believe, p. 61 : Saxon Heptarchy, Kent, Sussex, West Saxons, East Saxons, East Angles, Mercia, and Northumberland. Everything during the Heptarchy is dark, confused, and uninteresting. I likewise read the article " Abaris," four pages, in Bayle's Dictionary. Bayle was a very great man, cool, candid, and philosophic (*w*).

(*w*) Bayle's *Historical and Critical Dictionary,* translated from the French of Pierre Bayle. The first edition was published

in 1696.   Bayle was bred a Protestant, being son of the Protestant minister at Carla.   He went to Toulouse to study, and
there attended the philosophical lectures of the Jesuits.   Some
discussions he had with a priest on religious subjects convinced
him, and he became a Catholic in 1669, but returned to Protestantism in 1670.   Abaris, the third person whose life is
given in the dictionary, Aaron being the first, was a Scythian,
about whom many fabulous stories were told, among others
that he was carried through the air upon an arrow, which had
belonged to Apollo.

No. 49, Tuesday, January 24th, 1797.—I wrote
two letters to-day, the one to my father, the
other to my uncle.   I am well satisfied with my
letter to my uncle, but that is no proof that he
will be so.

I read but little to-day, 20 pages of *Anacharsis,*
Vol. 2, 164—184.   I have nothing to remark
on this portion of the work.   Nineteen pages
of Henry, Vol. 3, 61—80.   Egbert mounted the
throne of Wessex in the year 801; England was
united into one monarchy by Egbert in 827;
Alfred the Great began to reign in 871.

I read two essays by Hume, Vol. 1, p. 12,
the first [51] on taste and sensibility.   The
former he considers as useful, the latter as pernicious.   I differ with him in opinion.   I look on
both as great promoters of happiness.   The second
essay is on the liberty of the press.   Hume considers it in some instances as a nuisance.   He
had never weighed this subject with sufficient
attention.   He had never boldly contemplated the

advantages that would accrue to mankind was the press free from all shackles.

The works of a historian called Asser (*x*), who was the friend of Alfred, have come down to us. I am glad of it for the sake of the fame of the hero.

(*x*) He was the preceptor and companion of King Alfred, whose life he wrote, under the title *De Vita et Rebus Gestis Alfredi*, in 893. The authenticity of the work has been doubted, however, though it is generally believed to be genuine.

I will for the future write my thoughts in my Journal at an earlier period in the night.

No. 50, *Wednesday, January 25th,* 1797.—I went to the courts to-day. I attended in the King's Bench during the pleading of a Mr. Townsend in favour of the claims of Lady *Morgel* Denny on the Denny estate. At the age of fifteen she had joined her husband in levying a fine by which a debt of ten thousand pounds received a priority of claim on the estate to her jointure. As she is still under age, she has moved on a writ of error to reverse the fine. She is to be brought up for inspection of [*sic*] the seventh of February, as her nonage is to be tried not by a jury, but by the inspection of the court. The mortgagees made no appearance (*y*).

(*v*) This is the only mention in the Journal of any visit paid to the Law Courts by O'Connell before he was called to the bar. A " fine " was a fictitious proceeding in a court of law which operated as a conveyance of landed property, and was much used as a mode in which married women could dispose of their estates. Fines were abolished in England by the Act 3 & 4 Will. IV. c. 74, and in Ireland by an Act of the following year (1834); their place has been supplied by deeds acknowledged before the proper officer. Lady Morgel Denny, being under age, could not make an effectual disposition of any interest in real property, whether by postponing it to a mortgage or otherwise; hence the proceeding by writ of error to reverse the fine. The Dennys were the great people of Tralee, and owned large estates in Kerry.

I read to-day eighty-six pages of Henry, Vol. 3, p. 80—166. I have now come down in the narrative to the arrival of William the Conqueror in England, *anno* 1066. The history of England is dark, confused, and not very interesting. The monkish historians of this period are very doubtful evidence. They used no proper discrimination of character. With them every man is either a saint or a devil. They had no penetration, no taste, no judgment, no philosophy. How little of the last is there even at the present day in the world!

I read thirty-seven pages of *Anacharsis*, Vol. 2nd, 104—221 [*sic*], a description of Athens, the Piræus, etc.

[52] I read twenty-five pages of Bolingbroke, 383—408. Bolingbroke gives a great character of Queen Elizabeth. But he was an orator, and his description suits the purpose of his remarks (z).

(z) There is much truth, as well as much eloquence, in Bolingbroke's description of the character of this remarkable woman. It occurs in *The Idea of a Patriot King*. " Elizabeth," he writes, " was queen in a limited monarchy, and reigned over a people at all times more easily led than driven, and at that time capable of being attached to their prince and their country by a more generous principle than any of those which prevail in our days : by affection. There was a strong prerogative then in being, and the Crown was then in possession of strong legal power. Popularity was, however, then, as it is now, and must always be in mixed government, the sole true foundation of that sufficient authority and influence which other constitutions give the prince gratis, and independently of the people, but which a king of this nation must acquire. The Queen saw it, and she saw too how much popularity depends upon those appearances that depend upon the decorum, the decency, the grace, and the propriety of behaviour of which we are speaking. A warm concern for the interest and honour of the nation, a tenderness for her people, and confidence in their affections, were appearances that ran through her whole conduct, and gave life and colour to it. She did great things, and she knew how to set them off by her manner of doing them. In her private behaviour she showed great affability, she descended even to familiarity, but her familiarity was such as could *not* [*sic*] be imputed to her goodness. Though a woman, she hid all that was womanish about her ; and if a few equivocal marks of coquetry appeared on some occasions, they passed like flashes of lightning, and imprinted no blot upon her character. She had private friendships ; she had favourites ; but she never suffered her friends to forget that she was their queen, and when the favourites did, she made them feel that she was so."

I wrote to-day to Captain O'Connell (*a*) at Carrick-on-Suir. I shall be very impatient until I receive an answer.

(*a*) Probably Maurice Jeffrey O'Connell, of Latine, captain in the (English) Irish Brigade, who married the Liberator's aunt

Anne or Nancy (*The Last Colonel of the Irish Brigade*, i. 9). But there was a Captain Richard O'Connell in the Dutch service, "Captain Dick," an "engaging scamp," as Mrs. Morgan John O'Connell calls him. "He belongs," she says, "to the family of Sir Lucius O'Trigger and Charles O'Malley. He possesses every attractive Celtic foible from which my hero"—Count O'Connell—"was free. . . . His real circumstances are like those of a hero of Lever's. He is poor as a church mouse, but he counts kith and kin with the finest people, and is constantly going amongst them. His grandfather was a rich man, Geoffrey of the Great Herds (Sheaira-na-mo-Mor). His mother descended maternally from the O'Briens of Ballycorrig, a family sprung from the younger son of the famous Earl of Inchiquin, 'Red Murrough of the Burnings'" (*ib.* 211).

I wish I knew how to make a proper estimate of my own talents. But that is impossible. Sometimes—and this indeed happens most frequently—I am led away by vanity and ambition to imagine that I shall cut a great figure on the theatre of the world. Sometimes I fear that I shall never be able to rise to mediocrity. But this I always think, that nothing could shake the steadiness with which I would pursue the good of my country. Distant prospects rise unbidden to my sight. They are not unwelcome to my heart.

No. 51, *Saturday, January* 28*th*, 1797.—I read to-day forty-two pages of Henry, Vol. 3, 257—299, continuation of the history of religion during the second period. St. Dunstan, St. Oswald, and St. Ethelwald were the great patrons of the monkish institutions. Fifty-four pages of *Anacharsis*, Vol. 2,

p. 220—274. Epaminondas received his death-wound at the battle of Mantinea on the fifth of July, 362 before Christ. He seems to have behaved with rashness in hurrying forward on the flying Lacedæmonian phalanx. Yet perhaps that body of troops could be routed but by unchecked valour. He had been driven out of Sparta (which he had endeavoured to surprise) only a few days before the battle. During the fight that took place on this occasion Isadas, a young Spartan, beautiful as the god of love, armed only with a lance and sword, performed prodigies of valour. He [53] laid at his feet whosoever durst oppose him. Some days afterwards the Ephori decreed him a crown, and at the same time condemned him to pay a fine for having fought without cuirass and buckler. How much of pride entered into their decrees ?

Attica was divided into ten tribes, which were subdivided into one hundred and seventy-four departments. The citizens of Athens were a portion of these tribes. Each tribe chose annually 50 senators, and the same number of substitutes. These senators were chosen from the entire mass of the people by lot. One article in their oath of office was to commit no citizen of Attica to prison who could find bail, except persons charged with a conspiracy against the State or the embezzlement of the public revenues.

The senators of each tribe were to preside by lot. The four first presided for thirty-six days, the others for thirty-five. The presiding senators were called *prytanes*, and were supported at the public expense in the Prytaneum. Each tribe of senators was divided into five decuries and had ten *proedri*, or presidents. The seven senior *proedri* presided over the whole machine of government one day in his turn. The senators were allowed 9 pence a day.

When Epaminondas was setting out on one of his campaigns he borrowed fifty drachmas, or about £1 17s. 6d. of our money, in order to equip himself.

I read to-day sixty-six pages of Dr. Watson's *Chemical Essays*, to the end of the first volume, 283—349. Saltpetre is composed of an acid and vegetable fixed alkali. This acid is the aqua regia, or fuming spirit of nitre. Nitre is made in Spain, as in the East Indies. The French have for more than a century made it in great quantities, but not from the spontaneous productions of nature. Dr. Watson defends Livy for saying that Hannibal used vinegar to soften the rocks on the Alps, if these rocks were of limestone.

Paddy Hease (*b*) called on me this morning before I was up. We breakfasted and walked for a long time together. We talked of the diversions of Ivreagh, etc.

(*b*) Probably the same person as Paddy *Hayes*, mentioned below (p. 214). O'Connell was not particular about the spelling

of proper names, and it must be remembered that the letter
" e " in the mouth of an Irishman of that day was the phonetic
equivalent of " a " as now pronounced before a single con-
sonant followed by a silent " e." See above, n. (g), p. 127, as
to the Hayes family.

Sweet Eliza (c), let me again offer up to you the
tribute of my silent wishes. Now by myself, in the
lonesomeness of my heart I reflect on thee with
satisfaction and delight.

(c) See above, p. 175.

[54] I have been this day thinking on the plan
to be pursued *when I come into Parliament* (d). If
to distinguish myself was the object of my exertions
that would be best done by becoming a violent
oppositionist. But as it will be my chief study to
serve my country, moderation will be a proper
instrument for that purpose. Moderation is the
character of genuine patriotism, of that patriotism
which seeks for the happiness of mankind. There
is another species which is caused by hatred of
oppression. This is a passion. The other is a
principle.

(d) This is a singular sentence. How in the beginning of
1797 O'Connell could have contemplated entering Parliament
is not easy to understand. On February 12th, 1795, Grattan,
by arrangement with Lord Fitzwilliam, the Viceroy whose
recall had such disastrous results, brought in a Bill for the
admission of Catholics to Parliament. Lord Camden was
sworn in as Lord Lieutenant on March 31st, and Grattan's Bill
was thrown out by 155 to 48. Catholics were disqualified for

a seat in the Irish Parliament by the English statute
3 Will. III. c. 2, which enacted that no member of either House
of Parliament of Ireland should sit without making a declaration of disbelief in transubstantiation, the invocation of saints,
and the sacrifice of the mass, and taking certain oaths. The
usurped jurisdiction to pass Acts binding in Ireland was
renounced by the British Act 23 Geo. III. c. 28. But by
the Irish Act 21 & 22 Geo. III. c. 48, all statutes made in
England or Great Britain relating to the taking of any oath,
or making any declaration, in Ireland, were to be executed
in Ireland. By the Irish Catholic Relief Act, 33 Geo. III.
c. 21, s. 9, it is provided that " nothing herein contained shall
extend to enable any person to sit or vote in either House of
Parliament unless he shall have taken, made, and subscribed
the oaths and declaration, and performed the several requisites,
which by any law heretofore made and now in force are required
to enable any person to sit or vote."

O'Connell, in entry No. 58 below (p. 202), declares his resolution to enter Parliament, and defines his line of political
action.

No. 52, Friday, February 3rd, 1797.—I have been
so busy since I wrote the last number that I
scarcely recollect how to make an entry in my
Journal. I have since Monday morning attended
drill regularly ; I have since that day dined at the
Hall. Keeping the term is much more expensive
than I should have imagined. I read nothing this
week. Between the attendance at drill and that at
Commons the days slip away unnoticed (*e*).

(*e*) " Keeping the term " means eating the prescribed number
of dinners in the Commons' Hall of the King's Inns, and of
course paying the necessary fees. " Attendance at Commons "

means eating those dinners. O'Connell entered as a student at King's Inns in the Easter term of 1795, but did not commence to keep his terms until he settled in Dublin.

No. 53, Monday, February 6th, 1797.—Yesterday I appeared for the first time in uniform (*f*). I put on this day the undress jacket of the Lawyers' Artillery for the first time.

(*f*) It was scarlet and blue. The motto of the corps was " Pro aris et focis " (*The Liberator : his Life and Times,* p. 176).

I received two letters to-day, the one from my uncle, promising cash, the other from my father, with an order for ten pounds. The money from my father I must not accept.

I read unto p. 204 of the second volume of Watson's *Chemical Essays.* The greater part of these pages I read on Saturday. I read to-day a few pages of Henry's *Britain,* to p. 368, Vol. 3rd.

[55] *No. 54, Thursday, February 9th,* 1797.—I reassumed my studies this day, and can therefore make a more satisfactory entry in my Journal than I could have done for some time past. Though this was a parade day, I did not attend, as I was still troubled with the remains of a toothache by which I was confined yesterday.

I read to-day sixty-five pages of *Anacharsis,* p. 274—339, Vol. 2nd. These pages contain a description of the laws, magistrates, and manners of the Athenians. An Areopagite was punished, expelled from this body, for having crushed to death a small bird that had taken refuge in his bosom. The Areopagus maintained its reputation until the total ruin of the Athenians (*g*).

(*g*) Areopagus, the Hill of Mars, upon which sat the Athenian court before which were tried wilful murder, bodily injury with intent to kill, incendiarism, and poisoning. It was a tribunal of great antiquity, though supposed by many to have been created by Solon, who flourished 594 B.C. The Areopagus was also a council, empowered to interfere in matters affecting religion and morals, and at one time in the administration of public affairs as well.

I read fifty pages of Watson's *Essay*, 204—254, Vol. 2nd. These pages treat of calcareous earths. Quicklime [loses] about eight hundred-weight in the ton during calcination. It acquires by being exposed four or five days to the air about 15 cwt. in the ton. According to Dr. Watson's experiments, the calcined stone loses nothing of its original dimensions. Twenty pages of Henry's *Britain* (p. 368—388, Vol. 3rd). Master Henry, thou wast in sober sadness a dull dog!

No. 55, Friday, February 10th, 1797.—I read but little to-day, as I attended drill from two till four. I read, however, thirty pages of *Anacharsis*, Vol. 2, p. 339—374. The chapter which I read to-day treats of the religion of Athens. Oh, Religion, how much have mankind suffered [*sic*] to thee! It was thou who wouldst have caused the banishment, if not the death, of Anaxagoras because he believed in one intelligent supreme Being. But what shalt thou return for the life of Socrates, of the first of philosophers?

[56] Christianity has had her millions of victims. The great Moore fell beneath her axe (h). The innocent babes have bedewed her altars with their blood. As for the system of the Jews, murder and rapine were its first principles. Could not men be moral without such assistants? We are not permitted to inquire. The hue and cry is raised against the man who dares to investigate the claims of those *principles*, as they are called, which have caused the devastation of empires. Why should truth be so disagreeable to the human ear? Is it that her light would dazzle? No. Persecution springs from self-love. Those who do not pay the tribute of coincidence to our decisions become our most hated foes. We would tear them; we would devour them. Of all the animals that infest this wretched planet of ours that species of monkey called man is certainly the most absurd and unaccountable.

I read to-day a few pages in Henry.

(h) Sir Thomas More, sentenced to death, and on July 7th, 1535, executed, for refusing to take the oath of supremacy, or rather, perhaps, denying the competence of Parliament to pass an Act making the King supreme head of the Church.

No. 56, Sunday, February 12th, 1797.—I should

not write to-night but that I wish not to lose the habit of writing. I want a philosophic mode of thinking. Let me never forget the utility of possessing that.

I received this morning a note from Miss Upton (*i*), reproaching me with having *deserted* her. As long as the recollection of her remains in my mind I will be astonished at this event. How blind are unfortunate mortals to their defects. Miss Upton imagined that she had made an impression on me !

(*i*) See n. (*n*) to No. 44, p. 175.

I read to-day thirty-eight pages of *Anacharsis*, 374—412, Vol. 2nd. The description of Delphi is [57] the country of Phocis.

No. 57, *Wednesday, February* 15*th*, 1797.—I dined yesterday at Mr. Franks's (*j*). I should have written to my father. I wrote to Charles Casey (*k*) on Saturday.

(*j*) See No. 35 above, p. 152.
(*k*) A Cork merchant, to whom O'Connell's uncle Maurice, familiarly known as Hunting-cap, was in the habit of consigning his butter. There is a letter from him printed in *The Last Colonel of the Irish Brigade* (ii. 218), which shows the hostility which the business community felt towards the rebellion of 1798. The writer says he has no doubt that the rebellion will be put down in another week, and adds, "May we live once more to see peace and quiet established. We did not sufficiently thank God for the happiness we heretofore enjoyed."

I read a good deal to-day, but did not attend drill.

I read to-day ninety-two pages of *Anacharsis*, p. 443—475, the end of Vol. 2nd, and Vol. 3rd, p. 60. The last chapter of the second volume contains the description of an Athenian house and entertainment. The Athenians had a great deal in common with the French—with the French, I mean, of the monarchy. The changes which the spirit of the Revolution has effected or will produce are by me as yet undiscovered. Great and decided these alterations must be. Perhaps they will increase the resemblance between the Athenian and French people. Some of the traits may be lost ; others, and strong ones too, may more than fill the place of the first. The Athenians were refined and frivolous, polite and luxurious. The French possessed all these qualities. The Athenians loved liberty. Here the altered situation of the French has or may produce a resemblance.

The first chapter of the third volume of *Anacharsis* contains [an account] of the best system of Athenian education. This system is personified, if I may use the expression, by Lysias, the son of Apollodorus. The latter was the host of our traveller. I found some fault with parts of this plan of education, I do not now recollect with what. I admired very much the continual application that is made to the reason of the pupil. Authority claims nothing, argument everything. It may appear trivial to add—but nothing relative to this subject is trivial—that *our* young Athenian is taught to use both hands indiscriminately. The Scythians were in the habit of doing the same.

I read to-day sixty pages of Henry, p. 404—432, the end of Vol. 3rd, and to p. 32, Vol. 4th. The penal code of the Saxon, as those of the other fierce conquerors of Europe, assumed in the period here spoken of an aspect [58] terrible only to the poor. The rich enjoyed purchased impunity. The age was barbarous, it is allowed. Yet in *our enlightened* days the case is but little altered. The poor are still the principal objects of legal punishments. The crimes which they alone are tempted to commit are those which are distinguished with the chosen horrors of the modern penal laws. Gaming with endless chain of frauds and deceptions, debauchery, corruption, and inveterate profligacy, may, indeed, become topics of animadversion for moralists, but the accommodating hand of the law touches them not, or if they are punished the delinquent certainly is poor. But robbery and theft, which the *great* and rich are not exposed to commit, are placed in the front rank in the dreadful death muster which our statutes ordain.

Henry tells us not by whom the different ordeals were to be chosen, nor what circumstances regulated the choice of them. The common ordeal chosen by the clergy was the *crosned* (*l*). This consisted in swallowing a piece of bread and cheese properly blessed and cursed. The hot iron ordeals were the

privilege of quality.   The water ordeal was indeed
easily passed through.

(*l*) The *corsnæd*, or " trial slice," sometimes called the "cursed
morsel."   The dose of bread and cheese was administered from
the altar, with the curse that if the accused were guilty God
would send the angel Gabriel to stop his throat, so that he might
not be able to swallow it.   As fear or nervousness has the effect
of arresting the flow of saliva, the timid naturally were found
guilty.

I likewise read the Preface and sixteen pages of
L'Origine des Découvertes attribuées aux Modernes, par
Dutens.   The author has proved that Aristotle
knew the merit and ability of doubting, and that he
was of Locke's opinion on the mode of acquiring
ideas (*m*).   Plato was the advocate, and, I believe,
the first advocate, of innate ideas.

(*m*) Locke taught that ideas came by sensation and reflection,
none being innate.

I have not yet paid the tribute of esteem to the
author of *The Travels of Anacharsis*.   He does
indeed merit the loudest approbation.   He makes
his reader intimate with the great men, the laws,
customs [59], and manners, of Greece.

No. 58, Monday, February 20th, 1797.—I should
not write to-night but that I have been so negligent
for some time past.   Let me once more resolve to
be regular in inserting the thoughts of the day.

I was in the House of Commons this evening.
Mr. Pelham was not sufficiently recovered from the

fatigues of his journey from London to attend. There was therefore no business before the House. Sir Lawrence Parsons spoke for near half an hour on the necessity of putting Ireland into a state of defence which would render it secure from the attacks of invading foes. His oratorical labours do not rise to mediocrity. I too will be a member. Young as I am, unacquainted with the ways of the world, I should not even now appear contemptible. I will steadfastly and persevering attach myself to the real interests of Ireland. I shall endeavour equally to avoid the profligacy of corruption and the violence of unreasonable *patriotism*. Of real patriotism moderation is the chief mark (*n*).

(*n*) See No. 51 and n. (*d*) thereto. This is the only visit to the House of Commons recorded in the Journal. Sir Lawrence Parsons was the ancestor of the present Lord Rosse, and a descendant of a brother of Sir William Parsons, who was one of the lords justices during the Irish rebellion of 1641. Sir Lawrence was a man of liberal views, and strongly opposed the Union. Pelham, afterwards Earl of Chichester, was Chief Secretary to Lord Camden, the reactionary Lord Lieutenant, who was sworn in on March 30th, 1795. Pelham fell ill, and Castlereagh became acting Chief Secretary (see Barrington, *Personal Sketches*, p. 173, and below, p. 213).

I dined this day at Mr. Day's (*o*). I wish I had that smoothness which society bestows on its frequenters.

(*o*) The Days were a Kerry family, and friends of the O'Connells. One of them became an Irish judge early in 1798

(see below, p. 218).   It may have been with him, while still
a practising barrister, that O'Connell dined on this occasion.

I read to-day ninety pages of Henry, p. 52—142,
Vol. 4th, on learning partly and partly on arts ;
forty-two pages of *The Life of Turgot* (*p*), by Condorcet.   Turgot was one of the greatest men of the
age, as he was the first who applied the principles
of reason and justice [60] to the practice of government.   He was the first practising pupil of the
modern school of politicians.

(*p*) Turgot, the great Finance Minister under Louis XVI.,
was appointed in August, 1771.   He laid down as the
fundamental principles of his fiscal policy, " No bankruptcy,
no increase of taxation, and no borrowing."   He relied upon
economy and good management to restore the finances to a
healthy condition.   He re-established free trade in grain within
the kingdom, and authorised its importation from abroad.   He
proposed the abolition of the *corvée*, or compulsory labour, a
burden which fell upon the poor, and the imposition of a territorial tax, which would fall upon rich and poor.   He also
proposed the suppression of exclusive trading corporations.
He wrote against fixing the rate of interest, and expounded the
doctrines regarding a paper currency which have since been
generally accepted.   He carried his proposals for the abolition
of the *corvée*, the imposition of a territorial tax, and the suppression of exclusive trading corporations ; but these measures
raised against him an opposition in which the courtiers, the
privileged orders, the members of the industrial classes, and
the ignorant populace united.   This coalition succeeded in
poisoning the mind of the king against him, and despite of his
solemn and prophetic warning that kings who give themselves
up to the direction of courtiers should remember the fate of
Charles I., he was dismissed on May 12th, 1776.

No. 59, *Thursday, February* 23*rd*, 1797.—Certain
it is that I should have read and written much more
if I did not enter into any corps. Yet the recollection of having been in one will hereafter be pleasant.
It will be still more pleasant to be always able to
say, " I was a volunteer."

I spent the greater part of this day under arms.
We were taught the exercise of the cannon. We
carried our three-pounder from the ordnance stores
on the quay to a yard belonging to a Mr. McEvoy,
of the corps. Thence we *attended* it to another
yard near Merrion Square (*q*).

(*q*) " In this—the Lawyers' Artillery Corps—Mr. O'Connell
served as a private, and earned his share of the just credit
these doubly civilian soldiers acquired by the rapid handling
of their guns, equalling, as they did, the regular artillery in
their management " (*Life and Speeches of Daniel O'Connell*, i. 13).
O'Connell's connection with the yeomanry involved him in some
personal risk, owing to his refusal to be a party to those acts
of inhumanity which disgraced the wearers of the uniform of the
volunteer soldier of that day. It is told of him that while he
was posted as a sentry on one of the canal bridges he was
ordered, but refused, to fire on some unarmed country people
who were about after the hour permitted by martial law. On
another occasion he interfered singly to prevent an innocent
man and his wife from being dragged out of their bed at an hotel
in James's Street, Dublin, which was being searched for sus-
pected persons by a body of yeomanry of which O'Connell
was one. " He was in danger again in trying to save the life of
a defenceless man from a member of the Attorneys' Corps, who
was trying to cut him down because he was alone and helpless.
O'Connell received the sword-cut on the barrel of his musket,
and the deep indentation it made proved how fatal the blow

would have been if it had been received by the person for
whom it was intended. Mr. Wagget, afterwards Recorder of
Cork, was O'Connell's sergeant, and, happily for him, happened
to come up at the moment. A few words explained matters,
and he at once took O'Connell's part, but he only got rid of
the attorney by charging him with his halbert " (*The Liberator :
his Life and Times*, p. 241).

I read this evening thirty-one pages of Henry,
p. 200—231, Vol. 4th. The author gave credit to
everything positively asserted by good authority
without considering the improbability of the thing
related. For instance, he gives us an account of the
effects of poetry and music on a Swedish king which
to me appears false, or, if it is true, it must have
been the consequence of a deep-laid plot. Olavs (a
Swedish historian, I believe), is the authority on
which this tale is founded. Henry gives implicit
faith to the evidence of William of Malmesbury—
evidence which must in many instances appear
more than suspicious. I am often enraged while
reading Henry's work at finding so much knowledge unillumined by a single spark of philosophy.

[61] *No. 60, Saturday, March 4th*, 1797.—I have
often wished that I was a philosopher. I have
often wished it in vain. If philosophy illumined
my steps I should not for so long a time have permitted my path to remain unnoticed. But no. I
am more weak than a woman. Good God !

That man alone can be a philosopher who is
superior to all circumstances because he is prepared

for them, who regards with calm coldness the vicissitudes and changes of human affairs.

At this moment I know not why I should not shoot myself. I have the means at hand (r). Yet life—damn life! If the future resembles the past what is the advantage of living? I am not able to speculate deeply, as my senses are absorbed by a powerful cold. I express only the sentiments of the instant.

(r) This is the second time O'Connell contemplates the possibility of committing suicide (see No. 43 above, p. 176). But this time he may perhaps be excused on account of that " powerful cold " that absorbed his senses.

I read to-day several pages of *Anacharsis*, Vol. 4. I know not the number.

Tom Bourke (s) is in town.

(s) Probably Thomas Fitzmaurice Burke, major-general in the British service. He was born in 1776, and was the son of Redmond Burke and Joanna, granddaughter of Daniel O'Connell, of Darrynane, and Alison Sigerson (*Last Colonel of the Irish Brigade*, ii. 128). There was a Thomas Bourke an ensign in the " Second Walsh's " (English) Irish Brigade. His com- mission was dated May 25th, 1796 (*ib*. 191).

I am really tired with living. A revolution would not produce the happiness of the Irish nation (t).

(t) O'Connell's reason for holding this opinion appears in entry No. 36 above (p. 155) : " The Irish people are not yet sufficiently enlightened to be able to bear the sun of freedom·

Freedom would soon dwindle into licentiousness. They would rob; they would murder." At this time revolution was in the air. Lord Fitzwilliam was recalled in February, 1795; soon afterwards the United Irishmen were suppressed, and became a secret society; the Coercion Act, 36 Geo. III. c. 20, was passed, and Lord Edward Fitzgerald joined the United Irishmen in the following year; the French fleet arrived in Bantry Bay December 22nd; in the spring of 1797, Colonel Lake was sent over to take the command in Ulster, where he proclaimed martial law, seized two committees of United Irishmen, and suppressed the *Northern Star*, a Belfast paper, which was the organ of their party; the people were being rapidly goaded into rebellion by the outrages committed by the soldiery. Sir Ralph Abercromby, who succeeded Lord Carhampton as commander-in-chief in the end of 1796, writes in 1798 of the conduct of the troops, " Within these twelve months every crime, every cruelty, that could be committed by Cossacks or Calmucks has been committed here." One of the Nationalist papers of the day published the following " receipt to make a rebel " : " Take a loyal subject, uninfluenced by title, place, or pension; burn his house over his head; let the soldiers exercise every species of insult and barbarity towards his helpless family, and march away with the plunder of every part of his property they choose to save from the flames." O'Connell, when discussing with O'Neill Daunt the way in which Irish history has been distorted so as to reverse the characters of the two contending parties in the rebellions that had taken place in Ireland, said, " Many of the Orange scoundrels in 1797 rivalled the atrocities of Coote and his bloodstained gang "—in the rebellion of 1641.—" In that year Orange Sneyd made his guide, a boy, blow into his pistol, and while the youth's mouth was at the muzzle shot him dead. In 1797 Sneyd was standing at the door of Mrs. L'Estrange's public-house in Fleet Street, and wantonly shot a boy who had brought him a message " (*Personal Recollections*, ii. 130). He told Daunt an incident that occurred in the following year, when a friend of his and his two brothers were arrested by a magistrate, who

owed their mother £2,000 on a bond, and who threatened to
have them flogged and hanged if she did not release it. "Sir,"
said she, "if you were to treat *me* in that way, you could not
extort the bond from me, and I am much mistaken if they have
not at least as much firmness as their mother." The brothers
were tried before Judge Day, and, no witnesses being produced
against them, were acquitted; that is, no doubt, the bill
against them was thrown out by the Grand Jury. After this
they were again thrown into gaol through the machinations
of the same gentleman, but were released by the commanding
officer who inspected the prison; (*ib.* 133).

No. 61, *Sunday, March* 12*th,* 1797.—I sit down to
write to-night merely to renew the habit of keeping
this Journal.

I loaded the cannon twice to-day. It was the
first time that we had two cannon out (*u*).

(*u*) The cannon of the Lawyers' Corps of Artillery, the exercise of which he had been taught on February 23rd (see
No. 59, p. 204).

[62] *No.* 62, *Tuesday, March* 14*th,* 1797.—I read
to-day ninety-six pages of Henry, Vol. 5th. William
called the Conqueror landed in England September
the 29th, 1066. William Rufus commenced his
reign in 1087, and was killed in the afternoon of the
third of August, 1100. Henry the First died in the
year 1135. Stephen died in 1154.

Various were the crimes, manifold were the errors,
of the people of the day. The world is changed for
the better.

I have not that readiness of observation nor that

fluency of expressing my remarks which I heretofore possessed. Writing the suggestions of the
moment was of the utmost utility to me. It gave
me those qualities which I have already mentioned.
It confirmed my philosophy. Laziness prevented
me from daily practice. But I mean no longer to
be lazy.

I am reading *The Jockey Club* (*v*). Vice reigns
triumphant in the English court at this day. Vice
and error are the rulers of the practice of the
English Government. The English are become
besotted and slavish. The spirit of liberty shrinks
to protect property from the attacks of French
innovators. The corrupt higher orders tremble for
their vicious enjoyments.

(*v*) *The Jockey Club ; or, A Sketch of the Manners of the Age.* It
was published anonymously in 1792 in three parts, and went
rapidly through several editions. *The Jockey Club* is mainly a
merciless exposure of the vices and failings of people of rank
and wealth living at the time when it was written. The identity
of the persons alluded to is but thinly concealed by suggestive
letters. The King of England and the Prince of Wales,
Louis XVI. and his unhappy queen, noble dukes and wealthy
commoners, titled ladies and *other* ladies, statesmen and
politicians, judges and lawyers—all come under the unsparing
lash of the anonymous moralist. But he knows how and when
to award praise as well as blame. Speaking of Lord G. H.
Cavendish, he says, " The character of the Cavendish family
throughout all its branches is uniform, cold and phlegmatic, of
unsullied honour and integrity. . . . We do not believe that
the mines of Peru could seduce this nobleman to do a dis-
honourable act." He indulges in an encomium on the beauty,

the grace, and the virtues of the Duchess of Devonshire. He is very complimentary to Fox, but very severe on Burke—the last of the series of characters that he assails—whom he calls a "venal apostate." The most cruel of all the articles in the collection is that on Marie Antoinette. The writer reproduces all the shocking charges of immorality made against her, and winds up, "Thus we bid adieu to the immortal heroine of Mr. Burke's romance." It was, no doubt, the recital of these infamous accusations that drew from O'Connell the exclamation, "O tempora! O mores!" (below, p. 211), for Marie Antoinette's character is one of the latest portrayed. In a note the writer adds the following curious account of a practice that he says prevailed at the Queen's table. He mentions that there had been a machine lately invented in France for the execution of criminals called a guillotine, after the name of its inventor, and goes on to tell how a model of it used to be brought in with the dessert after the Queen's dinner, and figures representing the principal and most obnoxious "patriots," with a little phial containing a crimson perfume about the neck of each. The "patriot" was tried by some magistrate who was a guest, and condemned. He was at once guillotined, and the ladies and gentlemen present dipped their handkerchiefs in the perfume, exclaiming, "Ah, how sweet is the blood of 'patriots'!" ("Ah, qu'il est doux, le sang des 'patriotes'!").

[63] *No. 63, Wednesday, March 22nd, 1797.—* Thadee Duggan (*w*) set off this day for London. He means to go to the East Indies.

(*w*) This may be his fellow-boarder mentioned above (p. 49), or the kind friend who came to the relief of the two boys when they were stranded for want of money on their arrival at Douay (see p. 41). A Mr. Hugh Duggan was surgeon in "O'Connell's" regiment of the (English) Irish Brigade, and "Thadee" may have belonged to his family.

I have finished *The Jockey Club* (*x*). "O tempora ! O mores ! "

(*x*) See above, p. 209.

Henry the Second died on the sixth of July, 1189.

No. 64, Friday, March 24th, 1797.—I have spent four hours of this day in reading. My mind is tranquil ; my senses feel with precision ; my expression is accurate.

I love liberty—and this is a moment fit for indulging reflection on that subject—I love liberty as conducive to increase the portion of human happiness. A great deal of the misery of man can clearly be derived from the form of government under which he lives. Oppression harasses his faculties. Privilege confined by *accident* insults his understanding. His industry is consumed to support the follies and vices of men who help him not. When it is exclaimed that " the splendour of government must be maintained, " it should mildly and firmly be replied, " No, but the happiness of the people should be established." In fact, the only rational motive of forming a Government is the good of the forming parties.

I read to-day 100 pages in Henry, Vol. 5, p. 189—289. Richard the First died April 6th, 1199 ; John died 1216. Magna Charta was signed on Friday, July 19th, 1216, between Staines and Windsor, at Runnymede.

I read thirty-one pages of Gibbon, Vol. 2nd, p. 395 —425 [64]. St. George, the patron of England, was no other in all probability than George of Cappadocia, who was intruded into the see of Alexandria. He was slain in a popular tumult in the year 361. Lest his relics should be an object of worship, and that he should be converted into a saint and martyr, his body was burnt, and the ashes thrown into the sea or dispersed in the air. Vain precaution!

Julian the great died near the banks of the Tigris June 26th, 363 ; Jovian died February 17th, 364, Valentinian, emperor, February 27th, and Valens March 28th, 364.

Athanasius died May 2nd, 373.

I read a few pages of the *Cour de Berlin* (*y*), likewise of *Origine des Découvertes attribuées aux Modernes*, par Dutens.

(*y*) See above, p. 138.

No. 65, Saturday, March 25th, 1797.—I read to-day during more than six hours, and read with attention. I now insert the number of pages : 164 of Henry, Vol. 5, 289—453, the end ; 182 of *Anacharsis*, 389—469, the end of Vol. 3rd, and to p. 102, Vol. 4th ; 24 pages of Watson's *Essays*, 50—74, Vol. 3rd ; a few pages of *The Rolliad* (*z*).

(*z*) *The Rolliad* was a political satire published in a series of papers in the latter part of 1784 and the beginning of 1785, immediately after the great struggle between Pitt and the Coalition. It was named after Colonel John Rolli, afterwards Lord Rolli, one of the members for Devonshire, a friend of Pitt and the Court, and was a collection of pieces in prose and verse which were written on the side of the defeated Coalition, and were personal, and often coarse, but witty. Dr. George Lawrence, one of Burke's friends, is believed to have been one of those concerned in it.

Virtue, thou certainly art more than a name. Thou bestowest firmness and quietude to the heart of mortal, whilst thou exaltest his conceptions. I was going to say that virtue makes the judgment correct, the conception accurate; but it is, in fact, the effect of accurate conception and correct judgment.

After having, in the conviction of my soul [65], made this eulogium on virtue, let me tremble whilst I ask myself how much of myself entered into my desire or dread of a revolution. Oh, if I was possessed of virtue I would wish for the happiness alone of mankind. If I possessed virtue I should meet every event without shrinking.

Stuart seems to me to be a very valuable man (a).

(a) Stuart must be Robert Stuart, the future Lord Castlereagh, who in February, 1797, became acting Chief Secretary during the illness of Pelham, the Chief Secretary to Lord Camden, the Viceroy who replaced Lord Fitzwilliam in February, 1795. Castlereagh became Chief Secretary in November, 1798.

No. 66, *Tuesday, March* 28*th*, 1797.—I read to-day 279 pages of *Anacharsis*, p. 260—464, the end of Vol. 4th, and to p. 75 of Vol. 5th. Alcam was the only poet, I believe, of Sparta. The Doric dialect prevailed in that city.

Anticrates of Sparta, Macherion of Mantinea, and Gryllus, the son of Zenophon, disputed the honour of having terminated the existence of the great Epaminondas (*b*).

(*b*) He was mortally wounded in the battle of Mantinea by a javelin, which he did not allow to be drawn out until he heard that his army was victorious and his shield safe, as he was told that he would die as soon as it was taken out.

No. 67, *Friday, March* 31*st*, 1797.—I read yesterday 149 pages of *Anacharsis*, Vol. 5th, p. 75—224.

I read to-day 322 pages of *Anacharsis*, p. 224—476, the end of Vol. 5th, and to p. 70, Vol. 6th. I shall have this work ended before next Friday. I will then apply myself with the greatest diligence to Henry's *History of Britain*. When I have read *The History of Britain* to the end of Belsharo's work, I will resume Gibbon. This systematic mode of reading will, I believe, be of more utility to me than the desultory method which I have followed.

[66] I called on Paddy Hayes (*c*) to-day. We walked for some time together.

(*c*) Probably the same person as Paddy *Hease*, mentioned above (p. 192).

It is impossible for any young man at the present day to guess with probable success at the mode in which his existence will terminate. This opinion has been in my mind these two days past. I have in consequence been accustoming myself to consider death without shrinking. Much yet remains to be done before I can familiarise myself with the idea. But philosophy and the practice of theoretic virtue (where there is no opportunity for the real) may soon make me look upon all events as indifferent to me individually.

I must avoid disclosing my political sentiments so frequently as I do at present. It would be a devilish unpleasant thing to get *caged !* Nonsense ! *Liberality* can never become dangerous (*d*).

(*d*) As to the risk O'Connell ran about this time see above, p. 130.

No. 68, *Monday, May* 1*st*, 1797.—For near four weeks of the month of April I slept at Bennett's (*e*). His wife was brought to bed on the third, and he was absent on circuit. On the ninth I thought it was impossible for his wife to recover.

(*e*) Richard Newton Bennett (see No. 6, p. 78).

The state of affairs at present is not a little singular. We are probably at the eve of a great change in administration. Within the last week the Duke of Leinster was deprived of his place in the Hanaper Office.   He has, I am (f)

(f) The next two pages are missing, the sheet on which they are written being torn out all but a narrow strip sufficient to hold the threads which bind the sheets together.   Upon this strip fragments of words can be read.   The first consists of the letters " to," probably the beginning of the word " told."   It is not unlikely that O'Connell tore this sheet out himself, fearing that something which he had there set down might compromise him at a juncture when, as appears from the next preceding entry, it was dangerous to disclose one's political opinions.   The entry thus destroyed was a very long one, occupying part of p. 66 and the whole of pp. 67 and 68. The proclamation of martial law in Ireland in 1797 drove the Duke of Leinster to resign the command of the Kildare militia.

As we learn from the next entry, O'Connell left Dublin for his uncle's on June 23rd, and remained until the beginning of November.   He continued to reside at Mrs. Jones's until January 13th, 1798, on which day he resumes his Journal, after an interval of more than seven months.   From this time forward it is very irregularly kept.

[69] *No. 70, Saturday, January* 13*th*, 1798.—I left Mrs. Jones's this day (g).   Some other time I will descant on my reasons.   My heart is now sick.

(g) From Mrs. Jones's O'Connell went to No. 14, Trinity Place, a retired locality lying at the back of Dame Street and South Great George's Street.   The house, with a number of others in the same neighbourhood, was demolished some years ago to make room for what was called the New Market.   O'Connell's landlord was a man known to theatre-going folks in Dublin as Regan the fruiterer, and was a purveyor to Dublin Castle. O'Connell was an intimate friend of a respectable cheesemonger named Murray, who carried on business at No. 3, South Great George's Street, and on one occasion, about the month of March, 1798, at Mr. Murray's table, he was betrayed by the heat of a political discussion into some forgetfulness of his constant habit of temperance, and while returning home he went to the rescue of a poor unfortunate whom a gang of ruffians were persecuting. He was immediately attacked himself. He knocked three of his assailants down, but was then pinioned behind and beaten savagely in the face. His injuries compelled him to keep his room, and his landlord took the opportunity to warn him against committing himself politically, " detailing the dark hints rife in the purlieus of the Castle of the game the Government were playing in allowing the insurrection to mature while they kept themselves ready and had it in their power to lay hands upon its leaders at any moment " (*Life and Speeches of Daniel O'Connell*, edited by his son, John O'Connell).

Important events took place in the life of O'Connell in the interval that elapsed between this and the following number, notably his call to the bar. On March 1st, 1798, he wrote the following letter to his uncle Maurice, printed in the *Irish Monthly* (vol. x. p. 585). It is addressed from 14, Trinity Place.

" Dublin, 14, Trinity Place,
" *March* 1st, 1798.

" My dear Uncle,—I sit down to acknowledge the receipt of two letters from you since I wrote last, the one of the 9th and the other of the 13th ult. I have since received a letter from Mr. Casey covering £56 16s. 6d., a sum fully adequate to any increased expenditure, and greater, I will candidly confess, than my expectations. I should indeed have known your kindness sufficiently well to be certain that you would do nothing for me by halves. I know not how to return you proper thanks for this last proof of your attention. I have already exhausted all that language could express on such occasions. I will now only say that I hope one day to be able to show that your favours were not thrown away on ingratitude or inattention.

" You already know that the observations contained in your first letter were unnecessary ; but they were, and ever must be, interesting to me when I remember the affectionate prudence which dictated them. They were all so strictly just that I assure you no consideration would induce me to expose myself in any degree to the disgrace and ruin which they pointed out.

" By the subjoined account of the expenses attending being called to the bar you will see that the Bench have decided against returning the twenty guineas deposited for chambers. They have, however, been almost driven to the necessity of resolving to build. When the buildings are to be commenced is quite another matter.

" I have done myself the honour of waiting on Lord Kenmare. He received me with the greatest politeness. He has changed his intention of removing to another house.

" Mr. Day has actually been appointed to the vacant seat in the King's Bench. He cannot sit until his patent comes over from England, which will happen in a few days.

There is nothing new in the political world. The odium against the Catholics is becoming every day more inveterate. The Chancellor seems hardly disposed to leave them the privileges which they enjoy at present, nor does he conceal his opinion on the subject. Some of the Administration would fain lay at our door the distracted state of the country—a state which is partly the consequence of the ferment which reigns all over Europe, but chiefly, I fear, the result of the weakness and cruelty of their own measures.

> " I remain, with affectionate regard to our friends at
> Carhen, my dear Uncle,
> " Your sincerely grateful and dutiful nephew,
> " DANIEL O'CONNELL."

With this letter is enclosed · the following catalogue of " payments to be made at being called " :—

		£	s.	d.
Fine		5	6	8
Stamps . . .		10	0	0
Deposit for chambers . .		22	15	0
Treasurer . . .		4	0	0
Sub-treasurer . .		3	12	0
Clerk		0	8	0
Gown and wig . .		5	6	8
Term fee		1	2	9
Crier		1	2	9
Total .	£53	13	10

His memorial for call to the bar was presented on April 19th, 1798. The certificate at foot was signed by Dom(inick) Rice. From the records of the Prothonotary's Office of His Majesty's Court of Common Pleas in Ireland, it appears that " Daniel O'Connell on April 26th, 1798, came into the said court, and did then and there take the oath of allegiance."

There is no entry of the date of his call to the bar in the records kept at King's Inns, but we know from an entry in his fee-book, which is about to be quoted from the *Irish Monthly*, that it was May 19th, 1798, the day on which Lord Edward Fitzgerald was seized. That fee-book has unfortunately been lost or mislaid. The Editor has sought to trace it, but without success. That which he has before him is a copy made by O'Connell, for what object it is hard to conjecture. But apparently he treated the original as only a rough record, for in the copy this entry occurs under date January 10th, 1802 : " Dr. McCarthy *v.* John Segerson : case for opinion. See *Waste-Book*, p. 43." On the title-page are printed the words *The Lawyer's Fee-book*. Before the words " Fee-book " are written, in O'Connell's handwriting, the words " Daniel O'Connell, July 19th, 1804," and after the words " Fee-book," also in his handwriting, " No. 1." The body of the book is machine-ruled in eight columns, with printed headings : " Dates " ; " Names of Parties " ; " Business, Nature of," etc. With these explanations, we proceed to give the following extract from vol. x. of the *Irish Monthly* :—

" There lies before us at present a rather rough quarto filled entirely with O'Connell's handwriting. Even in the heading, ' Fee-Book No. 1, Daniel O'Connell,' his signature is very like the autograph affixed to his portrait, forty-six years later, in the cheap pictures which grouped together all the traversers of the State trials of 1844. As I transcribe the opening pages textually, I may premise that ' B. R. ' stands for ' Banco Regis,' or ' King's Bench,' and 'C. B.' for ' Common Pleas '; '34th G. 3 ' means the thirty-fourth year of the reign of George III.

" ' I was entered in Lincoln's Inn on January 30th, 1794, 34th G. 3. I kept one term in Gray's Inn. I was called to the bar on May 19th, 1798 (38th G. 3), Easter term.

" ' The judges then were—in Chancery, John Fitzgibbon, Earl of Clare ; in B. R., John Scott, Earl of Clonmel, William Downes, William Tankerville Chamberlain, Robert Day, Esquires ; in C. B., Hugh, Lord Carleton, Thomas Kelly, Alexander Crookshank, Mathias Finucane, Esquires ; in Excheq., Barry, Lord Yelverton, Peter Metge, Michael Smith, Denis George, Esquires.

" ' The courts were shut during part of Trinity, 38th G. 3, as a rebellion then raged. During the same term Earl Clonmel died, and John Wolfe, then Attorney-General, was appointed in his place, with the title of Lord Kilwarden.

" ' The summer circuit of the year 1798 was very late. I did not go to it, as I was confined to my uncle's house with a violent fever, of which I was near to perish.

" ' During the summer vacation, 1800, Lord Carleton, Chief Justice of the Common Pleas, resigned. John Toler, Attorney-General, was appointed to succeed him, with the title of Lord Norbury, but did not take his seat on the bench during Michaelmas term, 1800.

" ' Lord Norbury took his seat in Hilary, 1801, as did also Mr. Luke Fox as one of the puisne judges of the same court in the room of Justice Crookshank. Fox got on the bench as the reward of his vote on the Union question. He was in considerable business at the bar. Morose, sour, and impetuous, but a lawyer, he has risen from the obscure position of an usher to a school. Toler was a *pretty gentleman* at the bar ; on the bench he is ridiculous. The thing is fond of blood, and has often reminded me that " Nero fiddled while Rome was burning."

" ' Much was expected from Wolfe, now Lord Kilwarden ; but his pompous inanity is insufferable.

" ' In Trinity, 1801, Sir Michael Smith was appointed Master of the Rolls. He is a gentleman and a scholar, polite, patient, and attentive. Yet he is a very indifferent judge. Tedious to a fault, the business multiplies, and very little is done.

" ' At the end of the same term St. George Daly took his seat as one of the barons of the Exchequer in the room of Smith, now Master of the Rolls. Daly is extremely ignorant, knows nothing of the law, and has not the art to conceal any part of his want of knowledge. These qualities, added to a difficulty of enunciation, have brought him into contempt with the bar and country.

" ' But Daly rises into almost excellence when compared with Robert Johnson, who in the same term was made judge of the Common Pleas in the room of the honest old *brogueman* Kelly. Johnson to an equal want of knowledge and discretion with Daly adds a peevishness of temper which is as ungentlemanly in its expressions as it is undignified in his situation. I should not, for my part, put any confidence in the man's honesty.

" ' In Hilary, 1802, William Smith, son to the Master of the Rolls, took his seat in the room of Baron Metge, who has resigned. Smith was Solicitor-General. He is a man of logical head, and what is called in modern jargon a metaphysician— that is, a man whose verbal distinctions reach far beyond natural differences, and yet are well supported. I do verily believe Smith to be a man of talents, and a lawyer, but his private character is chequered by ill-temper and caprice, perhaps the effect in some measure of ill-health.

" ' On January 28th, 1802, John, Earl of Clare, Chancellor of Ireland, died, and he was buried this day, January 31st. He has been Chancellor since ' " ———

The entry breaks off abruptly here, and the date is not elsewhere supplied. As a matter of fact, Fitzgibbon, Earl of Clare, became Chancellor in 1789.

O'Connell got his first fee on May 24th, 1798, from James Conner, in a case of *Duckett* v. *Sullivan*. The fee was £1 2s. 9d.— that is, one guinea Irish currency—for drawing a declaration on a promissory note in a case in the Court of Exchequer. James Conner is no doubt the same person as the attorney who gave him the brief at the Tralee assizes in which he made a great hit in cross-examination, as described below (p. 225). As he mentions in the above entry in his fee-book, he did not go the summer circuit of 1798, and he did not get any business until February 3rd, 1799, when James Conner gave him another guinea fee for drawing another declaration. James Conner stuck to O'Connell. Of the seventeen fees that he got in 1799, ten came from Conner. One gets an insight into the state of society at the time from reading these entries. Under date March, 1799, Spring Circuit, Ennis, there appears " On behalf of Daniel O'Connell, petition for presentment for cattle houghed," and at Tralee, same month, a similar petition for another client. The petition in such cases was for compensation for the injury, to be paid by an assessment on the ratepayers of the district. At the same assizes at Tralee he had a brief on a prosecution for an assault by " John Segerson, of Cove," against " John Segerson James," the name " James " being added to distinguish him from some other John Segerson. This John Segerson James appears to have had a knack of getting into trouble with his neighbours, for under date July, 1799, Summer Circuit, Tralee, we have the entry "*John Segerson James* v. *John Segerson*, Ed.: brief for the defence in an information for sending a challenge."

Several of the men in the corps of yeomanry to which O'Connell belonged were United Irishmen, and O'Connell fearing that some officious person might implicate him in their disaffection, left Dublin in June, 1798, for Carhen. O'Neill Daunt gives, as nearly as possible in O'Connell's own words, an account of his journey and of what took place after his arrival : " Communication by land with the interior was cut off; so eighteen of us sailed in a potato boat bound for Courtmasherry. We each gave the pilot half a guinea to put us ashore at the Cove of Cork, where we arrived after a capital passage of thirty-six hours. I then went to Iveragh, and remained some months at Carhen."

Mr. Peter Murray, of the Registry of Deeds Office, Dublin, a son of O'Connell's host mentioned above (p. 217), gave to Mr. Fitzpatrick a different account of the circumstances under which O'Connell left Dublin on this occasion, which is narrated in *The Sham Squire*. Mr. Murray says, " I well remember O'Connell one night at my father's house, during the spring of 1798, so carried away by the political excitement of the day and by the ardour of his innate patriotism, calling for a prayer-book to swear in some zealous young men as United Irishmen at a meeting of the body in a neighbouring street. Councillor —— was there, and offered to accompany O'Connell on his perilous mission. My father, though an Irishman of advanced liberal views and strong patriotism, was not a United Irishman, and endeavoured without effect to deter his young and gifted friend from the rash course in which he seemed embarked. Dublin was in an extremely disturbed state, and the outburst of a bloody insurrection seemed hourly imminent. My father resolved to exert to the uttermost the influence which it was well known he possessed over his young friend. He made him accompany him to the canal bridge at Leeson Street, and, after an earnest conversation, succeeded in persuading the future Liberator to step into a turf boat that was then leaving Dublin. That night my father's house was searched by Major Sirr, accompanied by the Attorneys' Corps of Yeomanry, who pillaged it to their heart's content. There can be no doubt that private information of O'Connell's tendencies and haunts had been communicated to the Government."

It is difficult to reconcile this very circumstantial statement with dates and facts. It is impossible that O'Connell could have sailed from Dublin in the spring of 1798. He was in Dublin up to May 19th, when he was called, and on that very day Lord Edward Fitzgerald was seized. The 23rd had been fixed as the day on which the mail-coaches were to be stopped, and this was the signal for the rising. O'Connell got his first fee on May 24th, and he says himself that it was in June that he left for Carhen.

In the August of 1798 he had a severe illness, occasioned, as he told O'Neill Daunt, by sleeping in wet clothes. "Old Dr. Moriarty was sent for. He pronounced me in high fever. I was in such pain that I wished to die. . . . During my illness I used to quote these lines from the tragedy of *Douglas* :—

> " 'Unknown I die : no tongue shall speak of me ;
> Some noble spirits, judging by themselves,
> May yet conjecture what I might have proved,
> And think life only wanting to my fame.'

I used to quote these lines under the full belief that my illness would end fatally " (*Personal Recollections*, i. 48, 49).

During his illness his doctor told him that Napoleon, at the head of his army, had marched successfully across the wilderness to Alexandria. "That is impossible," said O'Connell ; "he cannot have done so ; they would have been starved." "Oh no," said the doctor ; "they had a quantity of portable soup, sufficient to feed the army for four days." "Ay," said O'Connell, "but had they portable water ? For their portable soup would be little use without the water to dissolve it." The doctor, glancing at the patient's mother, said in a low and satisfied tone, "His intellect at any rate is untouched."

O'Connell also gave O'Neill Daunt this account of what occurred after he got well :—

"After my recovery I prepared to quit Carhen to go off circuiteering. It was at four o'clock on a fine sunny morning that I left Carhen on horseback. My brother John came part of the way with me, and oh ! how I did envy him when he turned off the road to hunt among the mountains, while *I* had to enter on the drudgery of my profession. But we parted. I looked after him from time to time till he was out of sight, and then I cheered up my spirits as well as I could. I had left home at

such an early hour that I was in Tralee at half-past twelve. I
got my horse fed, and thinking it was as well to push on, I
remounted him and took the road to Tarbert by Listowell.
A few miles further on a shower of rain drove me under a
bridge for shelter. While I stayed there the rain sent Robert
Hickson also under the bridge. He saluted me, and asked me
where I was going. I answered, 'To Tarbert.' 'Why so late?'
said Hickson. 'I am not late,' said I; 'I have been up since
four o'clock this morning.' 'Why, where do you come from?'
'From Carhen.' Hickson looked astonished, for the distance
was nearly fifty Irish miles. But he expressed his warm
approval of my activity. '*You'll do*, young gentleman!' said
he; 'I see you'll do.' I then rode on, and got to Tarbert
about five in the afternoon, full sixty miles, Irish, from
Carhen. There wasn't one book to be had at the inn, I had
no acquaintance in the town, and I found my spirits low enough
at the prospect of a long stupid evening. But I was relieved
by the sudden appearance of Ralph Marshall, an old friend of
mine, who came to the inn to dress for a ball that took place
in Tarbert that night. He asked me to accompany him to
the ball. 'Why,' said I, 'I have ridden sixty miles.' 'Oh,
you don't seem in the least tired,' said he, 'so come along.'
Accordingly I went, and sat up until two o'clock in the morning,
dancing. I arose next day at half-past eight, and rode to the
Limerick assizes. At the Tralee assizes of the same circuit
James Conner gave me a brief. There was one of the witnesses of the other party whose cross-examination was thrown
upon *me* by the opposite counsel. I did not do as I have seen
fifty young counsel do, namely, hand the cross-examination
over to my senior. I thought it due to myself to attempt it,
hit or miss, and I cross-examined him right well. I remember
he stated that he had *his share* of a pint of whisky, whereupon
I asked him *whether his share was not all except the pewter*. He
confessed that it was; and the oddity of my mode of putting
the question was very successful, and created a general and
hearty laugh. Jerry Keller repeated the encouragement Robert
Hickson had already bestowed upon my activity in the very

same words : ' You'll *do*, young gentleman ! you'll *do* ' " (*Personal Recollections*, i. 119).

Jerry Keller was a noted counsel, as appears from an anecdote of him (*ib.* p. 121). No doubt it was he who signed O'Connell's memorial to be admitted a student of the King's Inns (see above, p. 52).

This extract is here given verbatim, but it is impossible to accept the narrative as correct in date. O'Connell fell ill in the month of August. A recovery so complete as to enable him to undergo such a journey as above described, therefore, must, at the earliest, have taken place some time in the autumn, and there are no sunny mornings at four o'clock at that time of year. Besides, there were at that time in Ireland but two circuits : the spring circuit, which commenced in March, and the summer circuit, which commenced in July ; and however good law business may have been then, it is difficult to suppose that the summer circuit lasted in 1798 far down into September. Moreover, O'Connell told O'Neill Daunt that his first circuit was in 1799 (*Personal Recollections*, i. 231) ; and in an entry in his fee-book, quoted above from the *Irish Monthly* (vol. x. p. 587), he says, " The summer circuit of the year 1798 was very late. I did not go to it, as I was confined to my uncle's house by a violent fever, of which I was near to perish." There are no circuit cases entered in O'Connell's fee-book that summer. Probably, therefore, the incidents narrated by Daunt occurred in the summer of 1799.

However this may be, the prophecies that he " would do " were gradually but surely fulfilled. In 1798 he received two guineas, that is £2 5s. 6d. Irish currency, in two fees. In 1799 he received twenty-three guineas, or £27 3s. 6d., in sixteen fees. In 1800 he received one hundred and eighty-three guineas, or £205 0s. 6d., in seventy-seven fees, in 1801 two hundred and twenty-five guineas, or £255 18s. 9d., in one hundred and nine fees. In 1802 his fees reached £346 18s. 9d., in 1803 £465 4s. 9d., in 1804 £715 9s. 9d., in 1805 £840 12s. In 1809 his receipts had steadily risen till, in that year, they reached £2,736. By the end of that year he had made

O'CONNELL.

Statue of O'Connell by Hogan

In the City Hall. Dublin.

From Photo by W Lawrence, Dublin.

altogether £11,531. In 1812 his fees came to £3,028, and in 1814 they had increased to £3,808, an immense income for a junior at the Irish bar. In little over sixteen years he made more than £28,000. The year before emancipation, though he was still a staff gownsman, he made the enormous sum of £8,000 and upwards, "an amount," as he says in his letter to the Earl of Shrewsbury, "never before earned in Ireland by an outer barrister."

O'Connell was most careful in keeping his fee-book. The columns are carefully added up, and the results brought forward. The receipts of each year are calculated, and the increase each year over the preceding, and the total of the current and previous years, brought out. This has led the writer in the *Irish Monthly*, and those who have copied from that publication, to exaggerate the income made by O'Connell during the first few years after his call to the bar, they having put down these totals as the receipts during the current year instead of that and previous years.

O'Connell's fee-book No. 1 ends on November 26th, 1805. His fee-book No. 2 is missing, but in some blank pages in the copy fee-book No. 1 his total receipts for each year down to 1814, inclusive, are given. Fee-book No. 3 covers the period from December 17th, 1806, to July 11th, 1809. In it he gives the names of the judges then on the bench. Among them were John Philpot Curran, Master of the Rolls, and Lord Norbury, Chief Justice of the Common Pleas. He mentions that three of them, Chief Justice Downes, Mr. Justice Day, and Mr. Justice George, were on the bench when he was called. Recording the retirement of Ponsonby from the chancellorship on April 30th, 1807, he remarks, "Ponsonby was, to say the utmost for him, but a *decent* judge. He was extremely courteous to the bar, and attentive to arguments, but nothing seems to me *now* clearer than the necessity of being a good *practical* lawyer in order to become a good judge."

There is one leaf of a subsequent fee-book in existence, a loose leaf, containing entries of cases from May 29th, 1829, to January 11th, 1830. His total fees during this interval

amounted to twenty-two guineas, earned in thirteen cases.   On
one page of this leaf is the following entry : " Trinity term,
1829, I did not attend, being employed at the freehold registry
in Clare."   He went the summer circuit, and at Tralee got
one fee of four guineas, and two of two guineas.   At Cork
he got one fee of three guineas.   These were his total earnings
on that circuit, and were probably the last fees he ever received.
Such were the pecuniary results of his devotion to the cause of
Ireland.

Fagan says (vol. i. p. 20) that the first case in which
O'Connell distinguished himself was at the Cork assizes, an
ejectment on the title brought by Mr. Charles Connell, of
Clover Hill.   The defendants were represented by Harry
Deane Grady, who handled the plaintiff so severely that he
horsewhipped Grady when he came out of court.   The matter
was brought before the judge.   " Mr. O'Connell defended his
friend in so masterly a manner," says Fagan, " that the young
gentleman escaped, while the counsellor's defence gave the first
impulse to his professional advancement."   The fee-book
No. 1 contains the following entries, which appear to have
reference to this case : " March 26th, 1803, Cork county,
case of Charles Connell " ; "February 12th, 1804, opinion on
ejectment brought " ; " March, 1804, Cork county, lessee of
Connell v. Purcell, motion to reinstate record " ; "August 17th,
1804, case of Charles Connell for advice," and under the
same date " Lessee of Connell v. Denis Purcell, draft deed of
compromise."   It would seem from these entries that the case
never was tried, and having regard to the income O'Connell
was making in 1802, he must have been well on the road to
success before the incident narrated by Fagan occurred.   There
is an entry under date April 24th, 1805, " Case of Connell's
lands at Ballybrach," but this can have no reference to the
occurrence in question.   Up to April 26th of that year
O'Connell numbers the entries in his fee-book consecutively,
the last being 1,013, and the total of the fees £2,446 15s.   It
may be of some interest to compare with those of O'Connell
the earnings of another great Irish lawyer, John Philpot Curran.

His fee-book is in the Royal Irish Academy, and shows that he made only about forty guineas in his first year, but a few years after he was making over £1,000 a year.

It may be well to explain with reference to the trial at Tralee assizes above referred to that the practice in Ireland is for each counsel to conduct the examination or cross-examination, as the case may be, in turn, so that the examination or cross-examination of an important witness may fall to the lot of the junior counsel, and sometimes the opposite counsel may so arrange the order of his witnesses that the cross-examination of a very material witness shall be taken by the junior, as seems to have been the case when O'Connell held his first brief. He might have asked his leader to take it, or his leader might have asked him for leave to take it; but, unless in exceptional circumstances, the latter course is seldom adopted.

The only other incident occurring in the interval between this and the next entry of which we have any information is that, as he tells us in the next entry, he drank too much on the night of December 30th, 1798.

I left Dublin for my father's, or rather my uncle's, about the 23rd of June. I remained there until the beginning of November.

Since I have been in town and at Mrs. Jones's I misspent my time during the summer, and have done very little better since my return to town. I am now to take up the study of the law with all the ardour which my situation requires. I think I will persevere in the rigid execution of this duty. I never was more firmly intent upon anything. Yet such is the complexion of affairs that it must appear extremely doubtful whether I shall be called to the bar. But my heart is too sick for political disquisitions.

I have read five volumes and a half of Gibbon. In a few days I will have the whole concluded. It is an extraordinary, it is an admirable work. The genius, the critical acumen, the laborious research, of the author, are unrivalled. He has mended my style; he has improved my thoughts; he has enriched my memory.

The first crusade was preached by Peter the Hermit in 1095; it set off from Europe [70] in 1097, and conquered Jerusalem in 1099.

There were seven crusades. Louis the Ninth— St. Louis—led the two last. They were both unfortunate, and in the later he lost his life before Tunis. Their dates are 1250 and 1268.

In the year 1291 Acre or Ptolemais was taken from the Latins. It was the last place they possessed on the coast of Syria.

" Satis—sed non super "——Nonsense !

No. 71, *Monday, December* 31*st,* 1798.—I now resume my Journal after a year of silence, a year which has been wretchedly misspent. My only consolation is that I have resolved to improve. Alas, it makes me sorrowfully to smile when I look at the pages of this irregular Journal, which are filled with good resolutions, and to sigh when I recollect how little fruit they have produced. But let me continue my Journal with regularity, and all must be well.

I have several resolutions formed. Let me give them vitality by committing them to paper.

My first resolution is no less than to be *virtuous*. This includes everything. Virtue would, I am convinced, be the pursuit of every individual did each but know that she alone bestows happiness. All my other resolutions are but emanations from this one. I know that to be virtuous is [71] to be happy. Everything that is contrary to our happiness is necessarily and of consequence contrary to virtue. For my definition of virtue is " that quality which produces happiness," as it seems to me that vice may be defined " that which produces misery." It is true that many, and indeed most, men are seeking unreal pleasure. But the gratifications of the hour are punished by the reflection, or the want, or the disease which follows. Thus, for example, many find a vicious pleasure in drinking. But punishment soon awaits them ; stupidity, sickness, and contempt are in the train of this gratification. How feelingly ought not I to write on this subject —I, whose head aches, whose stomach is nauseated, and whose reflections are embittered in consequence of last night's debauch. Oh, let me avoid with the utmost care the fatal vice of drunkenness. Let me continually arm myself with the conviction I now feel of its destructive qualities and of its consequent immorality. Let me for ever retain the salutary hatred which I now feel against this odious vice. My resolution is formed, and to the future pages of this Journal I appeal for the consequence (*f*).

(*f*) O'Connell kept the resolution recorded here. " In my

young days," said he to O'Neill Daunt, "it was deemed an essential point of hospitality to make guests drunk against their will, drink till they were sick. I was myself the first person who rebelled against this custom at Iveragh. After I returned from the Temple, I introduced the fashion of resistance, and I soon had abettors enough. It was fortunate for me that I never, while a youth, could drink more than three glasses of wine without being sick, so that I had my personal convenience to consult in aid of temperance" (*Personal Recollections*, i. 155). O'Connell was an enthusiastic supporter of Father Matthew's temperance propaganda. The sobriety of the enormous crowds which attended the "monster meetings" held in support of the repeal movement was not only a fact remarkable in itself, but conduced greatly to the order by which the meetings were characterised. This sobriety was largely due to the efforts of Father Matthew.

I must likewise become regular in my hour of going to bed and rising. I have been shamefully deficient in this particular. As a mode of correction I shall in future put down the hours of going to bed and rising.

[72] With this day closes the year, and with to-morrow the figures change. The artificial figures fixed by man serve to warn us of the flight of time. An hour and an hour, to-morrow and to-morrow, and the insect which inhabits this our anthill vanishes from our sight and is seen no more. Oh, Maurice, oh, my brother, how early in life hast thou forsaken me. Oh, accursed be the authors of the war, and accursed be the breeze whose pestiferous breath brought death to my brother. On the mountains of St. Domingo his

remains lie mouldering, whilst the negro trains his savage bands around, and the more savage white man hides his diminished head. Could I but throw myself on my brother's grave, could I even behold the spot where for ever his bones are laid, it were some consolation. Would I had never been born! Life is short and full of sorrow. Man is born to trouble as the sparks fly upwards (*g*).

(*g*) Maurice entered O'Connell's regiment of the (English) Irish Brigade, which was formed when the Irish Brigade was broken up (see above, p. 8). His commission is dated in November, 1795. He exchanged into Viscount Walsh de Serrant's ("Second Walsh's") regiment. He died in December, 1797. No intimation of his death was given to his parents, and the first news of it that reached any of his relatives was an announcement in the *London Gazette* of April 11th, 1798, that a Mr. McMahon had been promoted to a lieutenancy in Serrant's regiment *vice* Maurice Morgan O'Connell. This was read by Count O'Connell, who on making inquiries found that it was his nephew whose name was mentioned, and that he was dead. The Count wrote at once to his brother Maurice, so that he might break the sad news to the parents. The letter, dated April 16th, 1798, is given in *The Last Colonel of the Irish Brigade* (ii. 217). Lieutenant O'Connell was only twenty-one when he fell a victim to the pestiferous climate of the West Indies, the only place out of Ireland where a Catholic could hold a commission in the army! The Count, ever kind and considerate, pays a high tribute to the memory of this poor boy: "Notwithstanding the levity of his temper, he was possessed of a great stock of honour, honesty, and good-nature, and, had he lived to the age of maturity, would, I am confident, have turned out a man of real worth, and of very endearing qualifications." He then adds a passage which goes far to explain why it was that this headstrong and adventurous youth would not fall in with the views of his uncle and follow some lucrative but humdrum career: " It is impossible to reflect on his fate without lamenting that inordinate passion for the army which led him to pass into another corps without consulting any of his friends. It would seem as if there was a fatality that hurried him on to his own destruction." Maurice was evidently a born soldier. For him there was only one profession, that of arms, and wherever there was fighting he wanted to be in the thick of it. Of such stuff are great captains made ; but for one like him, if he clung to the ancient faith, the only use that England had was to waste him on some swamp or some jungle, where the most dangerous foe to be met was not the arrow that flieth by day, but the pestilence that walketh in darkness.

How dreary, desolate, and solitary would not a few more deaths make me. Yet the revolving years will bring them. Oh, God, oh, Eternal Being, of all Thy creatures man surely is most wretched. Thou art indeed inscrutable, and I adore Thee.

[73] *No. 72, Wednesday, January 2nd,* 1799.—I now commence another year. There appear no less than five in the title-page of this Journal. Alas, alas, it should have been long since concluded. I fancy this year at least will bring it to a close (*h*).

(*h*) It never was brought to a close. There are several blank pages at the end, though the Journal is continued at intervals down to June 4th, 1802. Next page is a reproduction, on a reduced scale, of the entry here printed, and is a specimen of the hand in which the Journal is written.

I went to bed last night at one, and got up this morning at eleven. Oh, shame ! shame !

The pursuit of happiness is the business of life. Yet how few know what happiness consists in.

No 72 Wednesday January 2d 1799

I now commence another year — there appear no less than five in the title page of this Journal. Alas, Alas, it should have been long since concluded — I fancy this year at least will bring it to a close

I went to bed last night at one & got up this Morning at Eleven ..Oh Shame! Shame

The pursuit of happiness is the only business of life yet how few know what happiness consists in. Truth is its ground work. Beneficence its only support. I wish to be happy yet I become less so every day. Day after day I lose that delicacy of feeling which for=merly governed my mind and action. Oh Truth shine once more on the head of thy Votary. Virtue thou alone canst give happiness. — Without thee Life is but a miserable burthen. Let me but be Virtuous and I must be happy.

I finished my notes of The tail out of Coke on Littleton to day and I read this evening part of Collins account of New South Wales. —

I dined to day with Bennett We talked much of the late unhappy rebellion. A great deal of in=nocent blood was shed on the occasion. Good God what a brute Man becomes when ignorant and oppressed. Oh Liberty What horrors are perpetra=ted in thy Name. May every Virtuous Revo=lutionist remember the horrors of Wexford!

D.C.   S

Truth is its groundwork. Beneficence is its only supporter. I wish to be happy, yet I become less so every day. Day after day I lose that delicacy of feeling which formerly governed my mind and action. Oh, Truth, shine once more on the head of thy votary. Virtue, thou alone canst give happiness. Without thee life is but a miserable burthen. Let me but be virtuous, and I must be happy.

I finished my notes of *Fee Tail* out of *Coke on Littleton* to-day, and I read this evening part of Collins's account of New South Wales (*i*).

(*i*) Collins's *Account of the English Colony in New South Wales* was published in 1798. It narrates the history of the penal settlement founded in Botany Bay in 1786. A number of transports sailed from England under the command of Captain Phillip, who was the first Governor. The voyage took eight months and a week. The author was one of the Government officials who accompanied the expedition. The work, which is illustrated, gives a very interesting description of the natives, and of their manners and customs, and of the productions of the country.

I dined to-day with Bennett (*j*). We talked much of the late unhappy rebellion. A great deal of innocent blood was shed on the occasion. Good God! what a brute man becomes when ignorant and oppressed! Oh, Liberty, what horrors are perpetrated in thy name! May every virtuous revolutionist remember the horrors of Wexford! (*k*).

(*j*) Richard Newton Bennett (see above, p. 78).
(*k*) The deplorable incident here referred to is probably the

massacre at Scullabogue on June 5th, 1798, where nearly two hundred and thirty unfortunate prisoners perished in the barn in which they were confined. When the rebels gave way at Ross, an express came to Murphy, one of those in command of the guard of three hundred men placed over the prisoners, ordering him to kill them. He refused to do so without a direct order from the General. Soon after he received another message to the same effect, with the addition that " the prisoners, if released, would become very furious and vindictive." Shortly after a third message arrived, saying " the priest gave orders that the prisoners should be put to death." The barn was then set on fire, and bundles of straw forced in to increase the flame. Very few escaped. One of them, who owed his safety to a priest, gave the foregoing account (Maxwell, *Irish Rebellion*, p. 123).

"There is every reason to believe," says Maxwell (*Irish Rebellion*, p. 126), " that this horrible atrocity occasioned to all but the lowest barbarians who were banded with the rebel forces feelings of alarm and disgust." Such conduct was certainly utterly opposed to the wishes and principles of the leaders of the insurrection. The first general proclamation issued to the rebels contained the following passage : " Soldiers of Ireland, remember your homes. Let the domestic hearth never be violated, nor the arms of the nation sullied by cruelty or revenge. Bear in mind that the weak and defenceless claim your protection, and that retaliation is only the weapon of the coward and the slave. Let this be engraven on your hearts, and let it be proclaimed to the extremity of our land, that insult to female honour, pillage, and desertion will be punished with death " (Teeling, *Personal Narrative*, p. 166). Almost the last act of Bagenal Harvey before he was deprived of his command was the publication of a general order containing the following clause :—" Any person or persons that shall take upon him or them to kill or murder any person or prisoner, or burn any house, or commit any plunder, without any special written order from the Commander-in-Chief, shall suffer death." And Roche also issued an address : " In the moment of triumph let

not your victories be tarnished with any wanton act of cruelty,
. . . neither let a difference in religious sentiments cause a
difference amongst the people " (Maxwell, *Irish Rebellion*, 126).
But the atrocities committed by the loyalists in the county of
Wexford were enough to drive an excitable peasantry to madness. The town of Wexford was surrendered to the rebels
without a blow. The garrison evacuated it, and " every unfortunate peasant whom they met in their retreat was butchered
without mercy. Age or sex afforded no protection. Women
and children were victims of their indiscriminate fury ; houses
were plundered and burned in their disorderly march, and even
the temple of divine worship was fired by their sacrilegious
hands " (*Personal Narrative*, 166). A specimen of what the
troops could do in the hour of their success is given by Mus-
grave : " A party of rebels got into a very good slated house at
the upper end of Mary Street "—Ross—" which the soldiers
having set fire to, the savages were *roasted alive.*" This may
be set off against the massacre of Scullabogue, which appears
to have occurred about the same time. Such atrocities on the
part of the troops were not confined to the year 1798 or to the
county of Wexford. In the year 1797 in Wexford alone
thirty-two Roman Catholic chapels were burned by the armed
yeomanry within less than three months, while the destruction
of private property kept full pace with this sacrilegious con-
flagration. Kildare, Wicklow, and other neighbouring counties
exhibited similar scenes of horror. The army, now distributed
throughout the country in *free* quarters, gave loose to all the
excesses of which a licentious soldiery is capable. From the
humble cot to the stately mansion no property, no person, was
secure. Numbers perished under the lash, many were
strangled under the fruitless attempt of extorting confessions,
and hundreds were shot at their peaceful avocations for the
wanton amusement of a brutal soldiery. The torture of a
pitch-cap was a subject of amusement both to officers and men,
and the agonies of the unfortunate victim, writhing under the
blaze of the combustible material, were increased by the yells
of the soldiery and the pricking of their bayonets, until his

sufferings were often terminated by his death. Torture was inflicted without mercy on every age and every condition—the child to betray the safety of the parent, the wife that of the husband ; and the friend and the brother have expired under the lash rather than betray those that stood in that sacred relation towards them (Teeling, *Personal Narrative*, pp. 131—133). Examples of cruelty practised on the unfortunate peasantry, some narrated by O'Connell himself, are mentioned above (p. 207).

O'Connell's attitude towards the revolutionary party at this time is thus described by Fagan (*Life and Times of Daniel O'Connell*, i. 19): " It is well known to those who recollect Dublin at the time that he not only held aloof from the revolutionists from hatred of their anti-religious and physical force principles, but wherever he had influence amongst young friends at the bar and in society he endeavoured to dissipate the wild notions which were carrying them into the vortex."

O'Connell was once reproached by two Americans with having censured the Irish insurgents of 1798. He replied that the scheme of rebellion was in itself an ill-digested, foolish scheme, entered upon without the means or the organisation necessary to ensure success. As to the leaders, no doubt, he said, there were among them some pure, well-intentioned men, but, he added, the great mass of them were trafficking speculators, who did not care whom they victimised in the prosecution of their schemes for self-aggrandisement (*Personal Recollections*, ii. 9).

O'Connell gave public expression to his views on this rebellion at the close of his career. In the famous debate in the Repeal Association which took place on the resolution expressing abhorrence of physical force, John Mitchell said, " The men of '98 thought liberty worth some blood-letting; and although they failed, it were hard that one of their sons should be thought unworthy to unite in a peaceful struggle for the independence of his country unless he will proclaim that he abhors the memory of his own father." This brought O'Connell to his feet. " He talks," said O'Connell, " of '98. Why, there were several good men engaged in the contest of '98. But alas! their struggle was one of blood and defeated in blood. The means they adopted weakened Ireland, and enabled England to carry the Union " (*Four Years of Irish History*, by Sir Charles Gavan Duffy, p. 339). In O'Connell's *Memoir of Ireland* (p. 25) he declares that the rebellion was almost avowedly, and beyond a doubt provably, fomented to enable the English Government to extinguish Irish legislative independence, and to bring about the Union. " But," he adds, " the instrument was nearly too powerful for the hand that used it, and if the Catholic wealth, education, and intelligence had joined the rebellion, it would probably have been successful."

John O'Connell attributed his father's hostility to the leaders of the rebellion of 1798 to his conviction that the insurrection facilitated Pitt in his Union policy. They in fact played into the hands of Pitt and Castlereagh. O'Connell, however, admitted that the people had great provocation to take up arms. " In Wexford," he said, " they were actually driven into insurrection by the insane cruelty of Lord Kingston, who since then had died in a strait-waistcoat. There was a sergeant of the North Cork militia named Tom the Devil, from the unheard-of atrocities he perpetrated on the peasantry " (*Personal Recollections*, ii. 9).

[74] *No. 73, Friday, January 4th,* 1799.—My reading this day consisted of law. I read *Blackstone and Cummin on Fee Tail*, and inserted many remarks taken from them in a book devoted to that purpose.

I went to bed last night at half after twelve, and got up this morning at a quarter after ten. When shall I correct myself of this sluggish habit? We will try to-morrow morning. Yet I fear this custom is stealing fast upon me. How much valuable time is lost by it. How much do my mind and my heart suffer by it. Well if it is now conquered.

I know not what subject to write upon. Yet I would fain eke out this page. I must therefore repeat what has often occurred to my mind and what I have already put to paper. I must again take notice of what I have lost in strength of mind, in love for virtue, and, after such subjects to descend low, what I have lost in conversation, eloquence. I have no longer my former fluency and happiness of expression, because I do not think with the intensity and accuracy that I used to do. The study of eloquent writers is of the utmost importance to him who would acquire a graceful and easy style. For my part, I always felt benefited by the perusal of Gibbon. A great deal of thought is expressed by almost every word that he uses.

In the course of another year I shall be a tolerably good lawyer. My present method of studying the common and statute law I believe to be the best. When [75] I have proceeded in it for some time I will commence equity on the same plan (*l*).

(*l*) It would be interesting to know what this plan was. That it was successful there can be no doubt, for although his strong points were cross-examination and power of persuading juries, he was an astute lawyer, as the following anecdote will illustrate: Hedges Eyre, of Orange notoriety, had invariably engaged O'Connell as his counsel. On one occasion a brother-Orangeman severely censured Hedges Eyre for employing the Catholic leader. "You've got seven counsel without him," quoth the sagacious adviser; "and why should you give your

money to that Papist rascal ? " The counsel on the opposite
side pressed a point for a nonsuit, and carried the judge, Johnson,
along with them. O'Connell remonstrated against the nonsuit,
protesting against so great an injustice. The judge seemed
obdurate. "Well, hear me, at all events," said O'Connell.
"No, I won't," replied the judge; "I've already heard the
leading counsel." "But *I* am conducting counsel, my lord,"
rejoined O'Connell, "and more intimately acquainted with the
details of the case than my brethren. I entreat, therefore, that
you will hear me." The judge ungraciously consented, and in
five minutes O'Connell argued him out of the nonsuit. "*Now*,"
said Hedges Eyre, in triumph, to his Orange *confrère*—" now do
you see why I gave my money to that 'Papist rascal'?" (*Personal
Recollections*, i. 176).

Here the Journal breaks off, to be resumed only after the
lapse of two years and a half, and to be then continued for but
four days, ending June 4th, 1802.

Some few incidents in his life during this interval are known.

In the year 1799 O'Connell became a Freemason, and was
afterwards Master of his lodge, No. 189. "It is true," he
wrote, "I was a Freemason and Master of a lodge; it was at a
very early period of my life, and either before an ecclesiastical
censure had been published in the Catholic Church in Ireland
prohibiting the taking of the Masonic oaths, or at least before I
was aware of that censure." O'Connell retired from the
Society of Free and Accepted Masons. "The important
objection," he wrote, "is the profane taking in vain the awful
name of the Deity in the wanton and multiplied oaths—oaths
administered on the book of God—without any adequate
motive" (O'Flanagan, *Life and Times of O'Connell*, i. 63).

During this year his professional income amounted to
£27 3s. 6d., as already stated above (p. 226). He went circuit
for the first time that year. A characteristic incident that
occurred on the occasion was told by him to O'Neill Daunt
while crossing the mountains of Kilworth on their way from
Carlow to Fermoy. Gangs of robbers had formerly infested
these defiles. "There was," said O'Connell to Daunt, "a

narrow causeway thrown across a glen which formed a peculiarly
dangerous part of the old road. It was defended by guard walls,
and too narrow for two carriages to pass abreast. The post-
boys used to call it a delicate bit, and a ticklish spot it surely
was on a dark night, approached at one end from a steep
declivity. My first circuit was in 1799. After the Cork assizes
I agreed to post to Dublin with Harry Deane Grady. When
we reached Fermoy we found the Inns quite crowded with the
judges, their suite, and their yeomanry escort, so that Grady
and I were forced to eat our dinner in the tap-room. Whilst
we were there a corporal of dragoons and three privates came
in. Grady and I were anxious to provide powder and ball for
our pistols, as we had to pass those mountains of evil fame
upon our journey, and with this purpose Grady turned to the
corporal and said, ' Soldier, will you sell me some powder and
ball ? ' ' Sir, I don't sell powder,' returned the corporal tartly.
' Will you then have the kindness to buy me some ? ' said
Grady. ' I believe the fellows who are licensed here are very
chary of it.' It was the year of the rebellion, and public confidence was not yet restored. ' Sir,' replied the corporal, ' you
may go yourself. I am no man's messenger but the King's.'
I soon afterwards whispered to Grady, ' I wonder, Grady, that
you, who have so much mother-wit, should have been guilty of
the blunder of calling the corporal " soldier." Did you not see
the mark of his rank upon his sleeve ? You have grievously
wounded his pride and turned him against us by thus under-
valuing him in the eyes of his own soldiers, whom doubtless he
keeps at a distance, and amongst whom he plays the officer.'
Grady said nothing, and in a moment or two *I* addressed the
offended corporal. ' Sergeant,' said I, ' I am glad that you
and your brave fellows had not the trouble of escorting the
judges this wet day. It was excellent business for those yeomanry chaps.' ' Ay, indeed,' said the corporal very civilly,
and obviously much flattered at my having called him *sergeant ;*
' it was well for those that were not under those torrents of
rain.' ' Perhaps, sergeant,' said I, ' you would have the kindness to procure me some powder and ball in town. We are to

pass the Kilworth mountains, and shall want ammunition. *You* can, of course, have no difficulty in purchasing ; but it is not to everyone they'll sell such matters.' ' Sir,' said my corporal, ' I shall have very great pleasure in requesting your acceptance of a small supply of powder and ball. My balls will, I think, just fit your pistols. You'll stand in need of ammunition, for there are some of those outlying rebelly rascals in the mountains.' Harry Grady was greatly amused at the brilliant success of my civility to the corporal. ' Ah, Dan,' said he, ' you'll go through the world fair and easy, I foresee.' Our warlike preparations, however, were not needed. The robbers did not attack us, and we got safely to Dublin " (*Personal Recollections*, i. 229). This anecdote affords an apt illustration of the application of the principle enunciated by O'Connell in the aphorism, " You will catch more flies with a spoonful of honey than with a hogshead of vinegar " (*ib*. 43).

O'Connell and Grady crossed the Kilworth mountains on that occasion. " It was a dreadfully wet evening," said O'Connell to O'Neill Daunt as they once ascended the same mountains. " My cousin, Captain Hennessey, commanded the company who had on that day escorted the judges from Cork to Fermoy. He was thoroughly drenched. He pulled out the breast of his shirt, and wrung a pint of water from it on the floor. I implored him to change his dress. ' Oh,' he answered, ' I shan't mind it,' and in that state he sat down to dinner. The result was, of course, a fever, and in three or four days he was a corpse " (*Personal Recollections*, ii. 56). No doubt O'Connell had a vivid recollection of what he had suffered the previous year from a similar act of imprudence. On January 13th, 1800, O'Connell made his first political speech, namely his speech against the Union. It was delivered at a Roman Catholic meeting held in the Royal Exchange—now the City Hall—Dublin. The resolutions were drawn up by John Philpot Curran. The chair was taken by Ambrose Moore. While the resolutions were being debated Major Sirr entered the Hall with a body of yeomanry, who grounded their arms with a heavy clash on the stone pavement. He asked to see the resolutions.

They were shown to him, and he read them. 'There is no harm in them,' he said, and throwing them on the table, quitted the Hall, attended by the yeomanry. O'Connell did not write the speech which he made upon this occasion, but prepared heads, a frequent practice with him. After it was delivered he gave the *Dublin Evening Post* a full report of it. The reader will find it in *The Personal Recollections* (ii., App. p. 326). In the course of this historic effort he summarised the reasons which induced the Catholics to hold the meeting. It had been stated, he said, that the Catholics were favourable to the Union ; that they were willing to sell their country for a price. The calumny was flung on the whole body, and the whole body should refute it. If their emancipation were offered in exchange for their consent they would reject it with prompt indignation. " Let us," said he, " show Ireland we have nothing in view but her good, nothing but mutual forgiveness in our hearts. Let every man with me proclaim that, were the alternative offered him of the Legislative Union or the re-enactment of the penal code, he would prefer the latter as the lesser evil. If any man be so degraded as to consent to the extinction of the name and liberty of Ireland, I would call on him at least not to leave to strangers whom he could not control the direction and management of his commerce and property." He moved the resolutions, which were duly seconded and passed. " It is a curious thing," said O'Connell to Neill Daunt, " that all the principles of my subsequent political life are contained in my very first speech. We met at the Royal Exchange to denounce the Union as Catholics. We had previously held private meetings at the house of Sir James Strong, who was active enough at first, but refused to be our chairman. So we made Ambrose Moore our chairman, a very worthy citizen. It was Curran who drew up our resolutions. They were very fiery and spirited in their original shape, but were modified into comparative tameness to suit the timidity of some of our friends in those days of terror and brute force " (*Personal Recollections,* ii. 110, 111). So true is it that all the principles of O'Connell's subsequent life were contained in his first speech, that in 1810 he said at a public meeting that, were the Premier " to offer me to-morrow the repeal of the Union on the terms of re-enacting the entire penal code, I declare from my heart, and in the presence of my God, that I would most cheerfully accept his offer " (Fitzpatrick, *Correspondence of Daniel O'Connell*).

The momentous question of the Union determined the future career of the great Tribune. It was the Union that first stirred him up to come forward in politics, he told O'Neill Daunt. But those who have read his Journal will have learned that long before he made this speech he had consecrated his life and his talents to the service of his country. As he says in a letter written to Walter Savage Landor in 1838, describing the influence of his surroundings on his dreamy boyhood, " I formed the high resolve to leave my native land better after my death than I found her at my birth."

His uncle Maurice was not pleased at his taking a public part in the discussion on the Union. Not that he approved of it, but that politics appeared to him to be fraught with great peril, and he would have preferred that O'Connell should have appeared on some question which would, in his opinion, have more directly concerned the Catholics (*Personal Recollections*, i. 202).

O'Connell was in Dublin in 1800, when the Act of Union was passed. " I was maddened," he told Daunt, " when I heard the bells of St. Patrick's ringing out a joyful peal for Ireland's degradation, as if it was a glorious national festival. My blood boiled, and I vowed on that morning that the foul national dishonour should not last, if ever I could put an end to it." Again he said to Daunt, " The year of the Union I was travelling through the mountain district from Killarney to Kildare. My heart was heavy at the loss Ireland had sustained, and the day was wild and gloomy. The desert district, too, was congenial to impressions of solemnity and sadness. There was not a human habitation to be seen for miles. Black giant clouds sailed slowly through the sky and rested on the tops of the huge mountains. My soul felt dreary, and I had many wild and Ossianic inspirations as I traversed the bleak solitudes. It was the Union that first stirred me up to come forward in politics."

An incident that occurred in 1801 will help to bridge the gap which separates this number from that which follows it.

"In the winter of 1801," said he, "I had been supping at the Freemasons' Hotel, at the corner of Golden Lane, with a jovial party. We were returning late, after having drunk a good stoup of claret, when a fire broke out in a timber yard and spread rapidly. I was provoked at the awkwardness of the fellow who was beating the ground with a pickaxe, but making no progress at getting at the waterpipes. I shouldered him away, seized the pickaxe, and soon I got at the plug ; but, instead of stopping then, I kept working away *con amore*, and would soon have disturbed the paving-stones all over the street, if I had not been prevented. Sheriff Macready, an old auctioneer, kept order with the aid of a party of Buckinghamshire militia. I was rather an unruly customer, being a little under the influence of a good bottle of claret, and on my refusing to desist from picking up the street one of the soldiers ran a bayonet at me, which was interrupted by the cover of my hunting watch. If I had not had the watch, there was an end of the agitator ! " (*Personal Recollections*, ii. 148).

His professional income in 1801 fell to £367 8s. 6d., owing to his having been absent from one circuit.

In the interval between the preceding entry and the next O'Connell removed to Westland Row. Macdonagh (*Life of Daniel O'Connell*, p. 45) says that he lived during all the years from 1798 to 1802 at No. 4 (now 33), Westland Row. The bar list published in the Dublin Directory does not give O'Connell's address until 1807, when it gives No. 1, Westland Row, which is continued until 1811. In the latter year Merrion Square first appears as his address. O'Connell seems to have at one time lived at No. 19, Lower Ormond Quay, for Count O'Connell addressed to him there a letter written on May 9th, 1801. He is delighted at Dan's success. On February 12th of that year he writes, " It is now time to congratulate you on your increasing success in your profession. Be assured, my dear Dan, no man living can take a more warm interest in you than I do, or shall exult more in any [thing] that can tend to raise you in the public estimation." In the letter of May 9th he bids farewell to his own hopes of distinction, and makes the Liberator the heir to his ambition : " Doomed as I am now to obscurity and idleness for the rest of my life, I have transferred my ambition on you, and do declare you from this hour debtor to your name and family for the lustre it was long my wish to attach upon them."

Well was the debt paid.

In these letters the Count charges Dan with some little commissions, which no doubt were duly executed. Mr. Crotty, of the county Cork, owed him £32 9s. 6d. Would Dan put him in the way of recovering it ? When he came through Dublin the last time he forgot to pay eighteen-pence to the hairdresser at the " Mail-coach " hotel, where he lodged. " His name is Daniel. He will remember me, and I request you will discharge my debt." He wishes Dan to call at the Heralds' Office, Dublin, and find out whether the coat of arms they were using in the family was conformable to that in the Office. He tells him of the death of Eugene McCarthy, already mentioned above (p. 71), and condoles with him on the loss of his friend Mrs. Murray, adding, " Though my acquaintance with her was very slender, yet I could not be indifferent to an event which would be very painful to you." He wished, moreover, that Dan should ascertain the forfeitures of Brigadier O'Connell at the revolution of 1690, " as a matter of curiosity, by which the situation and consequence of the family at that period may be ascertained. . . . I indeed must allow it to be of very little importance this day to ascertain what our ancestors have been more than a century back, but for one who, having lost all the bright prospects of my past days, *ne vis plus que mes souvenirs*, I am fond of indulging in dreams, particularly historical." These letters are full of the most touching expressions of affection towards O'Connell, and it is to be hoped that he gratified the wishes of an uncle to whom, next to Hunting-cap, he owed the opportunities which opened to him his distinguished career.

No. 74, Tuesday, June 1st, 1802.—I recommence my Journal rather to insert a detail of facts than to give way to desultory observations.

I will keep it as a monitor, to record my diligence or my waste of time.

I went to bed last night at half after eleven, and got up to-day at nine. I read 32 pages of *Cruise on Fines*, 44—76. I drew a declaration on common promises (*Almond* v. *O'Leary*). I read aloud 600 lines of *Paradise Lost*, to the end of the first book, and also 15 pages of Milton's Life, from 47 to 62.

Milton was born in London Dec. 9th, 1608.

I wrote seven letters.

No. 75, Wednesday, June 2nd, 1802.—I went to bed last night at half after eleven, and got up this morning at half after seven.

I prepared myself before I went to court to argue the case of *Gallway* v. *Rice*. But I should have argued it badly. In point of preparation I am but too negligent.

After my return from court I searched some authorities on the writ of *audita querela* for *Gorham* v. *Corneberry* (*m*).

I read some lines of the *Paradise Lost* aloud (2nd book).

(*m*) O'Connell is singularly reticent about his law cases. He mentions only *Gallway* v. *Rice*, *Gorham* v. *Corneberry*, to which he recurs in No. 76, and *Murphy* v. *Baldwin*. He was by this time in considerable practice. His professional income in 1802, as we have seen, was £346. *Audita querela* was a proceeding taken to prevent a judgment recovered in a civil action that had been satisfied by payment or otherwise from being enforced by execution. It was abolished by the rules made under the English and Irish Judicature Acts, there being a more speedy and convenient remedy available.

No. 76, Thursday, June 3rd, 1802.—I went to bed last night before eleven, and got up this morning at seven (*n*).

(*n*) This is a decided improvement.

I spent the day from that time till four in reading law. I pursued my researches in Gorham's case (*o*) [76]. Had I gone down to the assizes as well prepared as I am at present, we should not have been defeated.

(*o*) See No. 75 above, p. 249. In his fee-book, under date January 10th, 1802, the following entry occurs: " *Richard Gorham* v. *Adam Corneberry :* bill for an injunction." Under date 1802, Tralee, there is also the following entry : " *Lessee Corneberry* v. *Gorham,* on an elegit." This was evidently an action of ejectment tried at Tralee Spring Assizes, in which, owing to O'Connell's want of preparation, the plaintiff got a verdict.

I read *Cruise on Fines* to p. 95 (*p*).

(*p*) See No. 74 above, p. 249.

Friday, June 4th, 1802.—I went to bed last night at half after ten.

Got up at half after seven (*q*).

I was in court the far greater part of the day, though I made but one insignificant motion.

I drew part of the answer in the injunction cause of *Murphy* v. *Baldwin*.

(*q*) Here again we note an improvement.

The rest of this page is blank, as is also the whole of the following page, except for the number 77 which it bears on the right-hand corner at the top.

Would that the Journal had been continued through the strenuous years that followed! But the pressure of business must have rendered it difficult, though men almost as much absorbed in public affairs and private pursuits have adhered to the practice of keeping a record of the events of their lives and of the day. Yet those who revere the memory of O'Connell must feel thankful that in the heyday of his youth he kept a diary in which we can read his inmost thoughts, and find that at that early age he cherished those lofty ideals which inspired him throughout his long and arduous career.

INDEX

THE END

BRADBURY, AGNEW, & CO. LD., PRINTERS, LONDON AND TONBRIDGE.

The Cambridge Apostles

By Mrs. Charles Brookfield

In demy 8vo, cloth gilt, gilt top, 21s. net.
With twelve full-page plate illustrations.

The " Cambridge Apostles " were a group of brilliant
young men who, whilst undergraduates of that University,
formed an exclusive intellectual coterie, and took the name
of Apostles partly because they were twelve in number
and partly because they were pioneers of new ideas and
stood, so to speak, on the frontier line of progress. Mrs.
Charles Brookfield, encouraged by the great success both
in England and America of her book last year on " Mrs.
Brookfield and her Circle," has written with full access
to her father-in-law's papers a fascinating account of this
group of young men, nearly all of whom attained in one
direction or another celebrity in life. Tennyson, Hallam,
Lord Houghton, Archbishop Trench, Maurice, Kemble,
Charles Buller, James Spedding, John Sterling—were
some of the members of this famous set.

Mrs. Brookfield and her Circle

By C. and F. Brookfield

CHEAPER EDITION

In 1 vol., demy 8vo, cloth gilt, gilt top, with 4
photogravures, 10s. 6d. net.

" These letters and anecdotes here collected are so rich
and abundant that the most copious extracts must give
an inadequate idea of what they contain. In Mrs.
Brookfield's circle dulness was unknown. Her friends
were all interesting, not for their position, but for themselves. It would be difficult to find in this same compass
so much which though only meant to be ephemeral is
really worth preserving as these pages preserve. . . .
An almost ideal picture of what society properly understood may be. . . . Mr. and Mrs. Brookfield do not seem
to have known any uninteresting people."—*The Times.*

LONDON: SIR ISAAC PITMAN & SONS, LTD.,
NO. 1 AMEN CORNER, E.C.

The Life of Froude

BY

Herbert Paul, M.P.

NEW AND REVISED EDITION

In demy 8vo, cloth gilt, gilt top, 16s. net.

" Mr. Paul's *Life of Froude* will certainly stand as one of the books of the year ; it is not only a brilliant piece of biography and a vindication by one of the most accomplished of contemporary men of letters ; it also possesses the profound interest which gathers round an attempt to interpret one of the greatest and most inscrutable of the Englishmen of the nineteenth century. Mr. Paul is here definitely acting as counsel for the defence. . . . with an eloquence and pungent irony which carry the reader through the whole volume."—*Daily News.*

George MacDonald

BY

Joseph Johnson

In crown 8vo, cloth gilt, gilt top, with photogravure frontispiece.

6s.

" Will be read with eagerness by thousands of Mac-Donald's admirers."—*Aberdeen Daily Journal.*

" Mr. Johnson has been enabled without prying into the private career of the man of letters or his family to give some personal details which are not generally known concerning Dr. MacDonald."—*Scotsman.*

" Gives us many pleasantly illustrative traits of his character."—*Manchester Guardian.*

" A most enjoyable book."—*Dunfermline Journal.*

LONDON : SIR ISAAC PITMAN & SONS, LTD.
NO. 1 AMEN CORNER, E.C.

Italy of the Italians

BY

Helen Zimmern

In imperial 16mo, with 31 full page plate illustrations,
6s. net.

A timely book, quite different in nature from any other work
on the subject. Miss Zimmern (for twenty years a resident in
the land) has sedulously avoided the style and purpose of the
guide-book, and aims, rather, to give the reader some idea of
Italy's real life and civilisation—the impulses, aims, hopes and
ambitions of the nation and her people, her present position in
the world of European thought, her contribution to the modern
movement, and her bequests to the fabrics of contemporary
science, art, literature and philosophy.

England's Parnassus

An Anthology of Anthologies

Edited by W. Garrett Horder

In fcap. 8vo, leather gilt, 3s. 6d. net ; cloth, 2s. 6d. net.

This book is an attempt to eliminate the personal equation
in the presentation of the best poems of the English language.
Nearly every previous attempt to present such poems is the result
of an individual judgment ; so strong is this that a student of
such anthologies can almost tell beforehand what each editor
will include—one is keen on form, another on ideas, and another
on the lyric element. It occurred to the Editor that a collection
gathered out of the finest existing anthologies, and to which
no poem would be admitted which did not secure at least
four votes, would be a finer presentation of English verse than
any existing collection. The result justifies this anticipation ;
at least this is the verdict of some very competent judges of
English poetry to whom the collection has been submitted.

LONDON : SIR ISAAC PITMAN & SONS, LTD.
No. 1 AMEN CORNER, E.C.

The Creed of Creeds

By the Rev. F. B. Meyer, B.A.

In crown 8vo, cloth gilt, 3s. 6d.

A series of brief expositions on the various clauses of the Apostles' Creed—probably the one statement of belief in which all Christendom could unite.

The New Idolatry

By Dr. Washington Gladden

In crown 8vo, cloth gilt, 3s. 6d.

A volume of discussions in protest against the commercialising of government, of education, and of religion ; and against the growing tendency in church and state to worship power and Mammon.

With an Introduction by the Rev. E. Griffith Jones, B.A.

The Child of Nazareth

By the Rev. Benjamin Waugh

In crown 8vo, cloth gilt, gilt top, with Photogravure Frontispiece. 5s. net.

The object of this book is to suggest that during the years He was being brought up, Jesus lived no still and silent life, but the active and fruitful one natural to all wholesome boys.

Essays for Sunday Reading

By John Caird, D.D.

With Photogravure Frontispiece.

In crown 8vo, cloth gilt, with silk register, 3s. 6d. net.

A collection of the scattered addresses of the late Principal of Glasgow University, perhaps the most popular preacher of the mid-Victorian period, on such practical subjects as Covetousness, Has the Gospel Lost its Ancient Power ? Married and Single Life, etc.

With an Introduction by the Very Rev. Donald Macleod, D.D.

LONDON: SIR ISAAC PITMAN & SONS, LTD.

No 1 AMEN CORNER, E.C.

ImTheStory.com

Personalized Classic Books in many genre's

Unique gift for kids, partners, friends, colleagues

Customize:

- Character Names
- Upload your own front/back cover images (optional)
- Inscribe a personal message/dedication on the
  inside page (optional)

Customize many titles Including
- Alice in Wonderland
- Romeo and Juliet
- The Wizard of Oz
- A Christmas Carol
- Dracula
- Dr. Jekyll & Mr. Hyde
- And more...

Lightning Source UK Ltd.
Milton Keynes UK
UKHW021559181119
353758UK00019B/4762/P